Tobacco Town
Futures

Tobacco Town Futures

Global Encounters in Rural Kentucky

Ann E. Kingsolver
University of Kentucky

WAVELAND

PRESS, INC.

Long Grove, Illinois

For information about this book, contact:
Waveland Press, Inc.
4180 IL Route 83, Suite 101
Long Grove, IL 60047-9580
(847) 634-0081
info@waveland.com
www.waveland.com

Frontispiece photo by author

10-digit ISBN 1-57766-708-5
13-digit ISBN 978-1-57766-708-7

Printed in the United States of America

7 6 5 4 3 2

To the children of Nicholas County,
who *are* its future.

**All royalties from this book are being donated
directly to the Nicholas County schools.**

Contents

Acknowledgments

My first thanks go to everyone in Nicholas County who collaborated in this research project by allowing me to interview them (sometimes repeatedly) and spend time learning from and with them. If I listed hundreds of names here, I would still be leaving people out; I might as well just append the Carlisle phone book. Thanks to *all* of you. I have had many mentors in Nicholas County, including my brother Rob Kingsolver and my sister Barbara Kingsolver as we were growing up there. I appreciate the long-term friendship and belief in this project of Catherine Sagraves, my high school English teacher, and her son Brian Canupp. I was his babysitter, and now he's my lawyer; that's how things work in a small town.

I am profoundly grateful to my grandparents, Roy and Louise Kingsolver, and my parents, Wendell and Virginia Henry Kingsolver. All four have been great mentors and friends in my life, sharing their time, insights, and skills. Dad saved his farm magazines for me, and Mom took the time to send me relevant clippings from the *Lexington Herald-Leader* for years, optimistic that one day they would be useful for this book. They have been. Thank you.

The National Science Foundation and the University of Massachusetts–Amherst supported this project early on through Graduate Research Fellowships, and much later, the Kentucky Oral History Commission helped me give something back to the community through a Nicholas County bicentennial oral history project in 1999, to which Annie Lorrie Anderson-Lazo, Susan "Taylor" Langley, and Mark Whitaker contributed as interviewers, and Steve Jackson as a videographer. Others who supported documentary research along the way included Robert Hughes, Laura Liger, Nancy Osberg, Julie Pheifer, and Sara Palmer (who followed William Emmons through the National Archives).

I thank Doug Bechanan and Carol Sparks for serving on the committee for the Roy and Louise Essay Contest on the Future of Nicholas County, several teachers for encouraging students to write essays, and the students for writing them. I also thank the editors of the *Carlisle Mercury*, the *Carlisle Courier*, and the *Lexington Herald-Leader* for permission to cite numerous letters to the editor and articles in this book.

As a scholar, I appreciate the many conversations from which I have learned, throughout the 25 years of this research project, with all of my faculty and student colleagues at the University of Massachusetts–Amherst, Lawrence University, the University of California–Santa Cruz, the University of South Carolina, and in the Society for the Anthropology of Work (especially Michael Blim, Susanna Donaldson, David Griffith, Charles Menzies, and Fran Rothstein). My dissertation chair, Sylvia Helen Forman, and members, Julie Graham and Brooke Thomas, each inspired me in different ways that have been useful in my academic career.

Others not already mentioned who have, in conversations along the way, helped shape this book include Laura Ahearn and Rick Black, Drue Barker, Tanya and Wendell Berry, Don Brenneis and Wynne Furth, Laura Cahue, Subhadra Channa, Nancy Chen, Sumi Colligan, Kamari Clarke, Lillian Wright Craft, Paulla Ebron, Pete and Carol Ekstrom, Shelly Errington, Elizabeth and John Fabel, Janina Fenigsen, Janet Fitchen, Dana Frank, Lisa Gezon, Susan Harding, Faye Harrison, Karl Heider, Steven Hopp, Mary Taylor Huber, Krissy Hudgins, Sue Hyatt, Paul and Claudia Isenhour, Alice Kasakoff, Art Keene, Paula Kingsolver, Mary and John Knight, Wendi Knight, Elaine Lacy, Tom Leatherman, Alison Leitch, Ann Magennis, Lisa Markowitz, Carolyn Martin-Shaw, Randy McGuire, Charlotte and Michael McLain, Brinkley Messick, Sandra Morgen, Olga Nájera-Ramírez, Mary Orgel, Annapurna and Loki Pandey, Stefania Pandolfo, James Peacock, Anita Puckett, Jennifer Reynolds, Ivelisse Rivera-Bonilla, Lisa Rofel, Michael Scardaville, Betsy and Mike Shally-Jensen, Kim and David Simmons, Marilyn Thomas-Houston, Anna Tsing, Jacqueline Urla, Gail Wagner, Hilda and Burton Whitaker, Brackette Williams, Lynn Wilson, Davida Wood, and Gail and Bruce Wright. My closest long-term colleagues in thinking through the issues discussed in this book, because of their similar work, have been Mary Anglin and Pem Buck, and they have been wonderful in talking this project through with me to its end. Tom Curtin has been great to work with as an editor, and I appreciate the contributions of Jeni Ogilvie and others at Waveland Press.

Finally, I would like to thank the rest of those who have been supportive in various ways during the last phase of this project, as I turned the piles accumulated in 25 years of research into this book: Sasikumar Balasundaram, Claudia Carriere, Charlotte Cassady, Jeannie Gates, Lenora Isenhour, Cat and Eric Keegan, Gloria Smith, Diane Wallman, Lois Wandersman, and my family (and intrepid colleagues in life), Mark and David Whitaker.

Tobacco Town
Futures

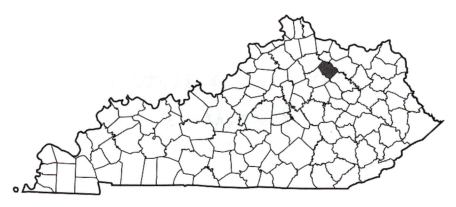

Nicholas County highlighted on the state of Kentucky map

Nicholas County (Courtesy Carlisle-Nicholas County Tourism, Inc.)

Chapter 1

Introduction

Stories of Globalization in a Tobacco Town

*E*very one of us is a storyteller, and everyone's stories are important. This book is about connections between individual and collective stories in a particular place—Nicholas County, Kentucky. Global stories about conflict, collaboration, economic success and crisis; hopes, anguish, injustice and justice; and courage and silence are connected to individual stories in any place. In a small community, more people tend to know one another's stories, thousands of them, for better or worse. All of us learn from each other's stories how to make do, when to speak up, what matters, and so much else, just as we learn from newspapers, books, television, radio, movies, billboards, the Internet, and magazines in the grocery store line. This book is about what Nicholas Countians, including me, have to say about globalization and how community decisions get made in the face of what the future might be like.

Globalization is a way of talking about the relationships, both social and economic, between people living and working around the world. We are most aware of those connections in moments of crisis, as when the U.S. mortgage crisis in 2008 affected economies around the world. We share a planet, as earthquakes and oil spills remind us, as well as a global economy. The geographer David Harvey (1990) has commented on the way time and space seem to be compressed by processes we call globalization, since technologies of communication and travel allow us to reach people and places much more immediately than used to be possible, and the world seems to be shrinking because of that. But not everyone has equal access to that closer reach of globalization.

We are increasingly linked to each other through the production, distribution, and consumption of goods and information, and it might seem that those links would help us understand each other's situations. Nicholas County garment workers were taken to Jamaica by their employers to see

1

where their jobs would go if they did not make their quotas, for example. But after the plant closed and the jobs did move away to other locations, that did not necessarily mean that Nicholas Countians were volunteering to pay higher prices for T-shirts made in other countries just because they understood that the labor was worth more than the price tag indicated. If people involved in global production were able to cross language, national, and cultural divides and compare experiences, it might make a difference; capitalist market logic, however, prevents exactly that kind of comparing notes by the lowest-wage workers to keep labor pools competing with each other. Several anthropologists (Kearney 1995 and Tsing 2000, for example) have called for closer research attention to the ways in which individuals across cultures define and experience globalization, instead of simply assuming we know what globalization means. For the past 25 years, I have been listening closely to the stories people in eastern Kentucky and other places have been telling me about globalization and other topics on their minds, and those stories shape this book.

The distance between rich and poor—both within and between countries—has actually increased in recent years, so globalization and the spread of shared growth-oriented capitalist goals (with increased profit as the bottom line) between nations does not necessarily mean improved job and food security for everyone in the world, just because we are increasingly interconnected. Everyone I have interviewed about globalization over the past 25 years in the United States, Mexico, and Sri Lanka agrees that it has its positive and negative aspects. The benefits can be selective, and the drawbacks can sometimes be catastrophic. Mr. Gowreesan, who lives on the east coast of Sri Lanka, for example, wondered after the 2004 tsunami in the Indian Ocean why television signals had been able to bring his community a cricket match all the way from New Zealand, but not advance warning of the tsunami headed for many hours toward Sri Lanka from Indonesia (TamilNet 2005). What good is globalization, then, he wondered, if that communication technology could not be used to prevent the loss of over 35,000 lives when the tsunami finally hit the shore of his country? Globalization has been going on for many centuries—long before it has gone by this name—and it is neither good nor bad in itself; it describes processes of spatial, social, and economic interconnectedness. The power over access to, and use of, the resources of globalization is what is contested, and that power is the reason for people coming to view globalization as positive or negative, or more likely some combination of both, in their lives.

Although everyone is connected to people in other communities through globalization, we do not make decisions as a global community; all global processes, and decision making, are somehow ultimately local. That decision making may happen, for example, at a meeting in the World Trade Organization headquarters in Geneva, Switzerland, or in parliament buildings or corporate board rooms, or in the Nicholas County courthouse or the living rooms of voters, but it is decision making that happens in actual places and conversations rather than in some vague stratospheric layer referred to as the "multinational" or "global." This is a simple point, but an important one, because if we know where and how decisions related to globalization on different scales are being made, and by whom, it is possible to see what is influencing those decisions and how directions change, or can be changed, as a result of a confluence of different (sometimes conflicting) interests.

Some decision making about globalization is intentional, as when trade agreements are negotiated, and some of it is more like a game of Scrabble (trying to make sense out of what turns up at a given moment). It is often possible to trace the particular conversations at the "global" level that result in local changes, and vice versa. One example of a local action that had a global effect was when the people of Cochabamba, Bolivia, said they would and could not pay the enormously high prices that Bechtel, a transnational corporation owning their privatized water system, imposed; this led to changes in Bolivian government and International Monetary Fund (IMF) policies. When the North American Free Trade Agreement (NAFTA) was being negotiated, I did research on the members of the negotiating teams for Canada, the United States, and Mexico and found that many of them had been to school together and shared a perspective supporting neoliberal economic policies; in considering their decision making about globalization, then, it made more sense to look at their similarities in vantage point (sometimes quite different from others in their own nations) than at their differences in nationality.

It is useful (as Gibson-Graham [1996] and Miller [1997] have pointed out) to think of global capitalism not as a single overarching entity or process but instead as a lot of different processes and networks, not all alike, in particular places that do have influences on each other. For this reason, in my long-term research on globalization, I have found it equally important and interesting to study and compare talk about globalization in many local contexts—whether that has been a farmyard in rural Mexico, with turkeys hopping on and off our laps during the conversation, or a national minister's, senator's, or bank executive's office, with other kinds of distractions and interruptions. Nicholas County seemed as good a place to me as any to study globalization, and I wanted to demonstrate in this project that the places imagined as "backward" or "in another time" (stereotypes of Appalachia that Batteau [1990] has traced and critiqued well) or otherwise detached from the momentum and decision making of globalization were every bit as much a part of those connected local and global processes as other sites around the planet.

People all around the world participate in multiple communities, wherever they happen to live. Susantha Goonatilake (1995:231) has noted that what we really need to be thinking about is how "these different communities, face-to-face, crossborder, and virtual, interact" and how individuals navigate citizenship in these various communities—some seen as local, some as global—to which we belong. A farmer I know in eastern Kentucky, for example, may be in the same hour chatting with colleagues in the European Union online about regulations for the marketing of organic tobacco from the

United States, then going outside to check on her children playing in the yard, and then going to the greenhouse to talk with a worker from Mexico about how the hydroponically grown tobacco seedlings are doing, working beside him along the rows of flats. She is shifting between roles and communities as she goes, engaging globalization on the farm.

Globalization is nothing new. As Frances Rothstein (2007) pointed out in her work following 30 years of changes related to globalization in rural Mexico, connections between communities far apart from each other have existed for hundreds and even thousands of years—what is happening is a change in the way power and labor relationships are configured between individuals, groups, and regions thriving or definitely not thriving in the current moment of globalization. Jane Nadel-Klein, another anthropologist, has made the excellent point that local communities should not be seen as static or as merely persisting through centuries of global capitalist connections, but that the identities, organization, and even existence of local communities have been emphasized or deemphasized, related to larger global patterns of demand for land, labor, and resources. Nadel-Klein (1991:502) says:

> I suggest that it might be helpful to look at localism not as paradox but as irony: global processes call localities into existence, but make no commitments to their continued survival. The irony lies in the fact that local identity is an unintended result of the global division of labor. When market forces make a way of life "marginal" or obsolete, communities don't die gracefully. "Local people" may oppose their own communal extinction. . . . An explicit link between place and political economy enables us to see how localism remains a highly salient, creative category, not merely a plaint to be invoked on behalf of those who live in out-of-the-way places.

It is interesting to think, for example, about the current resurgence of popular attention to locally grown or made food and other products in relation to the most recent widespread economic crisis that has brought neoliberal capitalist policies into question. Arif Dirlik (1996:22, 28) has noted that narratives demonstrating a growing "concern with the local as the site of resistance to capital, and the location for imagining alternative possibilities for the future," abound, but that we need to remember that the local is both "a source of promise and predicament," since there have been examples of both increased democratization and increased discrimination as localized responses to the current moment of global capitalism. I believe that by looking at the relationship between "local" and "global" in any place as dynamic, and by not assuming that local is static and globalization is animated, we can learn a lot about how people construct meanings of both "the local" and "the global" and act on them.

Cornelia Butler Flora and Jan Flora (2008:274) have written about the relationship between global and rural economies, and the patterns they discuss reflect discussions and decision making in rural Iowa, rural Kentucky, and many other traditional farming regions:

Most experts now agree that the world economy has changed and that the U.S. economy is restructuring in response to those changes. Features of the new global economy are that (1) the industrial economy is less dependent on the natural-resource economy, (2) manufacturing production is less dependent on labor, (3) the movement of capital is the driving force in the world economy, and (4) the development of instantaneous communication among knowledge centers around the world and the development of e-commerce have allowed for the physical separation of production and marketing components. . . . In this changing economic environment, rural communities need to diversify their economies, must be creative in locating market niches or finding new uses for existing resources, and need to develop regional, national, and international linkages that help local businesses remain competitive.

In Nicholas County, Kentucky, as in other places, people have been talking about encounters with globalization for some time. I attended a conference for local officials and businesspeople in the 1980s, for example, called "Kentucky Goes Global," to which former Secretary of State Henry Kissinger and the then U.S. ambassador to Canada, among others, were invited to help shape a strategy for dealing with coming changes in the state. The golden triangle in North Carolina was seen as a model for anticipating a more research- and information-based economy, and some were advocating for more links between universities and industry. Others were building industrial parks and hoping to attract more multinational corporations to rural Kentucky.

I went to one session in which county judge-executives (the highest elected county government officials) and other elected officials were being instructed by a fellow judge in how to discourage labor union organization to keep wages low enough to attract new industry. I was surprised to hear that local authorities were being encouraged to send letters directly to workers discouraging them from listening to union organizers; that was a lesson in power relations related to globalization. The competitive edge to capitalist globalization, since its logic is that someone has to profit from someone else's labor, means that everyone is hoping that the goose that lays the golden eggs will move to *their* industrial park, and the fact that there is still an empty nest in the industrial park next door, or that the goose has flown to Jamaica, is not discouraging because the logic holds its own hopefulness about success in the free market.

At the time I started listening to Nicholas Countians' stories about globalization in the mid-1980s, there were a number of stories to follow. Going back in time, probably the oldest story is geological: the county's hilly landscape is situated on the dividing line between the Lower Ordovician limestone, which supports the bluegrass to the west that strengthens the bones of thoroughbreds in the horse industry, and the Upper Ordovician shale, which signals the Pennsylvanian coal seams to the east. In many ways, Nicholas County is on an edge between different ecological and economic zones. It also sits on an historical edge between North and South; Kentucky was a border state in the Civil War, and in Nicholas County, many families, churches, and neighborhoods were divided. One funeral from that era was described to me in which a family buried two sons at the same time, each coffin draped with a different flag.

A more conventional way to describe this Kentucky community currently is that it has about 7,000 residents living in a set of communities, the largest of which is Carlisle—the county seat (with a population of over 1,500). A long-term story in which the county can be situated is that of rural-to-urban migration: as Kentucky's population grew from just over 2 million in 1900 to over 3.5 million in 1990 and the United States grew from around 180 million residents in 1900 to nearly 250 million in 1990, Nicholas County's population decreased from around 12,000 in 1900 to 6,725 residents in 1990 (Forstall 1995). Nicholas County lost about 1,000 residents per decade between 1900 and 1960, and the population has been fairly stable since then. This does not mean, of course, that people have not been moving in and out of the county.

Migration is part of the story people tell about identity, and census data—incomplete accounts in themselves—comprise one way of following stories about identity. In Census 2000 (see http://factfinder.census.gov), for example, 6,698 Nicholas County residents identified themselves as being white, 57 as black or African American, 17 as Native American, 8 as Asian, 41 as of multiple or other racial identities, and 45 as Latin American (27 from Mexico) and Latino. What does it mean to be the only person from Puerto Rico or Japan, for example, listed as living in Nicholas County by the U.S. Census Bureau? This book will follow not only dominant narratives but also narratives of those who tend to be "othered" in terms of identity or vantage point.

"Othering" is an anthropological term referring to the way a person or group might be defined as different, and even sometimes less significant, from the perspective of a group that is dominant in number or power. Class, for example, is a way that Nicholas Countians might be "othered," both as a whole group in relation to other regions of the country and through distinctions drawn within the community. The number of Nicholas Countians living below the poverty level (as defined by the U.S. Census) was around 19.5 percent in 2006, higher than the overall Kentucky rate of 17 percent and the United States rate of 13 percent, but there is also a dramatic income divide within the county that encompasses millionaires and a growing number of people who are unemployed. According to the U.S. Census Bureau, again, over 1,000 Nicholas County residents have no health insurance. In a farming community, off-farm employment is often more significant for bringing health insurance coverage into the household than income.

Nicholas County, as mentioned above, is east of the Bluegrass, or horse country, and in the very western edge of the knobs, or foothills of Appalachia. The land is divided into small farms, and the major cash crop has been burley tobacco (an air-cured tobacco, used mostly in cigarettes) for over 200 years. Tobacco cultivation has shaped the whole landscape, with fields carved into the clay hilltops or bottomland and barns with some of the boards swinging open along the sides to air-cure the tobacco when it is hanging up on the rails inside in the fall. It has also shaped community life, since lease agreements and labor exchanges bind neighbors and family together like baling twine, and the local economy was long tied to the annual issue of tobacco checks in January, since that was when many bills could be paid. The identity as well as the landscape of the county was linked with tobacco, equally a local and global crop, and that was seen by many late in the twentieth century as being on the brink of change with revisions to the 1933 Agricultural Adjustment Act that had set up the system of quotas, or "base," that tobacco farmers grew and could reliably market through collective warehouses in the region. Federal policies were about to change, and people were beginning to talk in the 1980s about what that would mean. Most Nicholas County families who farmed also had some members earning wages and health benefits off the farm in factory or service jobs.

At the same time that changes were said to be coming in the tobacco industry, 25 years ago when I began this research, changes were also coming across the southeastern United States in the textile industry. The major factory employer in Nicholas County, a combined textile and garment plant, was facing some big changes as well, as local ownership had shifted to multinational ownership and that nationally known underwear company was considering shutting down some of the small plants scattered across the hill country, including the one in Nicholas County. Kentucky's governor and chamber of commerce were trying to land the first Toyota assembly plant in the United States (a bid in which they were eventually successful), and Nicholas Countians were beginning to talk about whether they might get jobs at that plant, or at a satellite plant they hoped might be constructed in the waiting industrial park near the county landfill on the main road into Carlisle. If Toyota came, the argument went, then maybe there would need to be satellite plants further out where seat covers and other parts needed for the cars might be manufactured. All of these stories were about very local and very global processes at the same time, and I was interested in how people envisioned the future given the challenges being faced at that moment. I wanted to follow these stories not just for a little while, but for years, as the future unfolded and we (since I am a Nicholas Countian, too) could follow and learn from the threads of decisions made individually and together.

Recently, after a talk I gave on this work at another university, a journalism student asked why he should care about what people in a small tobacco-producing town were saying about the future over a 25-year period; what is compelling about that, he asked, when there is so much going on in the world that needs to be documented, discussed, and acted upon? I thought that was a good question, and here is my attempt to answer it, after thinking about it for some time. The residents of Nicholas County, Kentucky, have been weathering a tremendous crisis in their community: the loss of, or major changes in, not just one but multiple sources of employment. The combination of a guaranteed income from the tobacco crop, under the federal tobacco program, and work at the local textile plant gave families a sense of independence, identity, and a secure working-class or middle-class livelihood, much like that of auto workers in the upper Midwest. And like the crisis in Detroit and other communities tied to the auto industry, having livelihoods and identity anchored by one or two main sources of jobs means that if those jobs go, there are problems for the whole community that spill over into mortgage foreclosures, problems with the tax base for the schools, and young people facing the choice to either move away or be unemployed.

The crisis faced by auto workers in Michigan and tobacco farmers in Kentucky and textile workers in South Carolina is related to global restructuring of industry and trade stemming from neoliberal capitalist policies. Over the past 30 years around the world, neoliberal policies have encouraged (1) privatization of industries that used to be nationalized, or federally regulated, (2) the relaxing of "protectionist" trade policies that discouraged imports of goods produced for less than a nation's own workers could make them, (3) less regulation of the free market, or "business," by the state, and (4) increased responsibilities for the recipients—either through work or paying a larger percentage themselves—of public services (like the "welfare-to-work" program). Globally, the implementation of these neoliberal policies (largely designed by economist Milton Friedman, cf. 1962) has been through the shift toward privatization in many countries, structural adjustment policies attached to World Bank loans, and a series of world trade agreements like NAFTA (see Kingsolver 2001).

As I studied what was happening in Nicholas County, I realized that what was happening with the tobacco and textile industries was tied to these much larger patterns that affected jobs coming and going in different regions of the world, and that these were in turn situated within historical cycles. To understand that further, I looked at the ways in which industries in Mexico and the United States were in similar rhythms—with private, large holdings of agricultural land, mines, factories, and so forth (often with absentee, including international, ownership) in the 1800s giving way to populist movements and small holdings in the early 1900s, with increased state protection of citizen versus corporate interests and the encouragement of small-scale livelihoods. Nicholas County had at that time, for example, "the People's Warehouse" as one of the local marketing options for tobacco farmers, and the new Mexican Constitution of 1917 guaranteed *ejido* lands, community agricultural plots that families could use and pass down but could not sell to large corporations (so they would never again be forced to work on plantations for wages much too small to live on, the reasoning went).

The New Deal brought more populist protections in the U.S., like the Agricultural Adjustment Act of 1933, which established the tobacco warehouse collective marketing system, for example, and attached the marketing quotas for the crop to individual property deeds so the market could not be flooded by one large corporate grower, among other reasons. That was also a time of antimonopoly legislation, which began to be dismantled in the early 1980s as neoliberal capitalist policies were introduced into the U.S. mainstream. In the latter part of the twentieth century, the tide in many nations turned toward deregulation and reprivatization.

As NAFTA was being proposed and then passed in 1993, I interviewed individuals with many different class, gender, ethnic, racialized, geographic, political, and occupational identities in Kentucky, California, rural Mexico, and Mexico City for a book I wrote called *NAFTA Stories: Hopes and Fears in Mexico and the United States* (Kingsolver 2001). The main concern on many people's minds was how NAFTA would affect their particular jobs as it would go into effect, in stages, over the next 15 years. Workers in the shoe and communications industries were worried about the effects of NAFTA in 1994, for example, and most recently, corn farmers in Mexico and truckers in the United States worried as national protections on those industries were relaxed under the final stages of the trade agreement. Nineteen industries, including banking and utilities, were privatized in Mexico in preparation for NAFTA, and there was a credit crisis in Mexico (in which interest rates on credit cards, no longer federally regulated, went up to 200 percent, for example) that came a few years earlier than the U.S. mortgage crisis in 2008.

What I wonder as an anthropologist, in all this, is how individuals explain their particular circumstances, such as job loss, in relation to these larger national and transnational contexts. In 1994, for example, very few people had access to, or time to read, the 2,000-page NAFTA document, but nearly everyone I talked with had an opinion about it—how it might help them, and how it made them anxious—and there were stories of blame attached to it. Anti-immigrant sentiment always tends to go up, for example, during economic downturns. I believe that if more people in communities around the world could speak directly with each other about their situations, comparing notes, it would be useful in making sense of these larger events (like economic crises) that can sometimes seem inexplicable or make people feel helpless.

In 2004, as a Fulbright scholar, I went to Sri Lanka (the teardrop-shaped island nation off the southern tip of India) to study the tea industry in comparison with the tobacco industry and found that people were facing some very similar patterns: taking on the risks of being an independent contractor (which is what is happening with tobacco farmers in Kentucky) directly with corporations instead of having government regulation (as there had been earlier) of labor conditions and terms of sale of the crop. Similar changes in the garment industry have been experienced by workers in Sri Lanka and the United States, also, because of the international Multi-Fibre Arrangement, which expired at the beginning of 2005. It had regulated the import and export of garments between nations in order to protect some textile workers, particularly in developed nations; now the market is wide open, so global clothing production has shifted toward the sites of cheapest labor, which has affected a number of nations in the Global South as well as the Global North.

What I have tried to do in the university classroom is connect students in the United States, Mexico, and Sri Lanka with each other directly (using the Internet) so they can learn through each other's experiences and through doing research projects together, to encourage communication across global contexts. The majority of students cannot afford the time or the cost of international travel, but everyone can benefit from exchanging vantage points on everyday life in different places. This has been a long way around the barn to get to the question, as one might say in Carlisle, but my answer to the young man who asked me why he should care about the experiences of Nicholas Countians is that, among other reasons, he might be facing a tough job market when he gets out of school, and he could learn a lot from the way Nicholas Countians have mobilized and reassessed their personal and community identities and resources in the face of an employment crisis, and imagined ways to go into the future.

Fieldwork in Nicholas County

This book is based, then, on a long-term research project in my hometown: anthropological fieldwork 1986–1989, a county bicentennial oral history project in 1999, and ethnographic interviews in years in between, including a number of interviews in 2009. I am a cultural anthropologist, and what we mostly do (whether we call it ethnography or engaged listening) is ask questions and listen to people's stories and try to understand them within broader, comparative contexts. Culture is not something we see as fixed or measurable, exactly, but a shared sense of the way the world works that we construct collectively. That does not mean that we all agree on what is true, by any means, but we tend to agree on the general frameworks into which we have been socialized. Most people in the United States agree that the world is round these days, for example, but some of us think that it was created by God, some of us think it started with a cosmic explosion, and some of us weave versions of these stories together into individual beliefs.

I have always been interested in the way so many different notions of who and where we are, and what decisions we ought to make as a group, can be circulating at the same time and be believed in emphatically. Almost everyone's version of reality can be true at the same time, it seems, but they may have different consequences when implemented in the world—take the different implications of "hunting" or "poaching," for example. As Lisa Yoneyama (1999) points out, the very different versions we each have of remembering personal events and telling larger stories—narrative flexibility that can be convenient in many social contexts—are occasionally cut through by very specific historical moments that necessarily anchor all of our memories of that time and where we were, whether that was the bombing of Dresden or Hiroshima, if one was there, or the events of September 11, 2001, or the flooding after Hurricane Katrina in the United States. When and how does individual memory coincide with collective memory of crisis events? How are events seen differently as cause for celebration or lament?

Tobacco production, for example, has had paradoxical interpretations. As tobacco farmers have said to me, they know about the health costs of tobacco, but it has fed quite a few children in Kentucky and it has been hard to find any other cash crop that would do that. The end of the tobacco program (described in chapter 2) is not likely to be pinned in Nicholas Countians' memories to a particular day or week, since a series of policies—some providing for shifts to alternative ways of making a living—went into effect over several years, but with plant closings, there is a particular day when the factory is emptied and the doors are locked. How do individuals, comparing notes on shop floors, at dinner tables, in fields, after church, at the gas station, or in community meetings, anticipate and deal with such crises and place them within large-scale ways of talking about change, like globalization? That cultural process is followed in this book.

When our sixth-grade teacher at Nicholas County Elementary School asked us each to stand up and say what we wanted to be when we grew up, I said I wanted to become an anthropology professor. I still am not sure why, since I did not know exactly what anthropology was, but my family had lived for short periods in other countries (in Zaire, in Central Africa, for example), and I was intrigued by the differences and similarities I had seen in how people lived in and explained the world. Later, when I was working on my PhD in Anthropology at the University of Massachusetts at Amherst, in the 1980s, I decided to do my ethnographic fieldwork—a sustained period of research on one topic in a particular place, or set of places—in my hometown in Kentucky.

Accountability to those who were kind enough to share their stories with me was important, not only to me personally, but also to anthropology as a field. It is in our code of ethics. I thought that doing research in a place where many had known me for a lifetime would level out the relationship between "researcher" and "researched," which can sometimes be perceived as an unequal one, and that I would find ways to be accountable to many different perspectives represented in the work; I wanted to maintain long-term relationships in my hometown. In anthropology, we often say that one of our tools is to make the strange familiar and the familiar strange; in this project, I learned that there were many ways in which all of us can be insiders and outsiders and that we learn best through a combination of lenses. "Insider" and "outsider" research—being from the context and speaking the language, for example, or not—each has its own challenges, and since I had been away from Kentucky for some time before beginning this project, I was a bit of both.

Supported by a National Science Foundation Graduate Research Fellowship, I returned to live in Nicholas County 1986–1989 to learn about how people in one place talked about the future in the face of changes related to globalization, especially the possible futures of a "tobacco town" given the looming loss of the major cash crop. My parents and grandparents lived there. My grandparents had each grown up on farms in Nicholas County and had moved back there in retirement. My parents had grown up in Lexington, Kentucky, and had chosen Nicholas County as the place to establish my father's medical practice and to raise their children. My father has been a family practice physician in the county since the 1950s, transitioning to public health work and public service when he closed his private practice. My mother worked in his office and as a volunteer coordinator in the community, and I started working in my father's office on Saturdays when I was 10. In a rural medical practice, the whole family is involved. We knew as children (before cell phones) the urgency of answering the phone and radioing my father out on the farm if he was needed in the emergency room. I got to know the landscape of the county accompanying my father on house calls, waiting in the car and listening to crickets and tree frogs and smelling fresh-cut hay or tobacco. I also learned that farming was not romantic, since chemicals could cause neurological problems and there were a lot of accidents with machinery used on steep slopes.

When I moved back to Nicholas County, I chose to rent an apartment in Carlisle, although it was considered strange for me to live alone. My family lived out in the county, and I wanted to live in town to get to know people through different networks. I got to know people I had known all my life in new ways and met people I had not known before. There were various stories in circulation about why I had moved back (sometimes involving recovery from brain cancer or a nervous breakdown). One classmate said, "You got out of here; why would you come back?" I tried to explain my research project in different venues—including the local newspaper—and my interest in learning through participant observation, semistructured interviewing, social mapping, and archival research around the county. I worked as a substitute teacher in grades 1–12 in the Nicholas County schools during my fieldwork, volunteered with the new adult literacy project, and joined a clogging group that met at night after everyone got off work in their different jobs. Sometimes I worked in the fields, volunteering to help set tobacco or put up hay for cattle. I played piano for revivals around the county—there are over 100 small churches of various Protestant denominations around Nicholas County and one Catholic church in Carlisle. Playing religious music was a way to get to know different people, but it was also cause for suspicion about my own beliefs. Once someone I had known since the third grade spoke to the congregation—while channeling the Holy Spirit—about a nonbeliever being present and not welcome, and I realized he was talking about me.

I had many occasions to be reflexive, or to consider my own racialized, gendered, and class position in this research. One morning, about six o'clock, I was walking down Main Street to meet another teacher in the cemetery; she and I took walks there regularly, as did others (much like some might go to a gym for exercise). As I passed the stone wall in front of the courthouse, there was a young man sitting on the wall who had probably been drinking for a while. He said, "Got it made, don't ya?" I replied, "I guess so." I have thought about his question a lot, as a distilled class analysis. He was right—I had it made, in terms of food and employment security, and as much as I worked in tobacco fields beside others who depended on that crop for a living, I would not understand the experience of having no safety net if a crop failed or a plant closed. I got to know people in many different class positions and heard their stories, but I do not presume to fully understand how all those words and silences connect to individual experiences. I have learned that there are many Nicholas Counties.

"Placing" a Kentucky Community

Just as some people might see hills and others might see valleys in a landscape, there are many ways to talk about identity and place. "Where are you from?" is a question that people answer in myriad ways, depending on the social context and what they might want to emphasize or deemphasize in that context. "Insiderness" and "outsiderness" are manipulated a bit, by all of us, and we make choices as we "place" ourselves in conversation. Here is an example. One summer day in 1988 I was in a day-old bread store in Lexington, Kentucky, about an hour from Carlisle by car, with my friend Mary Ann Moore. She had lived in Carlisle for over 60 years

Mary Ann Moore (photo by Gordon Burkett)

as a healer, a mother and grandmother, a worker, and an oral historian and activist in Nicholas County's African American community. We ran into another woman prodding loaves, and she said to Mary Ann, "I know you— you're from Carlisle!" Ms. Moore shook a mock-angry finger at the other African American woman and said "Not me—you know I'm from Sharpsburg." They went on to name people they might know in common from that neighboring community—through the AME Church there, and students the other woman had taught in school. Once they had "placed" themselves relative to one another in a larger social network, we parted ways in the aisles. That was when I learned that she had been born in another town and still went to church there. At another occasion, a wake in Lexington, I heard Mary Ann Moore tell someone she was from Carlisle when someone asked if she lived in another community.

In part, we identify ourselves in relation to place in terms that we think the listener might understand, depending on how well he or she knows the regional and social landscapes. Nicholas Countians have a variety of ways in which to situate themselves, or ourselves (I also shift the way I identify according to the context): Kentucky, the Midwest, the South, Appalachia, rural America, the Outer Bluegrass, or Nicholas County, for example. Within the county, residents might choose to identify as being either from Carlisle or from one of many smaller communities still thriving or long abandoned in the county: Abner's Mill, Bald Hill, Banta, Barefoot, Barterville, Blue Licks, Buzzard Roost (or Sprout), Cassidy Creek, Concord, Crayton, East Union, Ellisville, Fisher's Station, Flora, Goose Creek, Headquarters, Henryville, Hickory Ridge, Hog Jaw, Hooktown, Ishmael Chapel, Jackstown, Lake Carnico, Licking, Locust Grove, Mexico (a community rumored to have been ceded to that country because of the independence of its residents), Milltown, Miranda or Frog Town, Moorefield, Morning Glory, Mt. Carmel, Mt. Zion, Myers, Oakland Mills, Parks Ferry, Pleasant Valley, Rose Hill, Saltwell, Shake Rag, Silver Ridge, Stoney Creek, Summitt Station, Sunnyside, Taylors Creek, and Walnut Grove. These communities are scattered over Nicholas County's 208 square miles. Over time, these small communities' schools have been closed, as have most of their post offices, but several still have stores. Stories of their distinct histories and identities are invoked in various ways.

I learned about the significance of landscape in "placing" identity in Nicholas County as I drove Lorrain Irvin, an elderly friend, around the county with a tape recorder running between us one day. She pointed to one set of hillsides now in pasture and named off all the families that had populated those hills before the 1918 flu epidemic decimated the county. She had known those families, and still thought of that as a community. Some people talk about phantom limbs; I learned from Ms. Irvin that day that there are also phantom landscapes—buildings, neighborhoods, farms, and families that are no longer there but by which people may still navigate. There are lots of jokes in U.S. popular culture about rural people giving directions like "turn by the barn that used to be at the corner"; this happens in cities, too, but there is more signage. As I have gotten older, I find myself also navigating by buildings that used to stand and the homeplaces of people now deceased.

Applying notions of global reach, or David Harvey's (1990) "time-space compression," to very localized changes in technologies of communication and travel, the relationship between communities in Nicholas County have changed a lot over time. An elderly resident of Carlisle once described to me her early childhood in Ellisville; when the time came for her parents to send her off to school in Carlisle (seven miles away), she worked in a household there for her room and board, seldom seeing her family. Most of the dichotomies associated with globalization—e.g., rich/poor, urban/rural—play out in Nicholas County, too. Carlisle, though ranging over the decades somewhere between 1,500 and 2,000 residents, is called "the city," and there is separate city and county governance.

Throughout the twentieth century, there were many changes in the smaller communities of Nicholas County, largely associated with the consolidation of schools. In a 1999 oral history interview, Evelyn Brierly described her career as a schoolteacher at a number of schools, all within the county. "In 1924, there were as many as 45 of these schools located throughout Nicholas County. Three of these were black schools at Henryville, Moorefield and Headquarters" (Lane 1976:301). Ms. Brierly had to move away from her home community of East Union for her first job in 1938 as the teacher of 35 children in eight grades in a one-room schoolhouse at Cane Run. Two years later, that school was consolidated into another one, and that was the pattern as she taught her way through six of the many schools in the county. One-room schools were combined with larger schools until they were consolidated into a single elementary and high school for Nicholas County, which I attended and which continue to serve the county's population. The postscript of this book is written by students in the seventh, eighth, and ninth grade at those schools.

Versions of the past, imagined futures, and the social and spatial mapping of place, power, and identity are all connected. I think this process is best theorized through an activity that Nicholas Countians do all the time—"placing" one another amidst all these matrices. People have a powerful penchant for placing ourselves and others. It is how we tell where we are at any given moment in a maze of shifting contexts as we negotiate identities, livelihoods, communities, memoryscapes (like Ms. Irvin's), and landscapes. As Kathleen Stewart (1996) has pointed out in counterpoint to my notions of placing (Kingsolver 1991 and 1992a), people "displace" one another also. We know that it can sometimes take four generations or more to feel "at home" or accepted as local in a community, but it can also be possible to "place" an absolute stranger as somehow local. For example, I was once standing in line at the post office behind a couple who had come to ask where they should erect a rural route mailbox in the yard of their newly purchased home in the county. The postal worker at the window answered their question quickly, but the conversation went on for another 15 minutes. The three of them were "placing" one another. Strangers at first, they did not end the interaction until it had been established that the husband had once worked on a team with the postal worker's cousin in a factory in another county, and that the couple's new home was very close to that of the postal worker's son.

Placing is an important activity in Nicholas County, and elsewhere. I have seen people stand in consternation with each other until they had figured out some relationship, however obscure, historical, or contemporary, between themselves. Placing is a way of dealing with too many potential placements, or with "matter out of place" as anthropologist Mary Douglas (1966) might say, in a small town, and also a way of negotiating and mediating alliances and conflicts. Categories like "us," "not us," "belonging," and "not belonging" can be fairly fluid, and even class and racialized identities are negotiable except at moments when fixity suits a political project, like segregation. Marilyn Thomas-Houston (2005:129–130) has discussed the complex ways in which people negotiate the belonging, or place, of not just individuals but also groups and ideas, and the fact that being or speaking "out of place" can affect the value and power assigned by others to someone's identity or ideas.

People can, by "placing" themselves and others in particular ways, legitimize or delegitimize arguments and claims to authority. In Nicholas County, there is a great deal of heterogeneity and ample opportunity to establish affinity with or distance from an idea someone has, or a political project, by saying about the same person something like "we go to church together" or "well, he's not really from here." One way of thinking about the way we place ourselves and others in relation to ideas, like the development plans for Nicholas County discussed in later chapters, is to think of these as shared projects, or discourses, in which a person might participate. It is possible to participate in multiple discourses simultaneously, and since they may sometimes have contradictory aims, "placing" enables individuals to shift between different emphases regarding identity and relatedness. Two Nicholas Countians might emphasize in one conversation, for example, the fact that they are cousins, or work in tobacco together after work, and in another conversation or social setting the fact that they plan to vote differently in an upcoming election or that one is the other's manager on the shop floor in a factory in another county. Later in this book I will describe how different development discourses (e.g., the promotion of historical tourism or the recruitment of a multinationally owned factory) have gained or lost support in the community because of how these imagined futures and their advocates are "placed" in community life.

There are many Nicholas Counties, depending on who you talk with and in what context, and ways to envision the county's future. Figures can be invoked to describe Nicholas County as marginal to, or as having higher poverty rates than, central Kentucky, but it is also possible to think about the resources available to residents of Nicholas County—like family-provided child care—that are not available to many people in urban centers. Chapter 4, "How to Live in a Small Town," conveys what those I interviewed had to say about the skills required for, and the positive and negative aspects of, living in a small town. By including in this book what Nicholas Countians have to say about the many ways to think about their community and its future, my hope is that common stereotypes about small towns, rural America, tobacco farmers, and Appalachia will be challenged; that readers—however they are "placed"—will consider the ways in which communities are actively and constantly produced; and that rurality might be thought of more in relation to resources, choices, and skills than as a static background or backwater to cosmopolitanism and global decision making.

Rurality and Farming Identity and Practices

Today, rurality is being commodified as something desirable for urban residents wanting a quiet retreat or a "simpler life." There is a burgeoning back-to-the-land movement, particularly among middle- and upper-middle-class, college-educated young adults, as there was in the 1960s and 1970s. What is it that they are looking for in places that they may have themselves dismissed as backward or even racist in other contexts? What does marketing rurality as a commodity mean for the long-term residents of rural areas? With all the scales and types of farming, what does farming mean, as an identity and a skill set? These are some questions I have thought about for a long time, since I was part of an earlier local organic agricultural movement in the early 1980s. Between college and graduate school, I first worked for an organization of small farmers in Tennessee, Arkansas, and Mississippi selling produce cooperatively through farmers' markets in Memphis, and then I directed the Bioregional Project for the New Alchemy Institute on Cape Cod.

I have come to think of farming as a set of skills often passed down in families, enduring mobility and class mobility unless choice or circumstances cut those ties. I can see this in my family, and in other families, and over time I have seen how people draw on these skills when the cash economy is in crisis, as it has been recently in the United States. No matter how far we get from the farm, farming is never far from us, somehow. Our family story is not unlike that of many other Nicholas Countians.

All four of my grandparents were raised on farms in Kentucky. Even after they moved into the city of Lexington, they were urban farmers, growing and preserving their food—e.g., curing hams, canning the vegetables and fruit they grew, and keeping bees—until they died. My mother's father, A. R. Henry, who had started a business building houses, used land during the Great Depression that he had purchased for construction to grow a market garden and run a dairy, drawing on skills he had learned earlier in his life. My paternal grandparents, Roy and Louise Kingsolver, moved back to Nicholas County after he retired from the insurance business. My grandmother continued canning food into her 80s, and grew vegetables into her 90s. My grandfather enjoyed picking blackberries and fishing back in the county where he had lived with his parents as tenant farmers and then on their own farm. There were 15 children in their household, since his parents raised five children left by his older sister when she died, and they had 10 of their own, with nine living to adulthood. In the photo with my grandfather and his father is the team of horses they used to work tobacco and for every form of transport: Kit and Ball.

My father worked summers on his maternal grandparents' farm in Nicholas County and then moved to the county after medical training at the University of Michigan to become a family-practice doctor. He has learned a lot from people in the county during his practice. Other doctors in the region were also working land and raising cattle themselves, as were most school and government employees in the county. Sometimes my father's patients paid their bills in food they had grown or hunted if cash was in short supply. My parents have been growing their own beef, vegetables, and fruit organically for 60 years, and still do. Even though my brother and sister and I left the county for college and have not returned to live in Nicholas County with our families, we have each grown food organically wherever we could throughout our adult lives.

Mike Phillips, who has served as the Nicholas County Extension Agent for 33 years, says that he has seen many young people who grew up on farms in the county move to cities but still draw on their farming skills and identity

James C. Kingsolver, my great-grandfather (left), and his son Roy Kingsolver, my grandfather, with Kit and Ball (photographer unknown)

by getting jobs in secondary industries related to agriculture—farm equipment sales, for example. Lines between the rural and urban blur as people live on the farm (young people putting trailers next to their parents' or grandparents' farmhouses, for example) and commute to the city. There are many strategies for "placing" oneself and for making a living, and those have long included a mix of rural and urban contexts, even as a distinct county or rural identity may be emphasized as "home." Nicholas Countians may not have benefited as much as other regions from various booms, most recently the housing construction boom of the 1990s, but there has also, perhaps, not been so far for rural communities to fall in the "bust" cycles, since subsistence farming skills and noncash economic activities (cf. Halperin 1991) have served as a cushion in hard times.

One way to think of farming, then, is as a skill set and an identity. That equitable sense of farming identity, or Jeffersonian agrarian independence, has often overshadowed something that is also true: farming as a way of life in Nicholas County has usually depended on income from some off-farm sources and also on the unpaid or low-wage labor of some individuals. Most recently, those workers have been Latin American immigrant or migrant workers on the larger farming operations. They are often from farming backgrounds themselves and are using this work as a strategy to keep things going in their own homeplaces. Local farming identity and practices are always also situated within class relations and the global circulation of commodities (cf. Mintz 1985), as is discussed in chapter 2.

Roy Kingsolver (right) with Wendell Kingsolver, my father (photo by author)

Development: Planning for Tobacco Town Futures

The third and fifth chapters of this book, especially, are about the various ways those "placed" inside and outside Nicholas County have envisioned its future over time. Each of those plans for the future of the county is situated within larger (regional, national, and global) discursive projects defining development and development goals according to various bottom lines and long-term trajectories. Modernization, for example, was a project shaping livelihoods and identities (as well as loan structures) in many regions of the world. A modernization perspective views industrialized (often colonizing) nations as desirable for industrializing (often colonized) nations to emulate, and it measures development or progress by the generation of profit and profit-making structures. There have always been critiques of this model by those benefiting least from it, like enslaved or indentured workers. Most recently, critiques of modernization goals and widespread development strategies have focused more on assessing human welfare and long-term sustainability as the bottom lines for development rather than simply quarterly monetary profits reported to shareholders (cf. Sen 1992, Robbins 2008).

Development can mean many things to people, whether marked by literacy, food security, and infant mortality rates; a booming line of businesses on Main Street; or the power to control and make decisions about natural, economic, and social resources (including histories and identities). Just as some terms have been tried in the English language and have not been adopted widely, some plans for development have been tried and have not taken off. In the 1980s, for example, some agricultural experts were recommending to tobacco farmers that their equipment—especially tobacco setters—could be easily converted for tomato cultivation. It was not so easy, however, to find markets for fresh tomatoes at that time, or to convert the identity of Carlisle and Nicholas County from a "tobacco town" to a "tomato town." Twenty-five years later, tomato production is proving to be one of a set of strategies for diversifying agriculture, helped, in part, by the tobacco settlement money (from a lawsuit against cigarette manufacturers related to serious health effects) that Kentucky has used to seed projects in diversifying crops.

Rural development plans in Nicholas County today include growing tomatoes and other vegetables and creating local, regional, and national marketing niches for them, continuing production of beef cattle (which has always subsidized tobacco production), independent contracting with tobacco companies for those who do not want to shift to other crops, and plans in other industries, mostly tourism and manufacturing. The current national project to bring high-speed Internet access to rural regions means that "rural isolation" is less of a factor in terms of social media and telecommuting (or working from home in Nicholas County for a company elsewhere), although the road system is still a practical constraint to the flow of goods and people through the area. In the larger region, rural Kentuckians are increasingly employed in the global service economy, with call centers and Internet book-company shipping centers coming to Kentucky as garment factories leave. Stories about what these changes mean to Nicholas Countians in terms of livelihood and identity, and what they want to see happen in the future, are recorded in this book.

Documentation Dilemmas in this Project

The Internet represents new job opportunities for Nicholas Countians, but it has represented a challenge to me in this long-term documentation project. When I started this research, it was anthropological convention (and part of our ethical practice) not to mention the names of the people or places we were describing, so in my first publications on this project, I used pseudonyms for both Carlisle and Nicholas County. In the ensuing years, however, my older sister has become a famous writer, and it has become a lot easier to find people's hometowns on the Internet, ours included. Thus, I decided to use the name of the community here and to make it a book for Nicholas Countians; any royalties from its publication will go to the Nicholas County public schools for supplies. Residents of the county were kind enough to share their time and stories with me, and this ethnography—intended for local use as well as a national readership of university students in introductory cultural anthropology classes—is one way I can reciprocate. It includes my attempt to encourage young writers in the county. In 2010, I sponsored an essay contest on the future of Nicholas County (in the name of my grandparents, Roy and Louise Kingsolver) for seventh, eighth, and ninth graders in the local public schools. All 47 submissions were mentioned at the Nicholas County Fair. The winners, decided on by a committee of educators and community members, received savings bonds and the promise of publication, since those essays comprise the postscript to this book. I wanted the young people, whose future is being discussed here, to have the last word.

Because of the long-term nature of this project, I had a related dilemma when it came to whether to use pseudonyms for individuals interviewed. Some of the interviews were done under the ethical guidelines of anthropology protecting the anonymity of those interviewed (especially on politically and socially sensitive topics, for example) and some were done as part of a bicentennial oral history project. That project, "200 Years of Farming in Nicholas County," was done in the summer of 1999 (as the county turned 200) with a grant from the Kentucky Oral History Commission. I used that grant to invite two graduate students, A. L. Anderson and Susan C. Langley, to come to Carlisle to do oral history interviews with me. My husband Mark Whitaker, also an anthropologist, helped too. Steve Jackson, a graduate student who was learning to be a filmmaker, volunteered to come along and do some filming of a few interviews. At a Nicholas County Historical Society dinner, I gave a lecture on the history of those whose (sometimes unrecognized) labor had contributed to tobacco farming in Nicholas County over the past two centuries: enslaved Africans, Irish immigrants, migrant workers from farther east in Appalachia, unpaid kin and fictive kin workers, and most recently recent immigrants from Latin American nations. Afterward, we asked those attending the dinner who they thought should be interviewed in the oral history project, and we started with those names and added others that we thought would offer perspectives not represented in the original list of suggestions. Those tapes are in the state archives and the local museum, for use by others.

The oral history interviews were meant as a service project, and I do not draw on too many of those tapes in this book, but where I do, I use people's real names because that is the convention in oral history interviewing. In recent interviews, I have explained that I would be using actual community and individual names in this book. When I draw on earlier interviews, I honor the anonymity agreement made at the time, unless later permission to use a name has been given. Many of those I interviewed in the 1980s were elderly at the time, and have since died. In this book, then, I am using a combination of pseudonyms, real names, and generalized identities in association with quotes. (A generalized identity, for example, means going up several levels of generality in describing a person because he or she might be the only representative of his or her occupational or ethnic identity, for example, in the county and would be easily recognizable since I am now using the name of the town.) I am also using a combination of narratives to convey *Tobacco Town Futures:* interviews, letters people have written to local and regional newspapers over the years, and what I have learned through participant observation and consulting other sources.

Any shortcomings in this book are mine, and one thing about going "home" to Kentucky is that I will be sure to hear about them. I appreciate that long-term "leveling mechanism" at work. When I left town after living in Carlisle for two years of fieldwork in the late 1980s, to return to the University of Massachusetts, Amherst, and write my dissertation, a county official said to me, "You'll never do anything for us here. You're going back to the real world." This book is my attempt, after 25 years of going back and forth between talking with people in the United States, Mexico, and Sri Lanka about globalization and teaching anthropology in Wisconsin, California, and South Carolina, to do something for the county and to show that it is very much part of that same "real world."

The Landscape of This Book

As mentioned above, I am writing here for two main audiences: all Nicholas Countians and introductory cultural anthropology university students. The first group of readers might care more about individual names and details than the second (and will probably be able to "place" them), and the second group might be more interested in anthropological concepts than the first. I have tried to balance this, and to listen to my editor and avoid sticking citations in at the end of every sentence, like doorstops, which is how I tend to write anthropology. Those citations are easy to trip over, but I also believe they are important, since I write as a member of a larger scholarly community and want to acknowledge that. Other Nicholas Countians have published books about the county, for example, and I will reference those texts when possible. At the end of each chapter is a set of increasingly challenging questions for students, which might be used in discussion or for essay assignments at different levels.

The next chapter takes up what it means to be a "tobacco town," and follows discussions of the history and future of that global cash crop. The third chapter situates development plans in Nicholas County, including its recent redesignation as an Appalachian county, with new access to resources available through the Appalachian Regional Commission. The fourth chapter, "How to Live in a Small Town," is certainly not *my* advice, since I cannot claim to be all that good at it, but what I realized was an assertion of skills and resources, not scarcity, associated with small-town life in many of the conversations I had with those who agreed to be interviewed for this project. In that chapter, also, I talk about the valuing and devaluing of different voices and ideas, experiences of inclusion and exclusion in planning processes, and the question of whether young people are represented in community decision making. Several long-term plans for the county's future are followed in this book, and chapter 5 points toward what we might learn from this about facing current challenges, however a reader might construct a "home community" and its future. That concluding chapter includes stories of what has happened on several individual farms since the tobacco buyout. Throughout this book, you will see how people both emphasize and blur distinctions including inside/outside, North/South, local/global, rural/urban, developed/underdeveloped, white/nonwhite, self/other, and historical/current; I see the two abovementioned audiences as blurred, or overlapping, as well.

Questions for Students

1. How are you linked with other people in the world through production, distribution, and consumption? (Look at the labels on your food and clothing, for example.)
2. What are some negative and positive aspects of globalization affecting your community's future?
3. What can you learn from quantitative data (like the U.S. Census profile of Nicholas County) and qualitative data (e.g., information gathered through interviews)? How do qualitative and quantitative methods complement one another in social science research?
4. This project went through several ethical reviews, since it involved long-term research. What are some of the ethical issues you anticipate might be associated with a project like this, and what do you see as some ways to address them?

5. How might you be "placed"? Kirin Narayan (1993:671–672) says: "The loci along which we are aligned with or set apart from those whom we study are multiple and in flux. Factors such as education, gender, sexual orientation, class, race, or sheer duration of contacts may at different times outweigh the cultural identity we associate with insider or outsider status." Think about circumstances in which you have claimed "insider" or "outsider" status in relation to a place, identity, or organization, for example, and discuss ways in which identity claims and the perspective of narration are context-dependent.

6. Humans both produce shared cultural meaning and are shaped—sometimes constrained—by it (cf. Geertz 1973; Weber 1958). An interpretive theoretical lens enables us to examine the contradictory cultural discourses in which we may participate. A political economic lens focuses on the power relationships linked to control of capital and other resources. How do you see both perspectives being used in this book? What does each enable you to think about?

7. Minority voices, e.g., by sexual preference, citizenship status, or racialized identity are being heard increasingly in discussions of rurality (Murdoch and Pratt 1997:58). Keith Halfacree (2003:147) says: "Instead of trying to understand all rural residents in terms of Mr. Average, we need to recognise a number of *marginalized* groups. These groups—*rural others*—reflect diverse economic, social, cultural and other forms of oppression and discrimination." How have you thought about rurality in relation to "othering"?

Chapter 2

Tobacco

A Global Crop

$\mathcal{T}$obacco is a paradoxical weed. In the field, it has to be fed at the bottom and cut off at the top in order to make it produce the large leaves valued in a burley tobacco crop. In communities around the world, it both feeds the people who produce it and kills those who consume its smoked and "smokeless" products. Tobacco farmers are not naïve about that paradox. In this chapter, I

Tobacco crop in the field (photo by author)

will address the question of why tobacco production has been as persistent as this "noxious weed" itself. It was possible to see, even 25 years ago, that tobacco production in Kentucky would need to be cut, which was why I started documenting how people talked about that looming change, but many farmers told me they would keep growing tobacco until it "hit the wall."

Tobacco is a powerful global industry, and even as production in the United States is cut back, tobacco companies find new sources of both producers and consumers. Consumer lawsuits have contributed to restructuring the industry geographically, but not to ending cigarette and chewing tobacco production worldwide. The worldwide production of tobacco has not decreased, and the tobacco companies are benefiting from the neoliberal reprivatization of the industry. There are also secondary industries, such as research and advertising, which support and are supported by the tobacco industry.

For many, like farmers in Nicholas County, there has been a maze of information about the crop and its future to navigate. It has been very difficult to know which research reports to trust, which plans for changing the tobacco program to support, and whether to take a risk on contracting directly with tobacco companies after the dismantling of the national tobacco program. Farmers, tobacco company representatives, and politicians have not spoken with one voice in each constituency—instead, there have been many different arguments to wade through. One of them is the complex set of arguments about whether to produce tobacco at all in the United States, and whether stopping production in the United States would have an impact on the health effects of smoking, since tobacco companies do not stop producing consumer products as farmers in the United States stop producing the crop—they just contract for it elsewhere. This is no doubt a disappointment to health advocacy groups that pressed for the Food and Drug Administration to regulate tobacco and for a reduction in U.S. production of the cash crop.

It may have seemed like the recent Master Tobacco Settlement Agreement (discussed later in the chapter) stemming from consumer lawsuits against four major tobacco corporations would have been a victory for anti-smoking advocates. Although tobacco use slowed in the United States, it did not decline internationally since tobacco companies formed new markets in other countries to replace consumers lost in the United States. The agreement appears, from a global perspective, to have served the interests of the multinational tobacco corporations, which are free once again to contract directly with tobacco farmers. The farmers have little choice now but to take whatever prices the tobacco companies offer, absorbing the risks of—and much of the blame for—growing tobacco. The tobacco settlement agreement and the tobacco buyout program, stemming from the same tide that got NAFTA passed, are part of a much larger pattern of reprivatization of the U.S. and global economy. This could be thought of as a century-long cycle of privatization, nationalization and/or state regulation of industry, and reprivatization that many nations in the world have experienced.

A century ago, for example, the American Tobacco Company (ATC or the Tobacco Trust)—established in 1899 by James Buchanan Duke—became a monopoly by intentionally underselling one of its tobacco products, Lucky Strikes, in which burley was substituted for Turkish tobacco (Badger 1980:17); the ATC used profits from its other profit lines to buy up or shut down 250 other tobacco companies. Nicholas County farmers were among those producing the burley that the ATC was buying. In 1890, farmers in the county sold over two million pounds of tobacco, sealing it up in hogsheads (large barrels) and sending it out of the county by rail. Price wars and increasing tobacco monopolies led to a drop in the prices Kentucky farmers were paid from 8–12 cents per pound in the 1890s to 1–3 cents per pound in 1904 (Axton 1975:84–86).

In 1904, the Association (or Dark-Fired Tobacco District Planter's Protective Association) was formed in Kentucky and Tennessee. It was a "voluntary" cooperative warehousing system through which farmers would be given a small advance for their crops and then were paid in full after the Association had received payment for the tobacco from independent (non-Trust) buyers, some as far away as Italy (Kroll 1965:63). Organizers of the Association saw it as the only way to combat the monopolistic tyranny of the Trust, which was lowering its prices for tobacco steadily, but the Association became tyrannical itself. By 1906, Night Riders—groups of horsemen in intimidating hoods and robes—were carrying out vows to see that growers who sold to the Trust, or who did not belong to the Association, either joined the Association or saw their crops burned and worse, in the terrorizing night raids. Pem Buck (2001) has written about the Night Riders' actions in western Kentucky reducing the number of tobacco farmers—concentrating control of production—and solidifying racialized and class inequalities in land ownership and other aspects of community life that have persisted for over a century.

In eastern Kentucky, the Association was the Burley Tobacco Association, formed in 1907. My grandfather remembered the fear that tenant farmers, especially, had of the Night Riders since a year's living rode on the crop that might be destroyed. The local newspaper printed an account (Shepherd 1989b:6) of Night Riders confronting Hiram Hedges in Ellisville, Nicholas County, and shooting him after an argument. In 1908, a different tactic was tried by the Kentucky farmers: a widespread strike, called by Tracy Campbell (1992:77) "the only large-scale agricultural strike in America." Around 35,000 farmers refused to plant tobacco crops in 1908 because the ATC had boycotted their pooled crops for the two previous years. The strike was announced in Nicholas County, with the Burley Tobacco Association chairman saying, "The situation today is the most critical since the days of the Civil War" and that the only recourse was "the abandoning of the crop for 1908" (Campbell 1992:87). By November, the demands of the farmers' cooperative were met by the ATC, fighting its own battle within the Trust with one of the other companies rising to power: R. J. Reynolds.

The Burley Tobacco Association fell apart within a few years (Campbell 1992:95), but the Trust continued to buy tobacco in the growing number of small tobacco warehouses around eastern Kentucky. Nicholas County (having no tobacco warehouses now) had multiple tobacco warehouses a century ago, including the People's Warehouse and the Red Star Warehouse, names reflecting the more agrarian populist era of the late 1800s and early 1900s, with the Farmers Alliance and the Farmers Union. Alec Simpson, a resident of Henryville in Nicholas County, told an oral history interviewer in 1980 that he remembered four large tobacco warehouses full of activity in the early 1900s, with black and white workers working together loading hogsheads of tobacco onto the train cars. That was the time in which the population of the county was at its highest, with almost 12,000 residents, most of them involved with tobacco production.

Antitrust legislation in 1911 broke up the tobacco monopolies just enough for prices to begin increasing for the farmers, but then the Depression hit. New Deal architects took up the idea of limiting production and raising prices for tobacco as a way to keep the tobacco industry going (with the jobs that entailed) and the small farmers on their land. In 1933, the federal Agricultural Adjustment Act was passed, restricting the production acreage in seven crops including tobacco, and providing for some price supports—not with federal funds, but with federal regulation. The Supreme Court ruled that act unconstitutional, so it was replaced in 1938 by the Farm Price Stabilization Program, which limited acreage in production but called for an annual farmer referendum to maintain the program. In the 1960s, quotas were changed from acreage to poundage because fertilizers were enabling farmers to produce more tobacco per acre. Changes were made that started a shift away from the focus of the Depression-era legislation on keeping small farmers and tenant farmers on the land, since new legislation allowing the leasing of tobacco quotas enabled some Kentucky farmers to have larger operations; that, in turn, made it worth their while to turn to mechanization (Goodman 1993:200–201).

The Federal Commodity Credit Corporation was established in 1938 to loan cooperative warehouses the money to pay farmers in full for their tobacco; some of it could then be marketed later by the pool when the prices were better on the global market. Tobacco, like coffee, can be stored—unlike fresh vegetables—and storage can be used to advantage or disadvantage by both farmers and tobacco companies, since sale does not have to be negotiated immediately before the product goes bad, and there can be stalling tactics to change the price. In 2010, we have come full circle from a privatized market in which monopoly tobacco corporations dictated prices and conditions for the growers a century ago, through a more federally regulated program from the 1930s into the twenty-first century, to a reprivatization of the tobacco industry. That reprivatization, begun in the 1980s with other neoliberal reforms of the U.S. economy, enables large, multinational tobacco corporations to (once again) buy from growers individually—rather than through a cooperative—at the prices they say are globally competitive. I began my field-work in the 1980s when the first inklings of those neoliberal changes were being felt in Nicholas County.

An Afternoon in Tobacco in 1988: Storm Coming

Watching the dark sky through the storm door of their house, Farley Wayne Wright, his wife Imogene, and I had waited for Peggy Tilford to drive in from her job at the apparel factory in the next county. Imogene was not coming with us, so after Peggy arrived, there were three of us in the front seat of a sky-blue Chevrolet on our way to set tobacco on the Cromer place on that June day: Peggy, Farley Wayne, and me.

The Wrights and the Tilfords had each grown tobacco crops on the Cromer place the year before, and had done all the labor on both crops together. But this year, the Wrights were not growing a crop and Farley Wayne was being paid to help the Tilfords. Farley Wayne was also helping a number of other friends and relatives with their crops this season, for wages instead of exchanged labor. Many people were shifting over to paying relatives this year instead of trading labor. One farmer growing a tobacco crop on his own land told me that he had three sisters, three brothers-in-law, and two brothers who had always just "swapped around" to get their crops in, but this summer he was paying his relatives $3/hour, the going rate, for setting and topping the crop, and he would be paying them $6/hour for tobacco housing, like everybody else.

Imogene Wright had always helped with the field labor when the Wrights were pitching in on crops as a family—she had felt it was only fair—but now that the work was for pay, she chose to stay home and work on the house after her day of working in a service job. Besides, Peggy Tilford was Farley Wayne's first cousin, not hers.

When Peggy had driven up, we had jumped into Farley Wayne's car without her passing any time of the day with Imogene; this was definitely work, not visiting time. Also, Peggy's husband Jim and sons James Lee and Randy were already out at the Cromer place. Jim had picked up the boys at his mother's after he got off work from the textile plant in Nicholas County. Farley Wayne worked there, too, as Jim's manager.

The Tilfords and Wrights were combining farm and factory work, like most farming families in Nicholas County, organizing tobacco labor at night after work, which was getting harder and harder to do as the factories were instituting forced overtime to make their quotas. It was hard to plan ahead when no one knew when the shift would end, but family members were more likely to put up with that than other workers one might hire to help with a crop. Both the Wrights and the Tilfords had been in a lease agreement with the Cromer family for years, leasing the tobacco base that was attached to the deed of the Cromers' land by the 1933 Agricultural Adjustment Act. This was not a tenant farming relationship. There were not many of those in the county any more. Most people had their own house now and were attached in different ways to farmland through kith and kin and long-standing lease agreements, like this one.

The Cromers, a multigenerational farming family, were mostly interested in raising beef cattle, and they leased the tobacco base attached to various parcels of their combined farmland to the Tilfords for a tenth of the gross profits from the tobacco crop. At the time, in the 1980s, most people in the county using tobacco base, or quota, in this way to raise a crop would be raising it "on the halves," or for half the profits, giving half to the owner of the base instead of being allowed to keep 90 percent of the profits, as the Tilfords were able to do under their arrangement with the Cromers. Various calculations of fixed or percentage crop yields and uses of land, barn space, equipment, and water went into lease agreements, which might be passed down between generations. These types of agreements were increasingly made between widows who had moved into town and the few younger farmers who were taking on more and more "base" to try to be full-time farmers, also maintaining equipment that they could use to bale others' hay, for example. As passed-down equipment was breaking down, it was getting more and more difficult for part-time farmers to be able to afford to fix or replace it, so equipment arrangements were figured in along with labor in lease agreements.

Each year, both the person raising the crop and the person holding the deed with the tobacco allotment (if the person raising the tobacco crop and quota-holder are different people) need to show up at the local office of the U.S. Agricultural Stabilization and Conservation Service (ASCS) to prove the right to raise the crop and to be issued a marketing card, which then needs to be shown at the warehouse to demonstrate the right to sell the crop legally. In 1988, the going rate for leasing tobacco was around 60 cents per pound (or about half the market price). That season, about 800 marketing cards were issued in Nicholas County (one crop being raised for nearly every third household). "Chemical cards" were issued by the USDA (U.S. Department of Agriculture) Extension Service office in the county, certifying that the bearer was over 16 and had attended a class and passed a test about the safe application of chemicals in the cultivation of tobacco, but several young men commented on the irony of this process: they sat through a film telling them to wear gloves and masks when handling health-endangering chemicals; they got their cards; then they went out into the fields, and their relatives or other employers told them to apply the chemicals as they always had—without protection. Some people still burned the tobacco beds to prepare them (getting rid of unwanted seeds and larvae), but many "gassed" them with methyl bromide, a gas poisonous to humans, if they could afford the chemicals. Some farmers do not read, and the workers in the agricultural offices help them fill out the forms to get their market cards, the most vital piece of paperwork needed for raising the crop.

On our way to the Cromer place, Peggy asked Farley Wayne when he usually went to work. He said he was out the door by 6:10 in the morning, and was working by 6:20. He had worked nine hours that day, in the packaging area of the textile and apparel plant. I asked him how it had gone. He said, "About like every other one—I work hard all day. The more you do, the more they want." The local factory Farley Wayne and Jim worked in used to be a sister to the one where Peggy worked, in the next county over. A multinational corporation bought out the local plant, and the local owners bought out the plant in the next county over, seeing it as a better risk. That had ruffled a few feathers in Nicholas County, but the owners took a number of local workers with them to the next county when they took over that plant. Peggy said she had worked over there even before the shake-up.

Peggy said that she left for work at 6:45 each morning and was at her desk in the factory by 7:30. She worked in the office as a contact for one of the buyers, and it was her job to decide which "cuts" would be assigned to the floor (what clothing parts would be cut and sewn to meet the customer's order). She had to bring home a lot of paperwork, usually, but she said she did not bring home any on nights when the family was going to work in tobacco. She said she had stayed at work the Friday before until 10:30 PM, preferring that to going in and working her overtime on the Saturday of a holiday weekend.

Farley Wayne turned his Chevrolet off the main road and crossed two cattle guards, winding up the dirt driveway around the elder Cromers' home and on up to the field behind their house. Part of the arrangement between the families was that the Tilfords (and formerly the Wrights, also) could use their most fertile fields, their tobacco barns, and their 8,500-pound tobacco allotment, or "base," in exchange for 10 percent of what the crop brought at the warehouse after it had been stripped and sold.

This night of setting tobacco, for which we had come, would be the second of four needed to get the crop out. As we rounded the lower corner of the field, Farley Wayne remarked that the plants already set were "standing up good." That was taken as a good sign, since Jim had needed to reset his crop five times the year before. Tobacco plants are robust, but they can be finicky about being transplanted. It is not unusual to have to "set" the crop multiple times, and that is one of three most labor-intensive points in the burley tobacco cultivation cycle. (Those points are "setting," "cutting and housing," and "stripping"—putting the crop in the ground in early summer, cutting it at the end of the summer and hanging it on rails in the barn to be air-cured, and stripping the leaves off the stalk when they are "in case," or moist enough, in the beginning of winter to bundle for market.) Reasons for the crop failing to become a good "stand" of tobacco after being set may include the plants having been washed out, or having dried up, or the field not being prepared properly, but sometimes it remains a mystery to the grower why the crop has to be reset. New seedlings can be borrowed or bought, if a crop has to be reset more than the anticipated number of times, but a crop might be abandoned if the labor costs for setting numerous times represent too many diminishing returns on the crop, especially given other risks. We did not know it yet, on this afternoon, but 1988 would go on to be a drought year. Water was rationed throughout the county, ponds dried up, and hay was donated to Kentucky from across the nation. The odds were not favorable for this crop, but it did eventually make it to the barn.

Women, men, and children are all considered capable of pulling the young tobacco plants from the beds in which they have grown from seed, and "pulling" plants is often done in family groups, as Jim and the boys had done. For setting, at least three or, better, four workers are needed: one to drive the tractor, two to ride the setter, and any additional workers can follow the setter and check water flow and plant condition for the others, filling in any plants by hand that have been missed by the setter. Other jobs the extra workers can do to speed setting are to fill the tank on the tractor with water and additives, and hand bundles of plants to those riding on the setter so the tractor can just turn around at the end of each row without the three primary workers getting off the tractor or setter. The speed at which the tractor goes regulates the speed at which water is squirted onto the freshly set plants (so one drives more slowly in a dry season) and the speed at which the setter rotates. The two people riding the spring seats on either side of the setter, with their backs to the driver of the tractor, alternately lay plants, roots-first, onto the cupped ends of the mechanical setter's rotating arms. From the cups, plants are dropped into furrows, which two plow-like blades on the setter open and close.

The job that probably demands the most skill in setting tobacco is riding the setter. Since the two persons alternately feed the setter plants, one is a right-handed setter and one is called a left-handed setter; these need not correspond to whether a person is considered left- or right-handed. The two individuals riding the setter have to be matched in skill to be able to set quickly, or else the mistakes of the slower partner have to be covered by the person whose job it is to follow the setter, on foot, filling in the gaps in the rows with plants.

There have been, and still are, pairs of tobacco setters who are famed and sought-after in the region. Setting is one of the jobs in tobacco production (like stripping) that is not considered gender-specific. The skill of setting is usually taught in families, since children accompany parents and other relations to the tobacco patch from a very early age. One woman told me that she had taught all of her daughters to set tobacco, and some of them were left-handed setters and some were right-handed setters. She sets from either side, herself, so she could teach them both ways.

As we drove up the hill to meet Jim and the boys, Peggy said she thought the last crop they had set had not done well because of the soil. Farley Wayne did not offer a reason. He stayed quiet. It was not his crop. Along the top edge of the field lay the beds, the canvas thrown back from the ones where Jim and the boys had been pulling plants. Peggy asked Farley Wayne and me if we needed any lettuce. Farley Wayne teased her about "turning into a farm girl yet, learning to plant lettuce around the borders of the beds" under the tobacco canvas. We bumped to a stop next to the tractor, the wagon, and the pickup truck in which Jim, James Lee, and Randy were waiting for us. By this time, it had started to sprinkle on our windshield.

Jim and the boys had been pulling plants for three hours. They had made up 44 burlap bundles of 50 plants each, and these lay on the wagon around the base of the water tank. The boys, ages 15 and 10, said a little later that their father was a real taskmaster, wanting the plants to be "just so big and all the same," and they complained that he did not give them breaks. James Lee and Randy did not work for a wage, for a calf, or for half the tobacco check come December, like some of their friends did. They worked to add to the household income, and they were looking forward to their trip to Washington, D.C., when the factories let out for vacation, as much as their parents were.

Farley Wayne got out of the car and walked around the truck to lean on Jim's window. As Jim told Farley Wayne how many bundles they had ready and where the earliest-pulled bundles—most needing to be set—lay on the wagon, Peggy scooted over behind the driver's wheel and motioned for her sons to roll down the window of the truck. She asked, "What do you know?" To her youngest's reply of "Nothin'," she said, "Don't you have any opinion about anything?" Randy said, "Yeah, supper. I want a chili dog with a Coke at the Dairy Queen."

Peggy shivered. She had changed into shorts before she left work, but it was turning cool quickly. She and I watched the rain pick up and the lightning strike, first two fields away and then in the next field. Farley Wayne came back to the car, and we rolled up the windows and sat for a while. We waited 45 minutes or so for the rain to slack off. Farley Wayne joked that Jim was scared of lightning, but they both knew the danger of putting people and metal equipment in the middle of an open field in a thunderstorm. Farley Wayne was eager to get to work and to get the whole crop out during the weekend, since he had other people to help. At the factory, Jim answered to Farley Wayne and was responsible for making sure the department that Farley Wayne managed had all the parts it needed. Here, though, Jim was in charge, and Farley Wayne not only waited for the younger man's sign but also said several times, "You're the boss."

When Jim got out of his truck and mounted the tractor, we knew it was time to go to our posts. Farley Wayne and Peggy climbed onto the setter behind the tractor, Randy and I loaded their trays with plants, and James Lee filled the water tanks on the tractor from the big one on the wagon. This season they were adding an herbicide to the water, which was sprayed onto the plants as they were set. The chemicals also got on the hands of those of us following the setter, whose job it was to right crooked plants. The others told me the herbicide "really stinks," but "it cuts down on the hoeing." As the five of us set out on our first row, the clay sucked at our feet and the tractor wheels, and the sun had just about gone down.

Tobacco: Local Leaves in a Global Commodities and Labor Market

Thinking back to the statement by Jane Nadel-Klein (1991:502) I quoted in the introduction that "local identity is an unintended result of the global division of labor," it is quite possible to attribute the very existence of Carlisle and other small "tobacco towns" to the global commodity of tobacco. In the U.S. colonial era, tobacco was itself used as a currency. Two centuries ago, when Nicholas County was founded and Kentucky's role in the United States as a commonwealth was new, tobacco was a booming business all across this rural region. It is not too hard to imagine attributing agency to tobacco, like "King Coal," and watching it people the landscape for the purpose of propagating itself, even though the Native American and European American settlements around Nicholas County were actually founded to take advantage of the salt lick that had brought mastodons to the area earlier, and tourists later. Early Kentuckians, reliant on river travel, considered seceding from the U.S. and becoming part of Spain to make it easier to get tobacco and other products to global consumers by going down their rivers to the Mississippi and on to the Spanish-controlled port of New Orleans instead of going over the mountains and east (Shannon 1976:28). Kentucky's tobacco traveled in 1,200-pound hogsheads on wooden "river arks" (Clark 1977:15–16).

Nicholas County was global from its founding, in 1799. At that time, one in six of its residents was an enslaved African. The transatlantic slave trade, marketing humans as commodities, facilitated the production of other globally circulated commodities, like tobacco. The 1850 census rolls for the county, besides the unrecorded birthplaces of a number of Nicholas Countians from regions of Africa, documented immigrants who had come to the county from 25 states and eight other nations (80 from Ireland, 16 from England, 14 from Germany, two from France, and one each from Scotland, Canada, Jamaica, and Wales). This global/local community brought farming skills and knowledge of commodities markets from many places. The production of textiles, for example, has been a fairly consistent skill set in the community. In 1810, there were sheep eating the grass on the hillsides of Nicholas County down to the stone, and 312 manufacturing looms produced 58,898 yards of cloth. There were tanneries, distilleries, a gunpowder mill, and salt works; 21 tons of hemp were prepared for the global market in 1810, and 51,384 pounds of maple sugar. Diversified production, focus on a cash crop, and various mixes of cash/noncash economic strategies have cycled through the small communities of Nicholas County just as they have in the myriad other nodes of the global economic system.

Farmsteads grew in their diversity of production even as tobacco started increasing as a commodity toward the middle of the nineteenth century. In 1850, for example, the Nicholas County census rolls show that a farmer named Zachariah lived on a hundred-acre farm with his family, cultivating half of that land; they kept horses, cattle, sheep, and hogs, and produced 40 bushels of wheat, 1,200 bushels of Indian corn, 42 pounds of wool, two bushels of peas and beans, 12 bushels of Irish potatoes, 300 pounds of butter, one ton of hay, and 20 pounds of maple sugar (and that is just what they officially declared). One 1850 resident of Nicholas County, H. C. Myers, was a boarder and listed his occupation as "capitalist." Global capitalism, as a way of organizing both markets and daily lives in various local forms, was in a phase of expansion hand in hand with colonialism around the world, and that shaped life in rural Kentucky as much as it did the colonizing and colonized nations from which new Nicholas Countians had immigrated.

William Emmons, born in Nicholas County in 1846, told his life story to a WPA worker in the 1939 slave narrative oral history program (Rawick 1977:326–331). His service record is in the National Archives. Here is a summary of his story. William Emmons was born near Carlisle. His father, Boyd, was owned by Hiram Norton, and his mother was owned by the Riggs family. When William was seven years old, he and his mother were separated. William was sold to Roy Emmons, and his mother was sold to the Banister family, in Moorefield. Sometimes William was able to visit his mother and seven siblings. But his daily life was spent on the Emmons farm, and William lived with the Emmons name from the time he was bought to work there.

William Emmons recalled that on the Emmons plantation in Nicholas County, there were 1,500 acres and 15 enslaved workers who lived in cabins with three rooms each and five-foot-wide fireplaces. He told the interviewer that Roy Emmons neither beat the slaves he owned nor allowed them to learn to read. They were not paid for their work. Each year, they were given three pairs of shoes and jeans. Any other clothing they wore, they wove themselves.

William worked there until he was 18, when he left to enlist in the Union troops. His everyday jobs on the Emmons place included milking, driving stock to the creek when the ponds got low, and plowing. He attended an integrated log church in Carlisle, and—when it came to town—Dan Rice's Circus.

On September 5, 1864, William Emmons left Nicholas County on foot with several other young men. By that time, he was owned by Polly Emmons. William said some men tried to stop them, but they said they were going to enlist and went right on to Covington, where they signed up for the Union Army. He became a private in Company H, the 117th Colored Infantry organized that summer in Covington, Kentucky, across the Ohio River from Cincinnati. The Company H soldiers were trained at Fort Nelson and served at the siege of Petersburg and Richmond. They were at the fall of Petersburg, pursued General Lee's troops, and were present at the surrender of Lee and his army at the Appomattox Court House. William Emmons was wounded twice during the Civil War. His company was mustered out of service in Texas in 1867.

William Emmons moved to Ripley, Ohio, where he lived with his wife Sylvia, and then, after she died, his wife Eliza Cowin, with whom he had 12 children. He outlived all of them but one, Guy Emmons, with whom he was living when he was interviewed by the WPA worker during the Great Depression.

This is the story of just one of the approximately 500 African Americans who left Nicholas County between 1860 and 1870. When I took history classes in the county as a child, a hundred years later, I was taught that there had not been slavery in Nicholas County because flat, rich land was needed for big plantations and that our land was too hilly for that kind of farming. What had happened to the history of Mr. Emmons and so many others? How had that history been remembered and forgotten in different communities within the county? I did know as a child growing up "white" that there had been segregated schools before I went to the consolidated Nicholas County Elementary School and that there was a part of Carlisle that was called Henryville in which most of the residents identified as African American. The global history that forged the first African American Nicholas Countians' individual histories, however, was not connected to what we learned from each other, as children, about racialization and class and how those processes related to the social and physical landscape of the county. I did not learn until I was an adult that there were oral and written histories—one of them called "the book"—passed from generation to generation in Henryville. Among other things, they chronicled African American land ownership in the county (sometimes not matching the recorded deeds in the courthouse, since some of those deeds were oral, and that difference has been exploited at times).

What other global stories were told and forgotten over time? The story of global capitalism, with connections being made between people and places through activities of production, distribution, and consumption was of course related to the forced migration of Africans with many diverse languages, skills, and regional identities to the United States, and to Kentucky. Sidney Mintz (1985) and other scholars have written about the need for tobacco, coffee, tea, and sugar—largely produced on colonial plantations, and then as cash crops—to fuel the industrial revolution in Europe, since they helped workers get through extended shifts and repetitive tasks in factory jobs. Kentucky contributed tobacco to the global market in large amounts. By 1880, Kentucky had surpassed Virginia as the state producing the most tobacco and was producing twice as much tobacco as any other state; Kentucky was responsible at that time, in fact, for producing over 170 million pounds of tobacco—one-third of the nation's total production. In Nicholas County, in 1880, hogsheads of tobacco were selling at around $2 each, and daily wages for work in tobacco were 75 cents/day to produce the 800–900 pounds of tobacco per acre being grown.

After the nonwage enslaved labor system that had brought the migration of African workers to Nicholas County ended, and William Emmons and many other experienced farmworkers left the county, there were other migrations into the county to provide low-wage labor in tobacco. While small farms are thought of as self-contained units and farmers are thought of as working for themselves, Kentucky tobacco farms have always been related to global economic cycles. Farmers have taken on most of the risk but little of the profit in the global tobacco industry. Their fate has been tied to the fate of this global crop and to world events like the Irish potato famine and the collapse of the Mexican peso after neoliberal reforms, since those have been factors in the migration decisions of some of the workers who have ended up on Nicholas County tobacco farms. Of course, over the centuries, all of the residents of Kentucky—including the first Native Americans to use its resources—have been migrants or immigrants. But there have been waves of transnational migration in the past two centuries, since Nicholas County became a county, which have led to differences in nationality, language, accent, and racialized identity between many farmers and the farmworkers who might get work on farms at peak moments in the tobacco production cycle.

In the United States, since whiteness is constructed as the defining identity, powerful legal and political structures have encouraged white land ownership and access to capital. People defined in an arbitrarily racializing scheme as nonwhite or "other," often recent immigrants, have had less access to land or capital and have therefore often been identified as a low-wage labor force. There are, then, powerful cultural constructions that are built up through layers of everyday experience that associate the word "farmer" with "whiteness" and "farmworker" with some "othered" identity—either minority or migrant or both. In 2010, African American farmers won a class-action lawsuit against the U.S. Department of Agriculture for discrimination in farm loan programs; they had not been recognized equally as farmers. In Nicholas County, "farmer" tends to be associated with whiteness *and* maleness; the word "farmworker" tends to be associated with either minority identity, migrant status, or both. Like farmer, farmworker is a term usually associated with masculinity. People of all ages have worked in tobacco fields with farmers, however, and both farmers and farmworkers in Nicholas County have been of both genders and many racialized and ethnic identities (Kingsolver 2007:95).

On small farms, tobacco crops have usually been produced through labor networks of kin and friendship that would belie stereotypical distinctions between farmer and farmworker, but at pressing times in the production cycle, especially as factory shifts became more unpredictable, migrant workers have been hired to provide temporary additional labor (and that hiring process solidified the distinction). At different moments, those seasonal migrant workers have been predominantly from Ireland, from farther east in the Appalachian region, and from Mexico and Central American nations. Sonny Simpson, Sr., whose grandmother had been an enslaved worker in Nicholas County, said in a 1999 oral history interview: "Mexicans. They are the ones who do all the work around here now. You see them on the street. Farmers pick them up and they go out and do the farmwork."

Ten years earlier, in 1988, farm labor shortages had become a crisis in the region. Farmers had trouble finding enough neighbors and relations to exchange labor to produce their tobacco crops, and the flow of migrants from farther east in Appalachia was slowing down. A farmer in a county next to Nicholas County told a reporter, "Usually about this time, (field) hands will drift into my store from surrounding counties and Eastern Kentucky looking for work in tobacco. . . . But not this year, I haven't seen a man. There have been a couple of carloads of women, but not a single man" (Poole 1988). Other farmers in the region talked of using workers in work-release programs from regional jails to meet the critical need for skilled tobacco-cutting labor (Poole 1988).

A farm paper sent to tobacco growers advocated the use of skilled migrant farmworkers from Latin America: "The best hope for a larger labor pool lies in the use of migrant workers. If the use of migrants becomes wide-spread, it could ease the severe labor shortage that has plagued burley producers" ("Next Year's Leaf Crop" 1990). Some tobacco warehouse managers became the labor contractors for connecting Latin American immigrant seasonal workers with local farmers, some through the federal agricultural visa (H2A) program that authorizes workers to be on a specific farm, but most crews were recruited to work without H2A authorization on a number of farms, since few farms in the area were large enough to maintain a crew of farmworkers full-time. That is why family, neighbor, or temporary migrant labor had been pieced together, but that patchwork quilt of labor arrangements was fraying. One tobacco warehouse manager explained the shift in tobacco labor as being related to the new Toyota assembly plant (discussed in chapter 3) in the region:

> Kentucky tobacco growers, long concerned about threats to their industry from overseas, have this year found some imports they seem to like. They're imported workers, Mexican migrant laborers that have come into a few burley growing areas to provide desperately needed help in harvesting tobacco. "We simply can't find any help locally for this kind of farm work," explains Mike Ammerman, who contracted for a group of migrant workers to help farmers in Harrison and Pendleton counties. Ammerman, who with his father Bobby manages tobacco warehouses and operates farms, says the industrial boom in Central Kentucky fueled by the Toyota auto plant in Georgetown has virtually depleted what little labor pool existed in previous years. ("Burley Imports" 1989)

One of the first farmers in Nicholas County to hire workers through Ammerman's Warehouse was Elmo Myers. He paid $700 for their 45-hour bus trip from El Paso, Texas. They were originally from Chihuahua, Mexico. In Nicholas County, Myers paid them $4 an hour and provided food, and housing in a trailer. They had not worked in tobacco before. Myers said: "I treat them like one of the family, and they do good work in return . . . if it works out, I imagine more farmers around here will use them" (Shepherd 1989a).

I often heard farmworkers, whether tenant or migrant workers, referred to in Nicholas County as "one of the family." Susanna Donaldson (2009), an anthropologist studying tobacco farming in east Tennessee, has noticed that as Latin American immigrant workers are recruited by farmers to work in tobacco there, they are recruited through the same kin networks that used to exchange labor. As I was doing my fieldwork in the late 1980s, I found that kin networks of unpaid labor exchange were just beginning to break down, and friends and relatives were beginning to pay each other by the hour since every-one needed the cash, and they were competing with other kinds of work.

"Tobacco Town" Livelihoods

An older farmwoman once leaned over to me and said, "There's only one god around here, and that's tobacco." She immediately blushed and said, "Don't say I said that." Her name is safe with me, but she had a point. If not a god, tobacco serves in Nicholas County as what anthropologists call a "key symbol" (Ortner 1973): something that is referenced in many different ways in organizing and understanding social life. The landscape, material culture, social networks, economic cycle, and agricultural knowledge base of the county are all strongly linked to tobacco. Festival queens have been crowned on tobacco wagons; bills in many local businesses have been paid annually when the tobacco checks come in January; and tobacco even influences sporting events and art. Tobacco wreaths have been sent home with interna-tional travelers as aromatic souvenirs of the region, and tobacco-related items were placed in a time capsule buried in the community.

John van Willigen and Susan Eastwood (1998:1), in their book *Tobacco Culture: Farming Kentucky's Burley Belt*, say, "A burley tobacco culture exists. Men and women who raise burley tobacco share knowledge about tobacco production, a language with which they talk about tobacco, and even a sense of tobacco politics." Children share in that tobacco culture, too, as they are socialized into it. Tobacco companies and organizations feature families exemplifying tobacco farming values, or best practices, in their magazines. There are hotlines to call for tobacco prices, and weather reports seen and heard by everyone in the community are geared for tobacco growers. There are many ways in which institutions—banks, government agricultural offices, churches, and schools—have supported a "tobacco way of life." When I was in elementary school, children might be out of the classroom for many days at key moments in setting or stripping a tobacco crop. Today, children are much more likely to be working in the school's community garden started by David Wagoner, a local organic farmer, than at home helping in a tobacco crop, and the barn in which the vocational agriculture students in the high school used to hang their crop stands empty, perhaps to be populated by the school's goat herd in the future. Tobacco culture, even if referred to as static, is always changing in this region; many wonder if this time, the key symbol is setting like an amber sun and the many relationships and skills that have gone into constructing a "tobacco town" will be used to construct something else. The next chapter documents some efforts toward that end.

In 1987, one business owner told me, "We can sure feel the fall of tobacco in our cash register, and I bet you'd hear the same thing from any other business in Carlisle." It was getting harder to match loan payment cycles with the annual tobacco checks, and as noted earlier, labor exchanges among families and friends were starting to be for pay instead of for free. Tobacco skills were still highly valued, though, as in the regional tobacco-cutting contest held in Bourbon County on the hottest day of the summer (August 18, 1987:97 degrees). Mike Kenney, a Nicholas Countian, placed third in the contest; in the photo below, he is chopping a tobacco plant off at the base of its stalk, and his wife Barbara is putting a spear on the end of a tobacco stick onto which six plants are stacked and left stuck in the ground to dry until they are gathered up on a wagon and taken to a barn to be hung up on rails to cure through the fall. Mike and Barbara Kenney have been career school basketball coaches. The tobacco-cutting contest celebrated the athletic aspect of tobacco-cutting. On an average day of cutting tobacco, a worker might have to bend over 6,000 times to cut tobacco stalks, and both speed and accuracy are valued in the field. In the contest pictured, Mike Kenney averaged four sticks (or 24 tobacco plants cut) per minute. When he worked in tobacco in 1987, he was paid 7 cents per stick, and could earn $7.50 an hour, which was over twice the minimum wage at that time.

In Nicholas County, most of the jobs in the formal sector—e.g., teacher, judge, banker, maintenance worker, business owner, construction worker, doctor, cashier, factory worker, cook—have been held by individuals who were either farming or had a family member who did. Part of what has made Carlisle a "tobacco town" has been the fact that there is not a strong partition between the knowledge base and class identities of people in different occupations—those work-based identities, and the skills that go with them, are cross-cutting and overlapping (particularly in farming). I do not mean, here, that there are not socioeconomic disparities, or class differences, in Nicholas

County. In 1980, one-fifth of the county's population was living under the poverty line (one-third more than in the state as a whole). Further, these disparities were racialized: 50 percent of African American households in the county were living under poverty level 30 years ago. (The percentage of Nicholas Countians living under the poverty line has now dropped to 13 percent, which is 3 percent below the state average.) Twenty-five years ago, as I began this "tobacco town" documentation project, there

Mike (left) and Barbara Kenney in tobacco-cutting contest (photo by author)

were families in the community with far more than enough, like mine, and families in which parents had to either forego meals themselves—one mother told me she drank a lot of water on days she could not eat, to feel less hungry—so they could feed something to their children, or send the children to a neighbor or relative's house for a meal.

Both economic and cultural class distinctions (not always the same thing) have certainly been made by Nicholas Countians in reference to each other, sometimes in talk about different churches and communities around the county as well as in talk about individuals. As in many eastern Kentucky towns, there were class terms like "across the tracks" and "silk stocking row" that were still used rarely, but these terms had more salience in the social and physical landscape of the early 1900s. In the 1960s and 1970s, though, class distinctions were played down in "tobacco culture" just as they were in the nation overall during an expansion of the middle class.

For recent generations in Nicholas County, Stephen Resnick and Richard Wolff's (1987) notion of "class process"—a more fluid, or relational, way of thinking about the class positions individuals occupy at any given moment—describes community life better than a more rigid model of class, since people have been shifting between positions of control over work processes even during the same day. One example of this was when Farley Wayne, who was Jim's manager at work in the factory, was working that night for Jim in the tobacco field; he made sure to signal that by saying numerous times, "You're the boss." This shifting of hats and roles is common in Carlisle, and skills are valorized in ways that cut across more standard understandings of class position. My mother hired Mary Ann Moore to help her clean her house once a week, for example, and Mary Ann Moore hired me to make her granddaughter's prom dress because she knew that I had done sewing and cleaning work for people in Memphis while I was in college. The categories of "employer" and "employed" have been intertwined in many ways in the community, then, and the line between cash and noncash work has also been a bit fluid. Family members may pay one another for work, for example, and nonfamily members may do noncash work, especially caring work that would fall under "neighboring" (discussed in chapter 4).

I am explaining all this particularly for readers who may think of individuals as associated with a single job that would denote a specific class position. Just as "tobacco culture" has been constructed in very different ways at different moments, "livelihood" is negotiated and constructed all the time in Nicholas County (as in many places), and livelihood in this tobacco town often involves a mix of strategies (e.g., farmwork and factory work) for households, with a lot of different roles—which may fluctuate between what might be seen in dominant U.S. culture and media as "classed" occupations and identities. As I write in this book about how people have imagined "tobacco town futures," the tobacco town they are imagining slipping away involves this particular configuration of livelihoods and social networks, with employment opportunities in tobacco, textile, and service industries as part of the

for-cash strategies going into the mix. All of those options have been diminishing in the last few years (with the service sector—jobs in government and
education—being the remaining stable employer). Another way in which
"tobacco town" life is changing is that some professionals (health professionals, lawyers, and teachers) are commuting to work in Nicholas County, as are
some of the seasonal tobacco workers, so it is more likely in 2010 than it was
25 years ago for a person to be placed one-dimensionally in a fixed notion of
class and occupation.

Part of the traditional "leveling" work in Nicholas County that has kept
people from valorizing themselves too far above anyone else is what might be
thought of as "placing" play, which reminds people of other power relations
they may have in other aspects of their relationships. Twenty-five years ago,
for example, when many women in the county were working in the local factory sewing underwear or working in service jobs to bring health benefits into
farming households, one woman told me about her husband (in front of
him), "He can farm as long as I teach," playing with the primacy of off-farm
and farmwork in the household. They both laughed. Farmwork is not
accounted for by the hour, as off-farm work is, so household members in a
tobacco town have not been likely to compare their hourly wages. Steve Vice,
who was helping his father in the family dairy in 1987 as well as raising beef
cattle on his own farm and raising tobacco and hay crops said, "A farmer's
day is 16 hours" (Duncan 1987a:2). Many, like Jim and Farley Wayne, who
farm after hours worked in other jobs, see it as extra income as well as part of
a way of life.

Swapped labor has been embedded in experiences of kinship in Nicholas
County. When I asked one couple whether they were going to attend an event
at a nearby state park, they said no, they would be housing tobacco. "With
your family?" I asked Brenda. "No, mine," Norville said. "They contact me
three times a year—Christmas, when they need something, and when it's
time to house tobacco." I asked, "Does that suit you just as well?" "Tickles
me," he replied. He and his father had gotten closer lately working on
machinery together, which they kept at his father's place. He said that he had
spoken on the phone with his father for the first time ever a few nights before;
his mother had always been the one to use the telephone to call him, even
when he was away in the service. Like Norville, most people in the county
have access to land through a relative. The average farm size in the county is
currently 181 acres, with over 90 percent of farms being operated by individuals or families.

There is an understanding between family members and everyone else in
this tobacco town that farming tobacco has been a risky business, even with
the federal tobacco program in place to keep prices from falling too low at
sale time. Getting a crop to that point is not easy: some years there are diseases like blue mold or black shank to deal with. Some years, like 1988 and
1999, have been such severe drought years that counties in the region were
declared disaster areas and hay was donated from other regions just to keep

the cattle alive. In 1988, I attended a community-wide prayer service in which people from across the county, including government agricultural representatives, gathered to pray for rain. Other years have brought flooding, like 2010 (another year of being declared a disaster area). One young farmer, who was leasing a number of other people's tobacco base in the 1980s so he could farm tobacco full-time, told me:

> A farmer takes every risk that there is going. When he starts out he's got everything working against him, insects are against him, and if there are any price reductions, they are against him.

Using older equipment (which is what most part-time farmers have) on steep hillsides is a very real physical risk, in addition to the risks farmers take in the global tobacco market. Eastern Kentucky has one of the highest rates of tractor roll-overs. Recently, one farmer attributed his life to his family insisting on his starting to carry a cell phone. He was able to make a call after his tractor rolled over on him, and got help. Part-time farmers working at night, after full shifts in other jobs, are prone to injury from weariness, as well. Pressured by a coming rain, too many have tried to bale hay when they are too tired (or it is too dark) and had a limb caught in the hay bailer. Rolling hay rather than bailing it saves labor, but it also means that one person is likely to be out in a field alone instead of working with a partner who might be able to help in case of an injury. Health insurance—with risks from accidents and chemical exposure—has been a pressing need on farms, and as nonfamily members are increasingly employed on farms, questions of liability must be factored into the farming risks. As tobacco production becomes further fragmented, these risks might include questions of citizenship and access to health care for new immigrant workers, and whether the worker, crop grower, equipment owner, or land owner is responsible for paying for emergency care in case of injuries or illness (like green tobacco sickness, which can overtake workers who spend too long handling the growing plants because of nicotine absorbed through the skin). Even with all its risks, however, tobacco culture is something that most Nicholas Countians have not wanted to lose entirely.

Moralizing Tobacco

Changes in U.S. tobacco production are often explained, in public discourse, as being made in order to reduce consumption of tobacco products because of the now obvious health risks. I see market logic, rather than moral logic, however, as most responsible for the current structure of the tobacco industry. The moral discourse surrounding tobacco has certainly been used, though, to the tobacco corporations' advantage in restructuring the industry. Neoliberal capitalist principles of free market participation (decreasing state regulation of the market), emphasis on individual responsibility rather than any systemic responsibility for success or failure in the market, and a reduction of tariffs or taxes to facilitate the movement of products across borders (which has *always* been necessary in the production of cigarettes, blending different tobaccos from different countries because of different properties they bring to the mix) are very evident in the way the moral discourse around smoking has been framed. All of this information, sent in mailings to tobacco farmers and seen in news stories and advertisements, influences the positions individuals take—which may be framed as moral positions—on tobacco production, distribution, and consumption.

Although the fact that Kentucky "has the highest rate of smoking in the nation and the highest rate of lung cancer for both men and women" (Vos 2008) may be related to low political will in the state to either ban smoking or noticeably increase cigarette taxes, tobacco farming families do not automatically support smoking, and young people are both smoking at a reduced rate in Kentucky (Vos 2008) and weighing in on this topic. William Rawlings (2009), for example, a Nicholas County student in Miss Letcher's homeroom, published an essay in the local newspaper called "Destruction by Tobacco," in which he said:

> In Kentucky, where I live, raising tobacco is a big part of our way of life. Tobacco is how a lot of families I know earn their living. But tobacco doesn't just make money. It brings misery—and death. . . . There's lung disease like the emphysema that cost my Papaw his life. . . . Sure, tobacco is part of our way of life. Raising it provides money for families here in Nicholas County, Kentucky. The tobacco industry is big business in America. But I say it's time we found another business to get into. We need to get off this crazy train ride to death. I don't smoke or chew tobacco, and I urge my friends and classmates not to either.

There have been many letters to the local newspaper like William's, in which children write about relatives who have lung cancer but will not stop smoking. Sometimes health care workers write in, too. Steven Hirshberg, a respiratory therapist, wrote a letter to the editor of the *Nicholas Countian and the Carlisle Mercury* on October 25, 2002, advocating a less polarizing view of tobacco. He talked about having health problems from smoking for many years himself, and helping others to quit smoking, and said that in his work he had run into "the mistaken but widely held perception that to be anti-smoking is to be anti-tobacco industry." He noted the fact that 7,700 of 913,000 Kentucky smokers had died "prematurely from smoking tobacco," but also that "revenues generated from tobacco pay medical bills and premiums." Steven Hirschberg said, "I think we can think out of the box, take the 'one side/other side' out of the question."

In more polarizing moral arguments about the health effects of smoking and who is responsible for them, tobacco farmers, rather than tobacco companies, have often been portrayed as "evil." In a letter to the editor of the *Lexington Herald-Leader* (the regional newspaper read in many Nicholas County households) on February 12, 2000, for example, a resident of a community less farm-based than Carlisle wrote in to say:

I recently heard radio ads in support of Kentucky tobacco farmers. One part of the ad states that growing tobacco is a family tradition. So's being in the mafia, but that doesn't make it right. The ad also says that Kentucky tobacco farmers are proud of their product, known for its quality.

How can any tobacco farmer anywhere be proud that the product they grow has caused the deaths of millions of people worldwide, untold suffering and millions, if not billions, of dollars in medical costs? How can they sleep, how can they call themselves Christians knowing this? They should stop growing this poison and produce something we can all use: food.

When I started talking with tobacco farmers 25 years ago about the tobacco paradox, many talked about tobacco as both sustaining and killing people. One night a group of us were taking a break from clogging on a hilltop driveway with a breeze. (Clogging is an Appalachian form of line dancing—like Irish dancing in tap shoes.) Most of us were already tired from a day of work before we had started, but it was an exhilarating change to be double-toe rock-stepping to songs with a strong beat like The Oak Ridge Boys' "Elvira" and "Old Time Rock & Roll" by Bob Seger. During the break, Rita Sue Ritchie started searching through her purse for her cigarettes. Her 11-year-old daughter, Darlene, spoke up finally and said that she had hidden the pack. She said, "I hate the smoke and they're not good for you." Clay Johnson, leaning against a post, said to Darlene in his very even tone, "It ain't good for you, but it feeds you. I bet 65 percent of the young'n's around here is fed off it."

Clay's comment summed up the livelihood contribution made by this cash crop that was not proving to be replaced easily by alternative crops, including fresh vegetables. Some, like cucumbers and peppers, had already been tried and failed because the marketing had not been worked out well for products that were not as flexible about the time of sale as tobacco. Karen Slader said this about her family's attempt to grow bell peppers as part of an alternative-to-tobacco program encouraged by the agricultural extension service:

> Don't talk to Rocky [her husband]. He's awful burnt out. He can't figure out why farmers work harder and harder and can't make a living. We tried the pepper program year before last, and it was a disaster. We grew the peppers and took them to the collection station, and they told us that for what they wanted that week they were the wrong size and color, so we lost about all we put into it. It *seemed* good, because we could use the tobacco setter to put the plants out, but the *picking* was a lot of labor. A lot of the peppers were red and green together and there was a code of what the station accepted that Rocky and I couldn't figure out.

A local banker told me, "Whatever peppers the farmers bring in to the marketing stations would be the wrong color or size," to keep the price low. So no matter what they might think about raising it, tobacco remained the viable cash crop.

Several members of tobacco-farming families pointed to inconsistencies in the moral logic blaming tobacco farmers for smoking deaths but not blaming alcohol or illegal drug producers for deaths related to those products. One woman said to me in 1998, for example, "You don't go out and smoke a pack of cigarettes, get in a car and go kill someone. But they don't talk about alcohol that way. They should take all the money and use it to do something about the deadly hard drugs that are killing kids." Some have attributed those inconsistencies to perceived class differences in producers and consumers of cigarettes and chewing tobacco versus alcohol.

After church one summer afternoon in 1986, my grandparents stayed in Carlisle for a polite while, visiting me in my apartment; they thought it was ridiculous for me to live in town when I had family living a few miles away in the county. While Pappaw nodded off, after an especially large piece of chocolate meringue pie included with our $2.50 Sunday dinner at Garrett's Restaurant around the corner, I took a moment to be anthropological with Mammaw. I went into the kitchen to mix up some iced tea, as my grandmother lit up a Cost-cutter cigarette (she and her sister smoked into their 90s; I never took it up). I asked, "Mammaw, why do you think cigarette advertising is falling off and whiskey ads stay in the news?" She rolled a smoke ring and said, "Whiskey's for the rich men, tobacco's for all, honey. Henry Clay, all of them you hear of made Lexington, they made their money off distilling. Tobacco's always been grown by the little folks, so they'll keep the whiskey flowin' and take away tobacco." This was something that made as much sense to her as going to church on Sunday, or drinking the iced tea I handed her with a turn in the conversation. I guess she was right, because in 2010, the governor of Kentucky was trying to get an allowance for "whiskey tastings" through the legislature in time to be advertised for the World Equestrian Games coming to the Bluegrass in the fall, as the tobacco program continued to be phased out in the region.

Farmers in the 1980s often expressed the complexity of the moral dilemmas associated with tobacco production to me. Sometimes they put their hope in tobacco research being done on ways to make medicine or food out of tobacco—something that would not be harmful to people. Most, though, came back to situational ethics, like this farmer:

> You know, it's a terrible thing to say. We're raising a product—even the people you talk to that's raising this product, you ask every one of them if you think it hurts you. And more than likely they'll tell you: "yes, I think it does." The very first thing they'll come back with is, "I'd rather my child smoke a cigarette than smoke marijuana or drive drunk on the road."

The Kentucky Appalachian Ministry of the Christian Church in Kentucky and the Lexington Theological Seminary held Tobacco Church Workshops in the 1990s to help participants sort through "the special economic, social, spiritual and ethical dynamics of churches and communities in Central Kentucky who depend on growing or marketing tobacco for their primary economy" (*The Kentucky Christian* 1994). Former President Jimmy Carter, who encouraged dialogue between tobacco growers and health groups at the Carter Center, wrote that letters discouraging such interaction were sent to farmers by a tobacco company and that one tobacco company ally "publicly called the dialogue and cooperation between health groups and tobacco producers 'dealing with the devil'" (Carter 1998).

Tobacco companies have vociferously contested the regulation of tobacco by the FDA, something first attempted during the Clinton administration and signed into law by President Obama, and the companies have sent many mailings to tobacco growers to promote that same position (with notices that they are not to be quoted in print, probably because of the recent lawsuit). Coverage of the federal regulation of tobacco as a drug (because of nicotine's addictive properties) in company magazines for tobacco growers was overwhelmingly negative, focusing, for example, on the irony of its being signed into law by a president who smoked.

For William Rawlings (2009), who wrote the essay about "getting off this crazy train ride to death," and for so many other Nicholas Countians, the question that has needed practical answers rather than political rhetoric is: what *other* ways of life might be feasible in a "tobacco town"? In the rest of this chapter, I discuss local interpretations of the recent changes in the federal tobacco program and the global tobacco industry, and chapters 3 and 5 include discussions of alternatives to tobacco that farmers have tried.

Changes in the National Tobacco Program and Global Industry

Twenty-five years ago, rumors were circulating in Nicholas County about an end to the federal tobacco program being on its way. When I asked people in farming households how they were preparing for possible changes in the tobacco program, most of their answers were like these two. One full-time tobacco farmer told me, "I'll be here when everybody is gone. I'll be there 'til they make me quit. I guess it's just if you're a farmer, you're a farmer; if you're not, you're not. I mean that's just me. I wouldn't trade my life and job for any going." His wife, who was working several service-sector jobs, said, "You're either cut out for it or you're not. I told everybody [her husband] will raise the last stalk of tobacco in Kentucky. He'll have it in his hands when the whole program goes down the tubes." An older farmer told me, about raising tobacco, "It's sort of a heritage thing here. You know, it's inherited and you start when you're a little kid. And we have never come across anything to make us any more money. And we know that. And so we continue to stay here and strive and go with these programs."

Most farmers then attributed the coming changes in the tobacco program to government interference, rather than to the tobacco companies. One young woman helping her family with a crop and working a health care job in Carlisle blamed collusion between big government, big growers (outside the county), and global production for the changes in tobacco: "It's politicians killing us. They're taking tobacco away from the little farmers and giving it to other countries. Big farmers go to Australia, Jamaica, and Japan, where they raise tobacco or teach them to raise tobacco. And it's cheaper over there to grow it. So the politicians help the big farmers." She suggested that small tobacco farmers should form a union (something tried a century before, as noted earlier in this chapter).

An older farmer also placed responsibility for tobacco-related woes in political hands in the 1980s, but he added the tobacco companies. He said:

> Ann, it's the farmer that always gets hurt. It's the government together with these tobacco companies that get the money, and the farmer doesn't get it. You know, we raise tobacco. I don't like to, because I don't approve of smoking, but it's how a lot of people around here make their livelihood. After they took the net price supports off tobacco, it really hurt us—about three years ago. One year we got $1.93 a pound, and this year it was $1.63–$1.50 a pound after costs were taken out. Where does that 30 cents go? To the *tobacco* companies. And it's the government that gives it to them, or lets them take it, and you know they can do an awful lot with that money. You take that R. J. Reynolds company, and how much they were trying to sell that company for. They say they make 75 percent of their income from tobacco—and where does it come from? The *farmer*. It's the *farmer* that's hurt, every time.

Some Nicholas County farmers had been to eastern North Carolina to see the operations of larger-scale flue-cured tobacco farmers there. ("You should see the diamond rings on their wives," one told me.) Peter Benson (2008a) has written about the conditions in the labor camps in which workers, many from Latin America, live and the relationships between those workers and the large-scale tobacco farmers in eastern North Carolina. In Nicholas County, tobacco farms are much smaller, and the hiring of Latin American migrant workers is much more recent than in eastern North Carolina; there are no large labor camps, which can be either positive or negative regarding conditions for workers. In Kentucky, migrant workers are much more dependent on individual farmers for their wages and housing. There is also less state regulation of housing and working conditions, and less NGO support for Spanish-speaking farmworkers than in North Carolina.

One Nicholas County farmer, just having returned from a tour of a North Carolina cigarette manufacturing company, said this in the 1980s:

> It makes me sick. I go down there and I see all those blends. They put chocolate in some of those cigarettes. They put molasses in some of them. . . . And I automatically know what they're doing, you know. These guys go down there and you can eat off the floor in one of those places. They get a tremendous salary. I mean the people sweeping the floor and driving Corvettes. . . . And here we strive to make a living and they're making a killing off this product. And these [northeastern] states are making a killing off of it from taxes off this product.

In 1974, a class-action suit had been filed by six Kentucky farmers against tobacco companies for price-fixing (Axton 1975:131); 15 years later, farmers told me that they saw prices as being about the same at all the warehouses. Still, farmers assiduously expressed a preference for a particular warehouse and buyer (some of whom were Nicholas Countians themselves), and they hoped for a better deal in the coming year. Company, warehouse, and political contacts were all cultivated as carefully by the farmers as their tobacco crops, and they tended to keep those contacts secret. After their tobacco had hung in the barn to dry and then come "in case" (gotten moist enough to handle, since the dry leaves get brittle), farmers were anxious to get it stripped and sorted into whatever grades the tobacco companies wanted that year. Once they delivered the year's tobacco crop to the warehouse, it was insured; until then, most did not have any insurance on the crop, and whole crops have been stolen or barns have burned, with a loss for the year.

At the warehouse, buyers are not supposed to know whose crop is where (since tobacco is sold by lots, as auctioneers move down the long rows). I have been told, however, that it was not unusual for farmers to give "good faith" gifts of country hams or cases of bourbon to corporate buyers and that they, in return, might get a little better price for their tobacco at auction. That whole social system, like the system of labor and quota exchanges within the community, is changing—if not exactly obsolete, since relationships persist longer than ways of making a living—with the phasing out of the tobacco program in which a crop could be bought by "the pool" and kept in the warehouse for up to three years if the farmer did not like the price the tobacco company offered each year through the auctioneer.

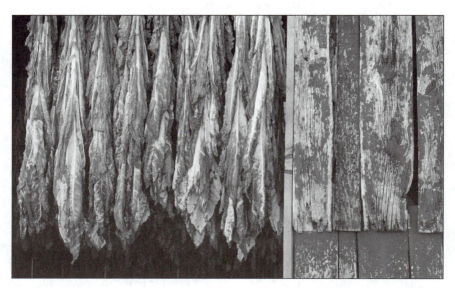

Tobacco curing in barn

The relationship between Nicholas County farmers and tobacco companies cannot be seen as necessarily oppositional, since some individuals have worn both hats. Howard Livingood is known for having navigated many community roles, including chairing the Nicholas County Board of Education through the consolidation of city and county schools, which he said was much more controversial than the integration of black and white schools had been in Nicholas County. Here is what he said in 1999 about going to work for a tobacco company:

> My life really took on a meaning about the same time I was appointed to the Board of Education. Within a year, a lot of things took place in my life. I accepted a call into the ministry, then I received a call from Brown and Williamson Tobacco Corporation to come and work for them. They said, "You've been recommended." I don't know how that happened, but I was recommended. I was hired by Brown and Williamson as a supervisor. . . . I grew up on a farm where we raised tobacco. I knew all about the raising of tobacco. And after I graduated from high school, I was drafted into the service. I spent two years in the Army. After basic training, I was selected for leadership school. . . . I attained the rank of Sergeant First Class and I was a platoon sergeant, and I spent most of that one year of Korea on the front lines. I was there when the war ended. . . . I went through a farm school, a government veterans' school. I learned how to grade tobacco. And then when the company called me, that was one thing they needed was someone that knew tobacco grades. Like I say, I grew up on the farm and then I was taught to grade tobacco, and then I worked with the company and then that was my responsibility to make sure the grades were right when they came in. . . . I worked with Brown and Williamson for 20 years, and I pastored a church part-time while I was working with them. . . . The church offered a five-year course of study. The company allowed me to go. . . . I went to Emory University for one year, during the summer, and then I found out that Duke University offered it a month earlier, so I transferred to Duke and I took a five-year course of study and a four-year advanced course. And the company let me go, and my salary continued while I was in school. I couldn't have beat that. It was an experience. . . .

Later, Howard Livingood took early retirement from the tobacco company so he could pastor full-time, which he did for 15 years in Nicholas County and then in other counties in Kentucky and North Carolina. He said, "I never used tobacco, and I wouldn't recommend anybody else to do it, but I have worked with it all my life, and I have a farm that raises tobacco now. My boys are raising tobacco [in Nicholas County]."

Howard Livingood's life story shows how work for tobacco companies has been interwoven, for some, with local roles in the community, often because of skills they have had coming from small-scale tobacco-farming families. So while some placed blame on big tobacco or big government for the changes coming in tobacco, those are not threads that can be spatially disentangled very well.

Many have written excellently about the recent changes in the tobacco program and its consequences (see for example Benson 2008b, Capehart 2003, Futamara 2007, Griffith 2009, Stull 2000 and 2009, and Swanson 2001). The two policies most instrumental in changing the tobacco landscape, economy, and social relations are the 1998 Master Settlement Agreement and the Fair and Equitable Tobacco Reform Act of 2004 (creating the USDA's Tobacco Transition Payment Program), or the "tobacco buyout" as it is called by most farmers.

The Master Settlement Agreement was reached at the national level with four tobacco companies to settle several class-action suits and lawsuits by individual states; those four companies, in exchange, could not be sued again over the same issue: promoting a product harmful to the health of consumers. Health risks from tobacco use had been publicized since 1941 (Axton 1975:118), but it took over half a century for tobacco companies to be held accountable legally for those health problems. The price of cigarettes went up almost 50 cents per pack as soon as the Master Settlement Agreement was signed, and those funds would help support the $1.5 billion the four tobacco companies (Brown and Williamson, Lorillard, Philip Morris USA, and R. J. Reynolds—many other companies have joined the MSA since the initial settlement) were required to pay over 10 years to help people stop smoking. The tobacco companies' representatives also promised to stop advertising campaigns aimed at minors, like the "cool" Joe Camel. Part of the award in the agreement was $368 billion from the tobacco companies, to be paid out over 25 years to 46 states (in Phase I) and an assessed fee of $5.15 billion on the companies that would go to tobacco growers to compensate them for the impact to their production caused by the Master Settlement Agreement (Phase II, or the National Tobacco Growers Settlement Trust), in payments over 12 years.

The Phase I payments went to states, and each state then had to decide internally how to use the money. In Kentucky, the Kentucky Agricultural Development Board was set up to administer those funds after the state's General Assembly voted in 2000 to dedicate 50 percent of the $3.5 billion Phase I funds through 2002 to agriculture, to help find feasible alternatives to tobacco; the other half of the money was used for health care and early childhood development. Tennessee, North Carolina, and Virginia also set aside substantial portions of the settlement funds for farmers and farming communities (Schipper 2001), although not with the same stipulations about alternative crops. The Community Farm Alliance, a group of Kentucky farmers already exploring alternative agricultural production and marketing options, was very influential in establishing the channeling of Kentucky MSA Phase I funds toward investment in alternatives to tobacco. Local agricultural officers helped tobacco growers in Nicholas County fill out the paperwork to receive their Phase II payments (divided equally between the growers, those owning the quota, and those owning the land on which the crop was grown); these payments were supposed to continue through 2010.

The Fair and Equitable Reform Act of 2004, or buyout, established the Tobacco Transition Payment Program to actually pay farmers to permanently give up their "quota," or tobacco allotment, from the Depression-era tobacco program legislation described earlier in this chapter. The payments were to be received between 2005 and 2014, through an assessment of nearly $10 billion on tobacco manufacturing and imports, but if a farmer wanted a lump sum it was possible to get one through a third party (using "successor-in-interest" contracts). For those facing a high debt load and layoffs in off-farm employment, the lump sum option was tempting.

The cooperatives through which tobacco has been marketed under that federal tobacco program were weakened by the settlement and the buyout, since they had been the buffer between individual producers and multinational corporations. Farmers can still sell directly to tobacco companies, for what the companies will pay them (and without the cushion of the cooperative to "float" them for a while and negotiate a higher price). Some farmers are growing under contract with tobacco corporations, and there are now both cooperative warehouses and independent warehouses through which tobacco is being purchased, either under advance contract or for whatever the current sale price may be when a farmer gets a crop to the buyers. In the burley tobacco region of Kentucky, the farmers taking the most risk in 2010 are those growing what might be thought of as "wildcat" tobacco crops, hoping to sell the tobacco to someone who has a contract (and possibly a better price than market price) but has underproduced and needs more tobacco to meet the contract.

Sales straight to buyers are not entirely new with the tobacco buyout; there have long been rumors of "black market" tobacco, but now the formal and informal markets have been collapsed together. In the first four years after the tobacco buyout, tobacco production increased in Nicholas County by almost a million pounds (from 2,176,200 pounds in 2005 to 3,072,000 pounds in 2008), but it had dropped by almost that much between 2004 and 2005, with the uncertainty about the future of the industry. In the same four years, 3,000 more head of cattle entered the mix on farms in Nicholas County, suggesting that people were branching out. Beef cattle have long been a kind of security "on the hoof" for tobacco farmers, as a calf could be sold off to pay extra hands needed at particular points in the tobacco cycle, and most of a herd could be sold off to pay back loans if a crop were lost entirely.

The language surrounding the restructuring of the tobacco industry, like many other industries in the United States and other nations in the current free-trade era, has been neoliberal. Tobacco grower magazines have recently been stressing efficiency and larger-scale production as positive attributes for tobacco farms.

The 2005 burley tobacco crop was the first since the 1930s to be produced without a "safety net," as some pointed out, and production dropped by about a third (between dry weather and the buyout) that year. Tobacco industry representatives wrote to tobacco farmers continuing to grow crops that the new independent marketing system would help them stay competitive in the global market and better meet the needs of their consumers. The editor of *The Burley Tobacco Farmer* (Gannon 1996:2), before the buyout, had used neoliberal discourse in talking about tobacco "rights":

> One resolution, however, that should be kept on the lists of those of us in the tobacco industry is the vow to keep fighting for our tobacco rights— the right to enjoy a tobacco product and the right to grow the leaf. This resolution should not be forgotten.
>
> In 1995, we witnessed the FDA trying to overstep their bounds by suggesting cigarettes be labeled as a health device, thus giving them the right to regulate the product as they see fit. Members from all segments of the tobacco industry flooded the FDA offices with written responses to the Clinton administration's proposed legislation. A lawsuit has even been filed questioning the FDA's jurisdiction on the matter.
>
> This was just one example of how the industry has fought together in response to an outside threat during these last few turbulent years. But we should all promise to promote and defend our industry every day throughout the year.

As mentioned earlier, health advocates might view the reduction in tobacco production as a victory, but so did tobacco company representatives who had found the federal protections of tobacco producers (having a price floor below which they would not drop) a hindrance to their ability to continue to provide shareholders with profits as global consumption and marketing practices shifted in the transnational industry. Peter Benson (2008b) describes the Philip Morris tobacco company taking health concerns into account in its latest approach to capitalist marketing. (The Philip Morris USA company supported FDA regulation, for example; not all companies did.) I believe that, through the transition in the tobacco program, U.S. farmers were "disciplined" (Foucault 1979) to take their risks on the open market like tobacco producers in nations of the Global South, including Malawi, India, and Turkey. This, then, was part of a much larger (and century-long) story about privatization, nationalization, and reprivatization in economic globalization.

How did Nicholas County tobacco farmers speak up in, hear about, and place themselves in that global story? One way was through talking directly with politicians. At many public events in Nicholas County, from fish fries to drop-ins at the courthouse, there are political candidates. For at least the past 20 years, those candidates for state and national office have had to take a public position on the future of the tobacco program. Several of them crafted their own plans, and may have been elected or not based on how people felt about those plans, as the spending of Kentucky's share of the settlement funds was being debated along with the federal buyout plan. Nicholas County farmers who read the regional and local newspapers could follow those plans that way, too, or online, as well as by talking with politicians in person.

In the 1980s, I talked with an older woman, Maude Ellington, who had long farmed tobacco. Like many farmers I have interviewed, she expressed a sense of loss of control over what was happening in farming. Her sense of who was in control of the agricultural industry was vague, but she did not place the responsibility on whoever might control the market—instead, she invoked the very neoliberal strategy of blaming the individual for not thriving in the free market. She said, "They don't want us to have tobacco." I asked, "Who's the they?" Ms. Ellington answered, "I don't know, but they want to bring in more of this foreign-grown tobacco and get rid of what's grown here." I followed up with, "Because labor's cheaper there?" and she replied:

> Yes, what's happened is we've priced ourselves out of a job. You see what happened to those people in Detroit who were working for $25/hour making cars? Now they don't have *any* job. It's people's own fault.

I have heard the role of the individual farmer, going along with Jeffersonian notions of agrarian independence, both saddled with responsibility for the current fragility of the tobacco market (as in Maude Ellington's words) and lauded. When tobacco quotas were cut back after the Master Settlement Agreement, Rod Kuegel, the president of the Burley Tobacco Growers Cooperative Association, talked about the threat posed to the cooperative by the experimental contract growing system that Philip Morris was trying out in 2000 in this way:

> It's a double whammy. . . . We've gone from family farm to partner to peon . . . I'm pretty sure I don't want to be their partner. This is the beginning of the end of the tobacco farmer's independence. (Patton 2000:A1)

Nicholas County farmers belonged to a number of organizations like the Burley Tobacco Growers Cooperative Association and the Farm Bureau that sent out statements on the settlement and the buyout, and the local U.S. Department of Agriculture extension agent, Mike Phillips, organized several local meetings with various stakeholders in the industry so that farmers could ask questions about the changes. In 1999, for example, there was a meeting held in Carlisle about the settlement agreement:

> The second floor courtroom of the Nicholas County courthouse was packed Tuesday night for a discussion of tobacco, what's happening and the effect what is happening may have on Nicholas County's farm producers and the whole community.
> Three of Nicholas County's five legislators at the state and national level were on hand for the discussion, and a fourth sent a representative from his staff. (*Nicholas Countian* 1999)

Going along with global neoliberal discourse in other industries—like clothing manufacturing, featured in the next chapter—around the time of the buyout, there started to be a big push for growers to improve the quality of their product for consumers. There were pictures in the paper of "trash" that was found in the baskets of tobacco: rocks, metal parts, and other "foreign matter" that would add to the weight but would be useless to the customer, in this case the tobacco companies buying the crop on the open market. Farmers were told to pay more attention to quality by tobacco producer organizations they belonged to, warehouse representatives, and government agricultural representatives in order to have a competitive edge in the world market. And, as in other industries, small-scale tobacco farmers received plenty of information about who their global competitors were and how their crops were doing.

As early as 1992, in a supplement to the *Carlisle Mercury* called "1992 Burley Sales," a USDA agricultural economist and the CEO of the Burley Tobacco Growers Cooperative Association explained to Nicholas Countians what was happening with global tobacco:

> About six years ago, American growers were told there was a world-wide shortage and that we had to grow more tobacco. . . . But at the same time, tobacco companies also encouraged growers in Brazil, Argentina, and Malawi to do the same thing. . . .
>
> Today, generics comprise over 30 percent of the cigarette sales in America, and these low-value cigarettes are being made from low-priced tobacco imported from low-cost-labor countries such as Argentina, Brazil, and especially Malawi. . . . (Greene 1992:5)

So when the buyout came over a decade later, many tobacco farmers in Nicholas County already had a sense of who their competitors were.

Politicians sometimes reinforced that sense of direct competition over the years building up to the buyout, as when Congressman Scotty Baesler sent out a letter in 1994 to his constituents in the Sixth District, including Nicholas Countians, in which he said: "Foreign-grown tobacco is one of the largest threats to American tobacco farmers because it is sold at cheaper prices. A provision in GATT known as Article 28 replaces domestic content legislation which was passed last year. Article 28 limits the annual import of foreign-grown burley and flue-cured tobacco into this country" (Baesler 1994). International policies, not surprisingly, have often been framed in Kentucky political discourse in terms of what they will mean for tobacco farmers. That did not lead, however, to a trust in politicians by tobacco farmers.

Wendell and John Berry (one brother a writer and farmer, the other the president of the Burley Tobacco Growers Cooperative Association) published a piece in the *Lexington Herald-Leader* that made an explicitly political economic argument supporting the tobacco program's purpose in maintaining small family farms and preventing them from becoming casualties of the global capitalist market. They characterized the free market logic behind the disbanding of the program protecting small farmers in this way:

> In other words, if farmers in the United States cannot undersell farmers working at slave wages in the Third World, then they deserve to fail. This is a different kind of economic justice. Asking the farmer (like the industrial worker) to produce more for less has always been the objective of the "free market" politicians, because farmers and wage earners don't give as large political donations as do the interests that exploit them. (Berry and Berry 1998:A17)

This analysis was in keeping with many that I heard from Nicholas County farmers, including: "It's politicians killing us," and "It's the *farmer* that always gets hurt." That did not, however, lead to a feeling of solidarity with tobacco farmers in other parts of the world.

The Tobacco Farm Quarterly, mailed free to tobacco producers, has a page on "world leaf news" in every issue. *The Burley Tobacco Farmer* has a similar page called "International News" in which there are short reports on tobacco issues in four or five countries (e.g., Turkey, Canada, China, and Brazil). Post-buyout neoliberal language of growing a quality product to suit the customer has been stressed in a number of articles on global tobacco production in the company magazines mailed to farmers. Those articles urge U.S. tobacco growers to increase competitiveness with growers around the world, working to produce what the tobacco companies want. Given the long hours worked and the approximately 20 percent functional illiteracy rate in Nicholas County, I am not asserting that every farmer sits down and reads every word of every tobacco publication that comes in the mail. But there is plenty of information on global tobacco production coming the growers' way—in the mailbox, through the media, and in conversations at the Southern States Co-op where supplies are picked up, at government agricultural offices, in social settings (when there is time to go to church or meetings), and with family members.

While some tobacco farmers have been very aware of their global competition, many consumers with whom I have talked have been little aware that each cigarette is a transnational product, with different varieties of tobacco (some grown in different countries) and curing methods giving different qualities to the blend. Burley tobacco, a variety of tobacco that has been cultivated in the hills of eastern Kentucky since the 1800s, is especially good—I am told—at holding flavorings blended into cigarettes. Jordan Goodman (1993:202) points out that U.S. consumers have been fairly oblivious to the place of U.S. tobacco in the multinational industry:

> In global terms the United States has been, in the postwar era, a declining player in tobacco production. . . . The lead has been taken by other countries, notably China, India, Brazil and Zimbabwe, on the one hand, and the countries of the European Community and Eastern Europe, on the other hand. One of the results of the changing geographical distribution of tobacco culture has been to allow for distinctly different modes of production, involving not only scale of operations and degree of mechanization but also differing social and economic relations between growers, on one side, and multinational tobacco corporations and the state, on the other. This diversity of tobacco culture globally has been a feature mostly of the twentieth century. Consumers of tobacco are generally unaware of this aspect of tobacco production, largely because manufacturing firms in the West have endeavoured to produce tobacco of similar quality over a large part of the world.

It is possible to stand in one field in Nicholas County and see tobacco as a small-scale, family farm cash crop, and in another field in North Carolina or Zimbabwe and see tobacco as an agro-industrial product with highly differentiated labor relations. Many people draw a firm line, I think, between agriculture and manufacturing (more culturally recognizable as industry), but it is very useful to consider tobacco in the same frame as automobiles, cell phones, shoes, and other transnational products produced by fragmented workforces who rarely compare notes with one another and can more easily be "managed" that way by those who control the manufacture and ultimate sale of the product, where most of the profit is gained. In the next chapter, agriculture will be put in the same frame with all the other industries being considered in development strategies as possible "tobacco town futures."

Questions for Students

1. I argue that the place I am from is constructed culturally in many ways as a "tobacco town." As changes come in the production of tobacco, changes in the conceptualization of identity and place are linked to those changes. Can you think of another place that is identified culturally with a particular industry? In what ways do people there face a culture as well as a livelihood challenge?

2. When you say the word "farmer," how do you think of it as gendered? Until 2002, the U.S. Census of Agriculture allowed only one household member to be designated "the farmer"; that person was usually male, even if both men and women worked on the farm. What other occupations, or particular work tasks, tend to be described as gendered? What are the implications of that for *everyone* doing those jobs?

3. Many others have written or talked about the tobacco paradox: a poisonous and addictive substance grown by people who rely on it for their livelihood (cf. Naipaul 1989:275). David Griffith (2009:440) has observed that "tobacco producers have been able to resolve the paradox between tobacco as moral and tobacco as evil by emphasizing production over consumption and pointing out production's socially beneficial ends." Can you think of other livelihoods or products that are considered to be morally or ethically problematic? How does responsibility for harm to consumers get distributed along the production/distribution/consumption commodity chain in different industries where consumers have been established to have been harmed by use of a product? What are the opinions of various stakeholders about the agency of the individual in deciding to consume a potentially dangerous product?

4. The editors and authors of the collection *Unfiltered: Conflicts over Tobacco Policy and Public Health* (Feldman and Bayer 2004) compared antismoking policies in a number of different countries (all considered democracies), and they found that both the laws and practices in relation to the laws differed across cultures, revealing different notions of the acceptable relationship between individual agency, or freedom, and state control. What do you think laws against smoking in different settings might tell you about the *cultural* context in which legislation is passed? As you think about cross-cultural experiences you may have had, how do laws about drinking age and seat belts, for example, differ across cultures, and how do the laws on the books compare with what people actually do and how they talk about that?

5. Lisa Yoneyama (1999) explores the difference between official accounts of the past, or "history," and individual accounts, or "memory." Think about the way I have described the "erasure of slavery" in eastern Kentucky in some official con-

texts and the persistence of memory in other accounts, like the WPA slave narratives and "the book" passed down in Henryville. Have you encountered differences between history and memory you could compare with this? What happens when official and unofficial histories differ? What does this tell you about history and power? How might you design a project comparing history and memory on a topic that interests you?

6. How do you think of your class identity? Patricia Hill Collins (2000) talks about a "matrix of domination" in which someone may have more power along one axis of identity, e.g., gender, but simultaneously have less power due to another dimension of identity, e.g., racialization. What factors go into your construction of a class identity? Think of examples in which one's class identity may be perceived as more multidimensional, or fluid. Then think of examples in which a person might be more constrained in the construction of class identity, as in the recent immigrants from Latin America to Nicholas County, because of their being "placed" in only one way, as low-wage workers (Kingsolver 2007:92). How can people in the latter group strive to convey the multidimensionality of their identity, despite what Peter Benson (2008a:596) calls "faciality"—the structural violence of overlapping power and perception as people look at others and "legitimize patterns of social subordination, economic exploitation, and spatial segregation"? As you navigate a particular day, think about when you have noticed a person's face more than his or her job, and when you have noticed a person's job more than her or his face (e.g., the hand that gives you change or the one that empties a trash can in the classroom). Write a brief analysis of these experiences.

7. James Peacock (2007:41–42) uses the term "grounded globalism" to emphasize the need to study globalization, not abstractly, but in specific local contexts. Howard Livingood experienced globalization through serving on the front line in Korea, working as both a producer and a company grader in the tobacco industry, and through training for his Christian ministry and serving as a pastor in a number of churches. In each of these roles, he had very localized things to do and networks to maintain, but he was also representing something more global (U.S. national interests through the Army, the multinational Brown and Williamson corporation, and both global Christianity and his denomination). In what ways do you have roles through which you can understand "grounded globalism"?

Chapter 3

Development Plans

Living on the Edge

*9*n ecosystems, edge environments—where a meadow meets the woods, for example—are the most productive. In human communities, living on the edge can mean either being marginalized or strategically participating in a number of overlapping environments, identities, and conversations. In this chapter, you will see how both of these have happened in east central Kentucky. Nicholas Countians have been marginalized (or left out) of development planning, feeling a lack of control as factory jobs have come and gone, tethered to the larger process of the deindustrialization of first the northern U.S. and then the Global North. The search for lower wages and nonunionized workforces in textiles and automobile production, for example, brought multinational corporate employers to southern states and then led them on to other countries. Nicholas Countians have *also* very actively and strategically used the position of being at the very outer edges of both the Bluegrass and Appalachian regions in crafting development plans and livelihood options.

By development, I do not mean the orderly progression from one identity to another, for example, "subsistence farmer" to "factory worker," as development was envisioned through nineteenth-century colonial capitalist discourse. Instead, I think of "development"

> as an active space of furious negotiation of identity, control of land and workplaces, and the myriad definitions of time and place implied in constructions of community and region. This negotiation is not random; there are constraints on the process of asserting one's own identity and desires in that we not only construct, we are also constructed, in powerful ways. . . . Development does not come somehow from "above," but is negotiated locally, regionally, nationally, and internationally. (Kingsolver 1992a:128, 133)

Practically, of course, development has to do with the investment of capital and who controls that process. Development discourses (or projects in imagining the future) embody what we believe about what it would mean to thrive, and for whom. Development ideas have come from outside and inside Nicholas County, and how those ideas get heard and acted on has a lot to do with how the speakers are "placed." The following is one example.

A Proposal Ahead of Its Time

Tom Hensley was born and raised in Harlan County, Kentucky, and his wife Lida Hensley grew up in Nicholas County. When he retired from being the regional manager of a number of Western Auto hardware stores, he and Lida settled on her family farm near a river at the edge of Nicholas County and started raising hogs. When he started talking with me in the 1980s about his proposal for a regional agricultural cooperative, walking energetically down the road to show me his hogs, he said people would still call him a mountain man sometimes, after 15 years of living in Nicholas County.

He was proud of his family and his livestock operation, which he called "mostly organic." He raised alfalfa, which is often plagued in that part of Kentucky by weevils that will eat the leaves of the plant into skeletons. Tom said that instead of spraying insecticide on the alfalfa crop, he just let his hogs into that field and they ate all the weevil larvae. He was good at solving problems like that.

I interviewed and visited the Hensleys over a number of years, and Tom wanted me to write about what happened with his plan. In all our conversations, I saw him get angriest about two things, his blue eyes snapping: what he saw as irresponsible use of government money (he was not a supporter of New Deal policies or "big government") and the foreclosures of small farms that he attributed to poor lending and mentoring practices and lack of well-thought-out business plans. Tom and Lida Hensley approached farming with strong business plans and said you just could not survive if you did not know how to manage a farm well. Twenty-five years later, Lida still lives on the place, with younger people farming it.

In 1985 the first Farm Aid benefit concert was given by Willie Nelson, along with John Mellencamp and Neil Young. Farm Aid was a touchstone for responses to the farm foreclosure crisis. One of those responses in Kentucky was the organization of the Community Farm Alliance (CFA). Tom Hensley attended those early meetings of the CFA in 1985 because he was mad. He had gone to a farm sale—one of those foreclosures—and watched as a family stood in their barnyard on a cold, windy November morning and watched their failed dairy operation being auctioned off. Tom shared with me what had made him so angry on that auction day:

> The father, mother, and all the children would see their cattle sold, the
> cows and calves they had cared for and milked. . . . These cows and

calves were a part of this family. They provided food for the table, clothes to keep the family warm, and much, much more. . . . Everything at this kind of auction is sold at a loss. What do they have left, you may ask. The answer is nothing but themselves and the clothes they own. . . . They have until January first to get out of the house they call home. I did not stay to see the last of the cattle sold. I really should not have gone to this sale. It touched me deeply.

A reporter from the *Carlisle Mercury* wrote, "Tom Hensley has a mission in life to help save the family farm—and he is telling his story to whomever will listen, and probably to some who won't" (Duncan 1987b:3). It is true that some people adamantly did not want to listen. I was at a political event in the courthouse one time in which a state legislator turned his back on Tom while he was describing his plan to help family farmers, and then walked out of the room. I did not run into many people who were neutral about Tom Hensley's ideas; they inspired about as much passion as he put into them.

The plan to help out family farmers in the region that Tom began to talk about with anyone who would listen stemmed from his vantage point as both a farmer and a retired businessman. "We export twenty billion dollars in food each year," he told me, "yet one out of five in agriculture in this country is unemployed. We import mutton, beef, pork, fish, fresh fish and vegetables." What he envisioned was a regional cooperative in which farmers had marketing contracts with large-scale restaurant and grocery chains in the area that would provide a guaranteed market for their crops, and nonfarm workers would have local jobs in the cooperative's processing plants and in distribution (as truck drivers, for example). He had strong negative opinions about "government socialism," like many in the cold war-era U.S., so when he talked about a cooperative he did not see it as a government-organized program to save farms but as a business venture that would work for everyone involved. In that spirit, he began with market research.

Tom Hensley talked with a manager of Kentucky Fried Chicken (KFC) and found out that most of the chicken used in the restaurants in our state, ironically, came from Georgia. The representative of the company told Tom that if he could get enough farmers involved to give them a steady supply of chicken (and of cabbage, for coleslaw), that would help KFC out, too, since they would not have to pay as much in trucking costs for whatever part of their supply was produced locally, and they made a commitment to buy from the cooperative. Representatives of a Kentucky-based sausage company also responded favorably to the idea of meat suppliers right in the same region. He found out that two-thirds of the milk supply for a local milk powder processing company came from outside the state, and that all of the potatoes for fast-food restaurants did. He believed that an economically viable market could be found for local agricultural products.

After talking with the KFC manager, the next step in Tom's market research was to look into the expense of constructing and running poultry houses. Poultry is not a significant part of the livelihood mix in that part of

Kentucky, at least not on a large scale, and the capital outlay and training necessary to go into poultry production would be substantial. Tom started collecting books about chickens, and talking with people at regional universities about chicken production. They promised to offer the farmers who joined the cooperative classes in financial management as well as agricultural and livestock production. Tom Hensley also started talking with a banker in the region who committed to putting up the initial capital for the construction of the poultry houses and the wastewater processing plant (so blood and feathers would not end up joining other factory effluents, already a contested issue in local rivers). For poultry, two houses are needed in rotation, and each one could cost $80,000–$100,000 to build in the mid-1980s. Tom worked out an agreement with the Kentucky Small Business Association in which they would provide small business loans that could be used to repay the bank's initial commitment, and payments would be made monthly on these so that no farmer was overwhelmed by debt. Here is how Tom told me (in 1987) he envisioned the cooperative working:

> What it amounts to, the way I had it planned, is for the producers, the truck drivers that go to get the chicken and the people in the factory must all share in the profit. There's not going to be a big I and a little you. . . . So once these loans are paid off and everything is free and clear, we will still contribute, and what we'll use this contribution for then, we'll put it in the bank; we'll let it draw interest on each person's percentage of his contribution and that will benefit his retirement when he retires, and every person will have a piece of the pie. There'll be no big I's and a little you.

When he could leave his own livestock, Tom started on a regional speaking circuit, making the rounds of Rotary Clubs, Chambers of Commerce, Farm Bureau meetings, county fiscal courts (legislative bodies of elected citizens, presided over by the judge-executive, making budget decisions for the county), and, as he said, anywhere he could get one or two people together to listen. He had parted ways with the CFA, and started calling his plan Kentucky Farmers First. He made it emphatically clear each time he spoke or wrote about the project that he was not running for office or aiming for any credit, and that the money spent on the development plan was his own. He wrote letters to the judge-executives in counties up and down the Licking River Valley (Bath, Montgomery, Fleming, Nicholas, Robertson, Harrison, Bracken, and Pendleton Counties); that region made sense to him as the geographical base for organizing the collective.

In each letter, he told the judge-executive what commitments had been made in other counties, and what was still needed as the plan grew to the scale he thought the cooperative would require to meet its commitments on the marketing end: 32 chicken farms, a hatchery, processing plants for meat and vegetables, grain farms and mills (to produce local feed), feed lots, a packing house, dairies, and quick-freeze and canning factories to process fresh local produce. He saw the cooperative as being able to provide jobs year-round, especially with the balance of vegetables and livestock. In a 1988 flyer for his Kentucky Farmers First campaign, Tom wrote:

> The next time you are in a grocery store, look around you. See how many items have their origin in Kentucky. Look at the meat counter, look at canned goods, look at frozen food. This tells my story better than I ever could. My plan will put thousands to work! My plan will save many family farms. My plan will produce revenue far in excess of its original cost. See my implementation plan attached.
>
> Almost every farmer can profit from my plan. The state of Kentucky can profit from my plan. Once we implement this plan, we will produce the food we use. We will produce the food for the school lunch program rather than import. . . . We can feed all Kentuckians Kentucky-produced food. Rather than import, we can export. Kentucky is within 24 hours of 75% of the population of this country. Look at the freight saved— exported in Kentucky trucks with Kentucky operators. . . . Let's go to work on this and don't stop until every pound of food that can be is produced in Kentucky. I need your help!

Tom was persistent in promoting his plan, including in letters he wrote to the editor of the *Carlisle Mercury*, like this one published on March 24, 1988:

> In keeping with my promise to you, to keep you and your readers informed on the progress of my Kentucky Farmers First Program. . . . We import 90 percent of the food we eat. Just think how many extra dollars this would generate for our economy, if we would start to produce the food we eat in Kentucky. [For] every item we import into Kentucky, the labor, tax, production, distribution, and all the supplies to produce this food is paid in another state. Our counties and state get very little of this dollar.

He went on to say that this would be a form of economic development that would benefit the whole region, and that he would soon be addressing the Kentucky Agricultural Development Foundation along with the lieutenant governor and others to talk about this proposal for development. "You can bet I'll kick the barn door open for the Kentucky farmer and his family," he told readers.

Four months after that meeting at the state level, there was one at the regional level in which political, agricultural, and business leaders came together from all the Licking River Valley counties that Tom Hensley was proposing cooperate. He had called them together to see how serious they were about getting to work on it, and he hammered that home:

> "The real factor here is time . . . we must act now. We don't have time to wait until 1990. . . . The drought we are going through is making things worse. Time is not on our side. In 1987, 40,000 farms quit farming . . . that's one every seven minutes," he told a hushed crowd. . . . "Economic development must begin on our farms." (Bond 1988)

There was another big regional meeting about the proposal in May 1989, in which the state agricultural commissioner, a U.S. Department of Agriculture specialist in cooperatives, and others gathered to discuss the feasibility of the plan in more detail. The potential for developing international markets and for bringing other products (including hardwood lumber) into the diversified mix were mulled over, as well as the recent failure of a large-scale vegetable growing and processing cooperative in the region someone else had tried. Participants in the discussion decided that failure was due to undercapitalization, and they talked about how to prevent that with better financial planning; the drought had also been disastrous to that venture.

Ironically, for a proposal intended to be grassroots by a person who was not very sanguine about the role of government in development, Tom Hensley's plan got more interest from state government than from local people. In July 1989, a USDA representative worked with Tom Hensley to assess farmer interest in participating in the cooperative by publishing a questionnaire in each local newspaper in the Licking River Valley to be returned to the judge-executive. The questionnaire asked detailed questions about the size of the farm, pasturage, livestock, woodland, experience in commercial vegetable and/or livestock production, and willingness to participate in the specific economic arrangements necessary for marketing through the cooperative. In September, Tom met with those who had responded with interest to the questionnaire to try to get the group off the ground. Unfortunately, Tom's proposal could not even get up a "run-a-go," as we say in Kentucky.

By then, I was living far away in the first of a series of states I would live and work in as an anthropologist: New York, South Carolina, Wisconsin, California, and back to South Carolina. I have a stack of letters Tom Hensley wrote to me in each of those states, as his hopes for the cooperative plan waned. Once he told me that it was hard to get 10 farmers (including himself in that group) to agree on the time of day. He was frustrated, also, by what he saw as lip service from politicians but little practical follow-through. In 1990 he wrote, "It is hard for one person to take on a project of this size with no help. Lida says to forget it and raise pigs."

Tom's economic development proposal, with its emphasis on regional planning along the river system, local food production, diversification of farming into numerous alternatives to tobacco with strong marketing contracts, and vertical integration of agricultural industry (controlling more of the distribution and sales, therefore more of the dollar, than with production alone) would fit right into 2010 conversations on the future of agriculture in Kentucky. Since he could envision how this could work 25 years ago, why was it impossible to make it happen? I think there were two main obstacles to his Kentucky Farmers First plan being implemented at the time: the challenges of being multiply placed as a speaker, and the emphasis at that moment in state and local development discourses on county-level competition rather than on regional collaboration in development plans.

Local knowledge can be devalued in many Nicholas County contexts, but that does not mean that outsider or expert knowledge is automatically trusted. As someone born in Harlan who became a local hog farmer, Tom Hensley and his proposal were situated as both "insider" and "outsider"—I heard them talked about both ways in the community. One factory worker talking about the development plan said that Tom did not have enough local contacts, meaning power, to pull it off since he was an outsider to the county. She said, "It's *who* you know to get behind it and everything." An industrial recruiter, not from Nicholas County, saw Tom Hensley as a local isolationist who was against neoliberal policies of free trade. Even though Hensley had framed his proposal in terms of supply and demand, the industrial developer said:

> I've heard of the plan, and it scares me. Because people are listening to him. . . . Isolationism on a state level is ridiculous and impossible to implement. He is completely and tea-totally ignoring the two basic economic principles of supply and demand—that you're gonna buy it where it's cheapest, no matter what. . . .
> On one hand, he's saying no, we shouldn't give farmers a subsidy, but on the other hand he's saying no, farmers shouldn't purchase a product where they want to. His policies are that you buy it in Nicholas County. . . . Let the market decide what's going to happen.

A businessman in Nicholas County blamed the farmers for the failure of the plan:

> It's another good idea, but the farmers here really don't *want* to do anything different. . . . It'll have to be a whole new generation that *wants* to try something different as they're starting out. . . . People are scared of change.

That new generation has come, 25 years later, as discussed in the final chapter. Tom Hensley did not live to see it, but since he said he did not want credit anyway, he would probably be glad to see *anyone* taking an interest in local agriculture and regional planning. The rest of this chapter follows *other* local proposals for the future of Nicholas County—situated within state and global discourses of development.

State-led Development Planning

In 1943, the Committee for Kentucky was formed to "promote a better understanding between the local community and the state so that our citizens can better understand how the local community fit into state development," as Harry Schacter (1949:182), the Committee's president, explained it. Committee members were volunteers representing business, industry, agriculture, education, labor, and other sectors. They drew on state networks ranging from the Girl Scouts to the Congress of Industrial Organizations (CIO) to implement their goal of getting Kentuckians to discuss the problems and potential of their communities in order to, ultimately, "make a strong America." Members divided the state into nine districts and covered the state, operating out of a trailer with a movie projector, a loudspeaker system, and a library of resources on what community meant (Schacter 1949:184). As you can see from the illustration below, the aims of the Committee for Kentucky fit into a larger project of industrial boosterism across the rural southeastern United States, which recruited both manufacturers to come to that area and rural workforces for those factories. In the 1940s and 1950s, global industry was being reconfigured, and particularly the southern states of the U.S. were booming with capital investment.

Consumerism was being encouraged to match the emphasis on manufacturing. One Nicholas County resident, Dorothy Neal, described her job as a home extension agent in the 1950s as including giving demonstrations of new electric appliances (time-savers) that could be used in the home. Those time-savers included kitchen appliances like washing machines. Dorothy Neal recalled that when she first came to Nicholas County to give demonstrations, there was one large frozen food locker—where people in the community could put their frozen vegetables—in the downtown building where her husband and his brother would later run their grocery and general store, but then individual households began to get electric freezers. Some Nicholas Countians can still remember when the New Deal Rural Electrification Administration strung lines across their farms, and their homes got first a single light bulb, then an icebox, then a radio. The growth in home appliances is one example of what was fueling consumer demand in the United States for the products of the rapidly expanding manufacturing industries.

The 1947 Report on Manufacturing by the Committee for Kentucky recommended the formation of local chambers of commerce and conducted community inventories of conditions for recruiting manufacturers; it also

8. COMMUNITY CONDITIONS
DO WE WELCOME FACTORIES?

The attitude of Kentuckians toward manufacturing varies. Some people are lukewarm, fearing increased wages for farm and other labor, unsightly plants, a "foreign" element, unemployment and relief costs during depressions, and a break with our agrarian heritage. But more people appear favorable. New plants are usually exempted from city taxes for a five-year period and occasionally a building is furnished on a subsidized basis. Under a 1946 law, city governments may issue bonds to make available such buildings.

Illustration from Schacter (1947, p. 19)

listed the advantages and disadvantages of attracting industry that might come up in community discussions. As Allen Batteau has noted in *The Invention of Appalachia* (1990:143), those speaking up against the recruitment of industry, particularly low-wage manufacturing jobs, to rural areas were often portrayed as stubborn individualists or backwards hillbillies resisting modernization rather than as having legitimate grounds for resisting, or even intelligently discussing the merits of, development plans.

As I have followed development discussions in Nicholas County, I have heard a range of opinions expressed about both local and state industrial recruitment strategies. Ambivalence toward, and critical engagement of, development discourse is ongoing. There has not been a clean sweep by the modernization ideology promoted in the illustration above. In the 1950s, though, there was definitely a positive response in Nicholas County to the community development initiative set in motion by the Committee for Kentucky. In a 1952 copy of the *Carlisle Mercury* (on page 2), I found this report on local community development organizing:

> The meeting Friday night at the courthouse concerning a community development contest is one which should be attended by all those interested in the advancement of Carlisle and Nicholas County.
>
> A great many improvements in Carlisle and Nicholas County have been made over the past few years without the aid of any centralized active body. . . . The meeting is open to everyone. No one is definitely in the organizing seat. It is hoped that the meeting will attract a large gathering of civic minded businessmen, housewives, farmers, and others who in the past have given of their time and energy to work for a better community. . . .
>
> As a medium of dispensing information in this community *The Mercury* would like to urge everyone to be present. We feel that an organization of this type would go a long way toward benefiting all segments of population in our city and county and therefore directly affects your future welfare.

The disavowal of any centralized planning or leadership is probably related to cold war ideology, which was busy growing in the column next to this one on the same page of the *Carlisle Mercury*. That column cautioned those who had admired socialist speakers like Norman Thomas to remember that socialism and communism were twin enemies of democracy. Thus, community development meetings in Carlisle were privately, not state-, funded and had no apparent leadership. That practice changed in the state-led development planning of later Kentucky generations, in which strong leadership has been viewed as a necessity rather than a liability.

Thirty years after the Committee for Kentucky had been organized, Kentucky Governor Julian Carroll's (1974–1979) administration set up Area Development Districts (ADDs) to channel federal funding *into* regions, and demographic and other data *out* of regions, for the purpose of development (which at that time largely meant the creation of manufacturing jobs). The ADDs were set up loosely along the same physical and ideological lines as those earlier Committee for Kentucky regions. They are often named by features of the landscape that might be promoted through tourism, like the Bluegrass ADD, the Gateway [to the mountains] ADD, and the Buffalo Trace ADD at the edges of which Nicholas County sits (it is the furthest east county in the Bluegrass ADD). If residents of the ADDs were polled, many might not know of the existence of these regions, or the counties that comprise them. They have administrative importance in state development conversations, but counties, as political units, have much stronger salience for the people of Kentucky. County-level politics have usually trumped regional planning efforts, as illustrated in the failure of Tom Hensley's attempt to organize a plan across county lines.

The creation of Area Development Districts meant that rural development would be mediated by the state, so that individual communities like Nicholas County would not be negotiating directly with multinational corporations or federal agencies. The ADDs marshaled development discourse into a single state narrative used to attract capital to the state. The largest such recruitment effort, in the late 1980s, was landing the first Toyota assembly plant, offering Toyota an incentives package of $125 million. The state was asserting control over internal development discourse because it was in competition with other states for such deals, and Kentucky administrators needed structures like the local and state chambers of commerce and the Area Development Districts to unify recruitment strategies and public relations representations of communities as potential industrial sites.

In the 1980s, when Tom Hensley was talking up his Kentucky Farmers First plan, the Kentucky Chamber of Commerce (KCC) was encouraging competition between localities as part of a larger development project. This took the form of the Certified Cities program. Volunteers in each community prepared applications to submit to the KCC for Certified City status, and the applications could be several hundred pages long, as Carlisle's was in 1986. The required format included information on economic development, community organizations, community planning, utilities, downtown revitalization, and community appearance. The document was basically a resource inventory that the Kentucky Chamber of Commerce could, in turn, use in recruiting manufacturing employers. The KCC questionnaires, as part of the application, asked for specific information about land for possible use as industrial sites (e.g., acreage, price, zoning, utilities, roads, available capital) and about the labor supply (e.g., average wages, unemployment, union activity). With state assistance, the Carlisle Chamber of Commerce prepared a brochure in the 1980s called "Your Company is Special in Carlisle/Nicholas County." The portion on the labor force read:

> There are no unions in Nicholas County—they're not needed. Low cost of living allows a workforce to offer you the most reasonable manufacturing wage in the region. They're eager to make you a part of their community and anticipate the benefits accrued from mutual appreciation and service.

A film made to promote industry in Nicholas County at around the same time promoted a female workforce available for manufacturing work because of the way households combined farm and factory employment locally. One speaker in the film said:

> It's a good farming area, which we think is a benefit to our company because we look at the female industry as being a part of subsidy to the family income and due to the fact that it *is* a farming area, then we think it is a good labor market for us to contribute and stay here in Nicholas County.

Notions of agrarian independence contribute to members of households with mixed livelihood strategies, including farm and service or industrial work, not seeing themselves as *primarily* an industrial workforce. One may be thought of as self-employed on the farm, even if ultimately producing a crop for a multinational corporation like R. J. Reynolds. As noted above, this was utilized in state and local industrial recruitment strategies.

A great deal of care, thought, and time has gone into preparing a series of comprehensive plans for Carlisle and Nicholas County since 1967. A major goal expressed in each plan has been to develop more local sources of employment in business and manufacturing so that fewer people would need to commute out of the county for work. The 1993 Strategic Area Development Program for Nicholas County emphasized a regional approach and effective use of technologies in the planning process, reflecting a shift in state emphasis from insular to linked planning processes among Kentucky's 120 counties.

Residents of Nicholas County had worked hard in compiling the applications for Certified City status, which was granted in 1991. Spud Marshall, the executive director of the Nicholas County Industrial Authority, was appointed by Kentucky Governor Brereton Jones in 1992 to one of the new development roundtables across the state; the charge of the roundtables, bringing industrial authority, chamber of commerce, and economic development representatives together, was "to prepare Kentucky's communities for their maximum growth potential and to enhance existing business services" (*Carlisle Mercury* 1992:2). Sometimes Nicholas Countians have been invited, as Spud Marshall was, to participate in regional discussions of development, and sometimes forums have come to Carlisle.

In 1993, there was a series of meetings at the Carlisle City Hall to get local feedback for the Kentucky Strategic Area Development Program, or Kentucky 2001, organized through the Bluegrass ADD. Some of the county's development challenges discussed in the meetings were the net export of Nicholas County workers each day to other counties (which retained their sales tax dollars, for example) and the comparatively high poverty and unemployment rates in relation to state levels. Long-term plans to address infrastructural problems (e.g., new water lines and a widened road to counties with more off-farm employment opportunities) were discussed, along with growing plans for tourism in the county (Mullins 1993:1, 3). Sometimes, as in

Kentucky 2001, the conversations about development that have been sparked by visitors have provided comparative information and support for ongoing local efforts.

In 2007, working with the recommendations for the county compiled in the Kentucky Association for Economic Development's Community Assessment Report, a citizens' group met at the Carlisle Methodist Church to plan their work as the Carlisle–Nicholas County Community Assessment Core Leadership Group, within which four volunteer groups were formed to focus on local community development, local education, local cooperation, and local tourism opportunities. Each group had a volunteer coordinator, plus a leader to help coordinate the work of all four groups. An article in the *Carlisle Mercury* urged further citizen participation "in an effort to move Nicholas County toward a more secure, happier, and brighter future. . . . The groups have no political agendas and elected officials are actually forbidden from participation among the various groups. The members of the Industrial Board will also have extremely minimal roles" (Mattox 2007:10).

Each of the community development organizing efforts over the past five decades has involved some of the same individuals, and some new ones. Although the endeavors of separate groups may seem to be disconnected, they are all connected to an ongoing community development discourse in Nicholas County engaging state, national, and global trends and encouraging citizen participation in development planning.

In 2009, Lorraine Garkovich, a University of Kentucky professor of Community and Leadership Development, gave a workshop in Carlisle that helped rekindle the Carlisle Chamber of Commerce, which has had periods of strong activity and dormancy, in part depending on leadership and time commitments. As the Nicholas County Industrial Development Authority and the Carlisle Chamber of Commerce have been organized and reorganized at different moments, they have occupied an important community role in galvanizing practical conversations about the economic future of the community. They also carry expectations within state-led development. When I had asked one of the state representatives for our region in 1988, for example, about the possibility of agricultural processing industries, as tobacco seemed on its way out, he told me that the state takes initiative in getting industry to Kentucky, but that it was the responsibility of communities to promote themselves as a location.

There have been a number of local development initiatives articulating with state and regional efforts like the Certified Cities program. Carlisle representatives attended the Kentucky League of Cities Annual Conference in 2003, for example, to compare notes with 800 other representatives of city government. The Kentucky Long-term Policy Research Center has prepared publications geared to development efforts, including: *Reclaiming Community, Reckoning with Change: Rural Development in the Global Context* (Smith-Mello 1995), encouraging more strategic industrial recruitment—e.g., employers providing training that might leverage workers out of their low-wage jobs—

and *Farms, Factories, and Free Trade: Rural Kentucky in the Global Economy* (Schirmer and Taylor 1995:15), which noted that Nicholas County was highly dependent on import-sensitive industries, specifically textiles, and explained the global free trade environment affecting local jobs. Such planning documents were available within state-led development discourses but were not consulted widely in Nicholas County.

A small group of volunteers from the business community along with elected officials, with some turnover over time, have worked on applying for grants through the Area Development Districts; those grants have been vital to sustaining city and county infrastructure. A key factor in local development initiatives has been how the wind was blowing across Kentucky regarding discouraging or encouraging community-level cooperation in development planning. In 1994, for example, the status Carlisle had won in 1991 as a Certified City was changed to Certified Community, and the emphasis of the program shifted from competition between cities to partnerships between communities in attracting industry.

In fiscal court discussions over the years, Nicholas County government officials have expressed the painful investment decisions to be made between future development and current critical needs, and the Nicholas County Industrial Development Authority has not always been seen as an affordable investment, even with its potential for bringing future dollars into the community. There have sometimes been questions in the community about what, and how much, the Industrial Authority was actually doing, due to its expressed need to keep its activities somewhat secret because Nicholas County might be competing with surrounding counties to be the site for a manufacturing plant, for example. There is currently a Carlisle–Nicholas County Industrial Authority, and an industrial park near the landfill at the edge of town is available for recruiting industries.

Development dilemmas faced in the rural southeastern U.S. may be usefully compared to those faced in the Global South, given some of the long-term structural barriers to development in each region. In 1987, for example, Kentucky was importing toxic waste from 31 states and Puerto Rico; it was a development strategy focused on the short rather than the long term. Residents of the county next to Nicholas County became concerned about the contents of compacted garbage being imported, for a fee, from New York and New Jersey. They already had a nuclear waste dump shut down in 1977 still containing "4.75 million cubic feet of garbage, most of it radioactive" (Chriss 1988:A1, 12). However, when they tried to stop the importation of northeastern garbage in 1988, they were unable to do so because it was ruled to be a protected commercial item under interstate commerce laws. As the state turned from such strategies as toxic waste importation to the information economy, it became evident that the information highway did not stop at everyone's door: in 1987, 400,000 Kentuckians (including 43 percent of Nicholas Countians) were reported to be "functionally illiterate" (Roser 1987). This made higher-paying jobs, recruited through the centralized application systems favored by multinational employers, much more difficult to get than local jobs in which it might be possible to use social networks to get around literacy requirements. Other development challenges were infrastructural, water being a central concern.

One county official told me in 1989 that being part of the 17-county Blue-grass ADD, even at its edge, would be helpful in addressing infrastructural problems like roads and water. He said, "Sure, each county is still looking out for itself, but there is strength in numbers and you can get things done within the region for each county that we couldn't get done if we were just crying out there by ourselves." Others expressed concern that the cities within the ADDs were diverting regional resources away from rural areas. A factory worker told me, "I can't figure out why all these surrounding counties are getting everything and Nicholas County is not getting anything." Allen Clay Stone observed in a January 11, 1996, letter to the editor of the *Carlisle Mercury:*

> We are at least twenty-five years behind the rest of our area. . . . Many of the young people joke about this town and county. They say, "give me my diploma and free complimentary road map so I can leave when I graduate."
>
> There is nothing wrong with the people here. We just need more to help people live better. We are a hill to almost mountain county with a few good farmers and modest industry. We have to do a great deal more to build bridges, roads, and water lines. This is due to the lay of the land in our area. Our needs are much different than most of central Kentucky.

Infrastructural needs led county officials recently to look east and uphill for partnerships and away from the Bluegrass, as described in a later section.

Paralleling these debates about regional development alliances were discussions of Kentucky's place in a global economy. In November 1987, nearly 900 businesspeople, community representatives, government officials, corporate leaders, and national representatives in the international arena gathered in Lexington for the Kentucky Goes Global conference. The explicit point of the conference was to educate local leaders in the specifics of competing in a global market. One speaker said, "We're in a struggle for survival. What brings us together internationally is economic reality, not an overarching humanitarian goal." Advice to small-community representatives included not investing in brochures to attract Japanese industry before learning more about the expectations for information and industrial sites Japanese investors might have, and making sure there was no union activity within a 50-mile radius of the industrial site being promoted. One speaker said that nothing was domestic anymore—that we had gone global long ago but were just now beginning to realize it in the United States, and Kentucky. That same year, officials paid $18,000 for a franchise of the World Trade Center so that there would be one in Lexington, Kentucky, to facilitate international marketing ties. Globalization was definitely mentioned in state-led development discourses, and transnational competition was brought home to Nicholas County workers when the local textile and garment plants, providing off-farm employment in many farming households, shut down and production went to other countries.

Many Nicholas Countians, not just those who attended discussions like the Kentucky Goes Global forum or who spoke with formal or informal authority, shared their analyses of the world economy with me. One night in 1987, the year the construction of the Toyota plant in Kentucky was announced, I was riding in a car with a family and the talk turned to a report the father had heard on television about the U.S. economy. He said, "It told how the majority of American money is now owned by the Japanese, and if the dollar falls, the Japanese put money in the Federal Reserve to pump it back up." His wife said, "The Japanese is taking us over." That unease about foreign control of the U.S. economy came up in a lot of local analyses of globalization, especially around that time.

For most people I have talked with in Kentucky, the words "development" and "industry" are associated with manufacturing, not with agriculture (which I see as equally an industry, and a multinational one at that). In Tom Hensley's development plan, however, the two were linked. At that time, Lieutenant Governor Brereton Jones also put agricultural industries into the same picture with other industries in a speech he made to the Mt. Sterling Kiwanis Club in May 1988, in a county near Nicholas County. He said that the total Japanese investment in the state of Kentucky was 1.8 billion dollars, and that was exactly the same amount that Kentuckians paid for food products imported into the state in 1987; he wanted to see the state invest in agriculturally related processing industries as well as manufacturing: "What's good for farming is good for Kentucky," he said. "We can't just go from administration to administration like a ball in a pinball machine . . . we have got to determine where we want to be in 15 or 20 years and how we're going to get there. . . . You've got to plan your work and work your plan," Jones said. In 2004, an agricultural extension agent in Sri Lanka I was interviewing about globalization said something similar: that the national investment in, and promotion of, garment manufacturing left the nation vulnerable to the vagaries of the global market in labor and textiles, but that Sri Lanka should have focused its industrialization on agriculturally related industries, to complement the strength the nation already had in agricultural production and knowledge. So this has been a global issue, and many regions have made the same development choices to invest in manufacturing clothing, for example, rather than to vertically integrate existing agricultural sectors.

Several attempts have been made to brand Kentucky products in the global market. Kentucky Fried Chicken is probably the most recognizable context for the word Kentucky around the world (there was one down the street from where I lived in the central mountains of Sri Lanka). But the state has tried out various slogans. Lt. Governor Jones encouraged marketing agricultural products with the "Made in Kentucky" label. I remember that for many years, in the late 1980s and 1990s, as I drove over the border home to Kentucky, the metal sign on the state line read "Welcome to Kentucky: Open for Business." Currently, there is a campaign to market local produce under the "Kentucky Proud" label. In this case, branding is part of the process of

bringing agricultural and manufacturing industries under the same development umbrella. The next sections follow three main development stories: textiles, Toyota, and tourism. The last one involves branding the history and
architecture of the community as resources for development have been more
broadly defined.

Textiles

Nicholas County's factories have been in the machining and garment
sectors; they have always been linked to global markets while providing local
employment, often with both owners and workers farming, as well. Lee Lynn
Machining, Inc., is a family-owned precision machining plant, for example,
that uses just-in-time processing (a post-Fordist Japanese-originated industrial technique that creates and supplies parts as they are needed). Textile and
apparel production has been one of the largest industries in the county,
though, and even more tied to the tides of the global labor and consumption
markets, especially the Multi-Fibre Arrangement (MFA), governing the
transnational textile trade from 1974 to 2005. With the expiration of the
MFA in 2005, protectionist policies ended, and both cloth and garments
could be produced wherever the market led those industries, which was
mostly to the People's Republic of China and Bangladesh. The late twentieth
century saw many sewing factories producing clothing for prominent multinational labels come to Kentucky, and then leave.

One couple from Bourbon County, Cliff and Carrie Shumate, left Hans-
ley Mills where they were working with Lonnie Giffin, and the three of them
started a garment factory called Giffin Manufacturing Company in Nicholas
County in 1948 with 50 employees (Wolf 1983). The Shumates' son Wayne
joined the company; he was production manager in the 1950s. The name of
the plant changed to Blue Grass Industries (BGI), occupied new facilities on
the main road into Carlisle, and then the plant—twin large buildings in
which cloth was made in one and apparel was sewn from the cloth in the
other—was sold in 1980 to one of the companies that at one time had the
largest contract with BGI: Jockey International. Wayne Shumate then
opened a new factory, Kentucky Textiles, in Bourbon County and some of
the Nicholas County BGI workers commuted there to work; others stayed
and worked for the new multinational management at the Jockey plant.

Wayne and his wife Kay raised their children Cliff and Paige in Nicholas
County. Cliff Shumate (the third generation in management) became the new
president of Kentucky Textiles in 1992. His sister Paige Shumate Short, the
vice president of new product development of Kentucky Textiles in 2000,
continued the family tradition of experimenting with new markets and products, creating a new cloth called HempSpun, mixing cotton, polyester, and
hemp fibers, which was made into garments that were sold to The Gap, Aber-
crombie and Fitch, and other buyers (Wall 2000:C1). Kentucky Textiles not

only manufactures products designed by the buyers, like Speedo bathing suits, but under Wayne Shumate's leadership, the company also originated a new line of one-size-fits-all leisure wear called "Sloppy Joes" (Nesbitt 1987) marketed locally and affordable for workers who manufactured the garments.

The Shumate family also raised beef cattle on a large farm, and Wayne and Kay Shumate started experimenting early with alternative products to tobacco that might work in the region, since they knew the marketing end well. Blackberries grow wild in the region, mostly along fence rows. (I have picked them for many a pie, first with my grandfather and now with my son.) The Shumates planted rows of domesticated (sweeter and larger) blackberries, opened a cannery, and started marketing blackberry jam (see http://www.windstonefarms.com). Their daughter Paige has recently collaborated with a health sciences researcher to explore the possible health benefits of blackberries (including combating colon cancer and inflammation).

I have talked with the Shumates about alternatives to tobacco over the years, and Wayne was interested in Kentucky products that could be connected with external markets. He knew it took more of a capital investment than most tobacco farmers had to switch to any other crop, which was why he and Kay felt it was important for them to start the innovation with their own capital long before state resources became available for alternatives to tobacco through the Master Settlement Agreement and the buyout program. Wayne also thought I was a little crazy for being so interested in this topic, and he started calling me "the blackberry girl" in the good-natured banter he kept up with thousands of people in and beyond eastern Kentucky.

As patron plant managers (local owners embedded in the community) of the largest factory employer in Nicholas County, the Shumates' relationship with workers was more complex than simply manager–worker. As Jane Collins (2003) has described, local owners of southeastern U.S. textile plants have usually forged relationships that appear more familial than the standard manager–worker relationships, with all the good, bad, and messy interpretations of family. Workers were dependent on the jobs offered by the factory and could not easily pick up and move to another shop floor if relations were strained. This was not just the case with Blue Grass Industries; it was a broader pattern of relating to employers in Nicholas County. In the textile factory, even after it was taken over by the multinational management of Jockey International, the family metaphor was reinforced through family–factory vacations (when the factory shut down production for two weeks in the summer), family–factory picnics, and gifts given for years of service (since cash given to family members in the United States is often considered less polite than a selected gift, unlike in some other cultures). One worker from Blue Grass Industries told me, "Wayne was fair to his workers," and described some of the gifts given by the management:

> Well, not only fair raises and things like that, but when you worked 15 years you got a $100 blazer and a watch, and when you worked 20 years you got this . . . silver service . . . and when you worked 30 years, you got

a diamond—and it was a huge diamond—so things like that. And we always had Christmas presents, and some of us got bonuses, I don't know if everybody did. . . . It was always awful welcome every year.

Jockey International carried on that tradition, and photographs appeared regularly in the local newspaper—as they had under local ownership of the factory—of workers with their service years and gifts (watches, clocks, globes, pins, pewter bowls, crystal bookends, etc.). Some workers would have preferred cash bonuses, but abandoning gift-giving would have revealed the labor and power relations the management was downplaying through the use of the family metaphor. The plant, especially when locally owned, also gave gifts to the community—shirts for a little league team and computers for a science classroom, for example.

One worker told me in the 1980s (after the plant was bought out by Jockey) that the turnover rate in employment at the factory was low, even after the very bad feelings that remained between groups of workers—and between some of the workers and the management—after the most recent of the three attempts to unionize the plant. He said, "I'd be tarred and feathered for saying so," indicating the heavy silence that prevailed in the plant and community about this, "but I'm still for a union because I think that's how workers get what they need." The group of workers that had voted against union affiliation, probably with the support of the management, made the group that had voted for the union carry a real coffin through the factory and dig a hole and bury it in the front yard, by the main road, the idea of forming a union silenced and buried for good. There were flowers and all. One worker said sadly to another that the fake funeral cost more than he was able to pay to bury his father. The family metaphor in a factory brings all the functional, dysfunctional, and exploitative aspects that can occur in families, including people spending time beside each other all day, not on speaking terms. Seeing relations in the plant as family relations, which has made some sense in tobacco culture because of the thick relationships between people in overlapping networks and even class positions, then, can make it more difficult to talk about class and power relations in the plant, as it did during the vote on unionization.

A member of the business community said that one of the problems with having more of a familial, or informal, style of management in the textile and apparel plant was that hiring through social networks (often tobacco and kin networks) meant that federal hiring guidelines were not being observed. After an African American worker won a hiring discrimination lawsuit against Jockey International, the factory started using the same regional hiring services that Toyota and other manufacturing companies in the region used. The businessman went on to say that a multinational corporate employer can sometimes have better conditions for workers because "they have factories in many, many other communities, in other states, other nations." On the other hand, because they can move so easily between contexts, they can demand a lot of the workers without loyalty to the community or responsibility to the workers as multiply "placed" individuals. Jockey's intentions were important to the community because the plant employed so many community members who were also part-time farmers.

Just as things were looking shakier for tobacco as a cash crop, there was concern in the 1980s that the multinational corporate ownership might mean the Jockey plant would close. Someone in Nicholas County government told me, "I'd rather have local, or at least *reliable* ownership of industry—not someone who'll come and soak you, and then go away." A woman who had moved her family in with her mother out in the country to save money said about an expansion of the Jockey plant: "I wish we didn't have to pay taxes for a new water line and then have people move in from out of town to take the jobs!" There was a sense that local investment in the industrial base should translate into local employment, even though people commuted from a number of counties to work at the plant.

In 1985, the Environmental Protection Agency expressed concern about the amount of sodium chloride in the effluent coming from the half of the plant in which cloth was made and dyed; that effluent went into a stream that was the next county's water source. In order to retain the 1,700 jobs at the Jockey plant, the state government revised water regulations so that the discharge was no longer in violation of water standards. "No one is talking, following last Thursday's special meeting in Frankfort between the governor, high placed Jockey officials, two cabinet secretaries and a state senator," reported the *Carlisle Mercury* (1986:1). "'In situations such as this it's sometimes better to say as little as possible,' Governor Martha Layne Collins told the *Carlisle Mercury* Friday afternoon."

Global tensions in the textile industry could be felt in Nicholas County as textile plants started closing down all around the state (all of the Fruit of the Loom factories, for example). Factory workers started telling me stories of deteriorating conditions at the plant. One woman I knew quit, saying, "It just got to the place where I couldn't keep my sanity or my self-respect, that way." Little plant loyalty remained; some workers were "wildcatting," or selling Jockey "knock-offs" directly for more than they would make sewing the same garments piece-rate. This is a common resistance and survival strategy among garment workers in free trade zones in the Global South (see Thomas 2009). Another friend, Gail, stopped by my apartment one day after work to use my phone. She said that her day at work had been rotten. Her machine had been slow, and she had been yelled at all day because of it. One winter day the power went out at the plant, and a worker told me that their pay was docked whenever there was a shutdown of the line like that, or if there was a shortage of orders at the plant, or if a worker was ill (there was no sick leave). When I asked Gail why the union vote had gone the way it had gone if conditions were getting worse, she said:

> Honey, we're too old to unionize. The factory workers out there have been there 30 years, a lot of us, and there's very little turnover. There's a

long waiting list for jobs. The men and women out there are loyal to the plant, and are too old to speak up. We never will. And Jockey tells us if we don't do just right they'll close the plant and step up operations in their plant in Jamaica. We've had girls from here [and she named them] go over there to train them in setting up that plant. And the line moves faster and faster here.

In 1988, the National Labor Relations Board ordered Jockey "and its officials to cease from harassing, threatening, and coercively interrogating employees about union activities or sympathies" (Hall 1988:1). After that, the layoffs started in a small way and grew: 10 workers in the knitting plant in the winter of 1990, and over 100 workers from the sewing plant in 1993. In 1995, when the Jockey plants shut down for some retooling, Nicholas County's unemployment rate shot to the highest in the state: 27.4%. In 1999, 326 workers were laid off from the sewing plant.

> Rumors of layoffs at the Jockey plant in Carlisle have been circulating for years, so Mayor Ronnie Clark figured the news wasn't good when two company representatives came to his office Monday. "I felt like 'this is it,'" said Clark. It was. . . . The Jockey sewing plant, the largest employer in Nicholas County, would close December 30.
>   "Everyone is a loser," said Clark, whose wife, Keneatha, worked at the plant and will be laid off. Clark blames NAFTA and increased competition from overseas for the loss of the jobs in Carlisle. "We bent over backwards to help them any way we could," said Clark. (Meehan 1999)

The article went on to say that some workers would be absorbed into the workforces at Jockey's sewing plants in neighboring counties, and that the knitting plant would stay open. The layoffs had gendered implications, since the knitting plant mostly employed men to make cloth and the sewing plant mostly employed women to sew it into garments.

In 2004, the knitting plant closed, with 137 more jobs lost in the county; Jockey kept about five workers in the machine shop between the two empty buildings for a while longer, and then closed its operations in Nicholas County entirely. As Jockey closed its sewing plants in Kentucky, it expanded production in its plants in Georgia, North Carolina, and the Caribbean. One of the reasons given was the Kentucky plant's distance from U.S. ports. The president of Jockey International at the time, Edward Emma, explained the "opening global markets" were responsible for the restructuring of the industry, with sewing labor being more affordable outside the United States. He said, "Jockey has waited longer than most of its competitors to make these changes, but the time has come to ensure that Jockey remains competitive in the years ahead" (*Carlisle Mercury* 2004:1). In 2000, the Carlisle–Nicholas County Industrial Authority bought the empty Jockey sewing plant, refurbishing it for a new industrial occupant (a paneling company). That startup did not get off the ground, nor did it have other prospects for its use. In 2010, it stands empty, but there are rumors of prospective occupants.

Toyota

Whereas people used to say that the Jockey plant held up tobacco farming in Nicholas County, now they say that about the Toyota assembly plant in Georgetown, Scott County (about a 30-mile commute each way from Nicholas County, via a narrow two-lane road on which the traffic moves at well over 50 miles per hour). One local farmer told me recently, "If it wasn't for Toyota, I don't know what people . . . I mean, that's kept people employed around here for almost a decade or more." There was a lot of hope for development in Nicholas County when Kentucky landed the Toyota plant. On the same December 19, 1985, front page of the *Carlisle Mercury* announcing the news that Kentucky Governor Martha Layne Collins (1983–1987) had announced the construction of the Toyota assembly plant, there was an article about the Carlisle Chamber of Commerce "gearing up for [a] piece of [the] action"; many surrounding communities were hoping to attract satellite plants to fit into Toyota's just-in-time supply model, for example, using the sewing skills already in Nicholas County to make seat covers for the new Camry cars produced in the Georgetown, Kentucky, plant. There were already over 100 Japanese-owned manufacturing plants around Kentucky, employing over 35,000 people, but the Toyota assembly plant would be far and away the largest manufacturer.

Governor Collins and her team worked hard to land the deal with Toyota. The state purchased the 1,600-acre site for the plant (for $10 million), prepared the site for development of the plant (for $25 million), and then gave it to Toyota for construction. Kentucky also committed to other incentives, including $33 million toward the training of workers for the plant (since this was not an automobile-producing region) and future tax breaks that totaled at least $125 million. The Toyota site was granted the federal status of a foreign trade subzone, which meant that the company would save $8 million per year because tariffs on imported parts would not have to be paid until the automobiles were sold, and tariffs on whole cars are less than on the component parts (Swasy 1987:A1). Toyota got proposals from 30 other states for the plant but accepted the bid from Kentucky. What was at stake? Jobs. There were 130,000 applications for over 3,000 jobs at the new Toyota plant. Kentuckians from 109 of the state's 120 counties were hired, along with workers from many other states.

There was backtalk around Kentucky about the deal, which was not uniformly welcomed. Here is a sampling of the many letters written to the *Lexington Herald-Leader* after the announcement of the Toyota deal by Governor Collins. David Warren wrote, "It's a shame that the citizens of Kentucky have to pay for all these incentives for new industries in our state to give to out of state people" (9/9/87). George Harris wrote, on August 21, 1987:

> Apparently, Gov. Martha Layne Collins isn't satisfied with the millions of
> Kentucky taxpayers' dollars she has donated to the Toyota cause. Now

she wants the federal government to donate $8 million to $10 million a
year on tariffs, which if enacted will take away thousands and thousands
of jobs from American workers. . . . If the Japanese had only known
when they tried to take this country by force that in 45 years there would
be people in politics such as Collins, Reagan and the U.S. Congress that
would give them the country, it sure would have saved a lot of lives, cost
and misery.

It was not uncommon for World War II anti-Japanese rhetoric to find its
way into anti-Toyota sentiments expressed in the 1980s. In another letter to
the editor of the *Lexington Herald-Leader*, Guy Deatherage wrote on August
14, 1987: "I think our present governor, having given great aid, assistance
and comfort to our old enemies, the Japanese, should be henceforth known
as 'Tokyo Rose' Collins."

These letters to the editor of the regional paper came from all around the
state, but I heard some similar reactions in Nicholas County at the time. One
farmer said that the state had "sold us out" to Toyota. A minister in the
county told me, "Everyone I've talked to resents Toyota and the Japanese." A
factory worker who had seen a Japanese robotics team at work in her plant
said, "They're like bees. They work different than us." A retired businessman
predicted that "the Japanese are going to take over the country and then lease
it back to us."

I ran across positive responses, too, in Nicholas County, especially since
the jobs at the plant were so needed. A professor of robotics at a regional university wrote an article published in the *Carlisle Mercury* that encouraged Kentuckians to move beyond skepticism and welcome assembly automation and
Toyota, as the way forward since the future of relying on tobacco and coal
was looking bleak (Masterson 1986:15). There was a lot of ambivalence
about how that scale of industrialization might change a place, and whether
something like the Toyota plant would even be really wanted in Carlisle. One
businesswoman told me:

> You stop and think about Georgetown [the site of the new Toyota plant],
> I believe if you go ask a lot of people over there, you go from house to
> house, I am just wondering how many people would say "yeah, open"
> with open arms. Because that turned that town completely upside down.
> Do you realize that Toyota's plant covers more square feet than the entire
> city of Carlisle? You could set the entire main area of Carlisle within that
> factory and still have room.

It was the case that there were some bumps in the road for Georgetown as
the Toyota plant was constructed, some of them having to do with roads
themselves, as there was debate over whether the corporation, the state, or
local government was responsible for improvements in the surrounding infrastructure (e.g., roads, waterlines, and schools) impacted by the $800 million
plant in the middle of the rural Scott County landscape. An article in the *Wall
Street Journal* published in 1991 summarized the impact of Toyota on the com-

munity as a "blessing and a curse: it creates jobs, but some fear domination by company, loss of small-town ways," as the headline read (O'Boyle 1991:A1). The increased traffic was a major concern for Georgetown residents. Only 11 percent of workers at the plant actually moved to Scott County to take jobs; 7 percent already lived there when they were hired, and the rest chose to commute to the plant from places like Nicholas County. Given the projections made at the time of the deal, though, it was hard for residents of Scott County to know what to expect. Toyota struck a deal to pay the Scott County schools $10.2 million over 20 years instead of taxes (Prather 1989:A12) as one way of compensating for the increased demand on local services. The increased revenues, according to Prather (1989:A12), added to tensions between city and county governments, which rejected a merger proposal.

Nicholas Countians began to apply for jobs with the Toyota Motor Corporation as the plant in Georgetown was being constructed; the three-hour application process included both written tests and interviews. As applicants waited to be called back, the plant grew. On October 6, 1988, former Governor Martha Layne Collins presided over the grand opening of the Toyota plant. I attended the opening tour of the facility with a retired Jockey plant worker and 60,000 other curious Kentuckians. Security was tight, to protect trade secrets. The roped pathway began with a tour through the history of Toyota auto production—a gallery of cars—and ended with free food, music, and balloons. People were moved along at a pace simulating the assembly line, affording rapid looks at a process in which rolled steel was stamped into parts, parts were assembled into bodies, bodies were painted and accessorized, and cars were prepared for shipment. The automation, directed by banks of computers along walkways overhead, amazed the crowd. Automobiles seemed to us to be making themselves, as they rode the tracks through their own production and circled overhead on what appeared to us as carnival rides. The size of the plant, more than 3.7 million square feet under one roof (Braden 1990:18), added to the surreal effect. Presiding over the entrance to the plant was a gigantic round, red papier-mâché head signed by all the workers, which we were told had been part of a teamwork exercise invoking a Japanese cultural symbol of group effort and promise.

Toyota management relied on that team spirit. The plant was not unionized. After some initial complaints about discrimination against minorities in hiring at the plant, Toyota spent $7.8 million on diversity hiring and buying from minority suppliers. Eventually, the local chapter of the National Conference of Christians and Jews gave Toyota a Brotherhood/Sisterhood award for its efforts to increase its hiring from within minority groups in Kentucky. A public image of partnering with communities was strongly cultivated by Toyota, which started a Volunteers in Place program, with workers giving hundreds of volunteer work hours in their own communities. Since the beginning of talks between the Toyota Motor Corporation and the Commonwealth of Kentucky, cultural similarities had been emphasized:

State officials say Kentucky and Japan have much in common. The Japanese "on several occasions have made comments about the similarities of values," says Sauer [Office for International Marketing in the Commerce Cabinet]. The Japanese cite Kentuckians' respect for tradition, the rural flavor of the people, their southern hospitality and their respect for each other. . . .

"They're interested in the same things we're interested in," [Governor Martha Layne] Collins said, like their family, their children, their homes and their jobs.

They study Stephen Foster's music. They know all the words to "My Old Kentucky Home" and they've heard of Kentucky Fried Chicken and the Kentucky Derby. (Braden 1986:7–8)

Toyota managers and government officials worked individually and sometimes jointly to get Toyota settled into the region culturally. Toyota symbolically moved into the famous Kentucky industry of thoroughbred horse racing by sponsoring the Toyota Bluegrass Stakes at the Keeneland race track. Lexington, Kentucky (not far from Georgetown), and Shizunai, Japan, became sister cities. The University of Kentucky, in Lexington, began offering evening classes on Japanese language and culture. The Japanese-American Society of Kentucky was formed in 1987 to promote good will and cultural exchange. Realtors in Scott County started putting up signs in Japanese, advertising property for sale. And Toyota Motor Manufacturing donated $2,500 to the Nicholas County Senior Citizens' Center in 1998. It looked like Toyota was staying in the state at a time when other manufacturers were moving out, and that built good will, also. The Toyota plant has become one of the most popular tourist destinations in the state.

In 1988, the *Carlisle Mercury* profiled a Nicholas Countian's trek across county lines and cultural lines (he was sent for training in Japan) to work at the Toyota plant:

Yes, there is a big world out there beyond Carlisle. Some of it different from Nicholas County, but much of it very similar if not the same.

One native Nicholas Countian was enabled to take the trip of a lifetime through being an employee of a new Kentucky industry and in doing so, gained appreciation and knowledge of a completely different culture.

Kirk Mattox, after much testing, earned a job as line supervisor in the assembly department with a title of team leader at Kentucky's newest industry, Toyota in Georgetown. (Mathes 1988a:13)

Hank Millerson is a farmer who also works at Toyota. He thinks that being a farmer was part of what got him hired at the plant:

Somebody right off the street couldn't stand it, I tell you. It's like housing tobacco every day. But . . . you're paid good, taken good care of, and you're interested in it. They'll do whatever it takes to see that everybody has got a good attitude toward work. . . . I guess it comes back to—you know, they pay you a good salary, good benefits, and have a bonus plan, a retirement plan.

Since Hank's other job, cash-cropping burley tobacco in a different multi-national industry, did not provide benefits, he needed the ones offered through Toyota. Sometimes the two jobs intensified at the same time, which was hard to take physically. Hank recalled one stretch of work at the Toyota plant, in the late 1980s, that lasted 19 days straight, with no days off and a lot of over-time. "Working over there and then coming home to house tobacco about three and a half hours a night—that was killing me." He was hoping that man-datory overtime would be cut back before calving season came. Hank said he was used to hard work, having grown up in farming. His mother worked at Jockey and farmed, too. At Christmastime, he said, when other families might be watching football, they would be stripping tobacco. Hank Millerson felt the combination of farm and factory work was vital to carrying on a way of life:

> There's not really a farm in this area you could live on. And pay for your groceries and your liquid fuel and your taxes and insurance. I mean just *live* there, and make a living and pay for the farm. . . . It's just an area that it takes a combination of four or five different things to bring in a little bit of money to make it here.

Putting Toyota into the livelihood mix meant more security than textiles as the twenty-first century approached, Hank Millerson and others found, but one local contingent was exploring another development option: tourism.

Tourism

A century and a half ago, Nicholas County was a national and interna-tional tourist destination—with a large spa at the Blue Licks Spring (a salt lick that had attracted mammoths long before tourists) and a bottling plant that shipped Blue Licks mineral water all over the world. Carlisle, too, hosted a lot of travelers as the train brought musicians, speakers, and actors through town to perform in Mozart Hall and spend the night at the hotel across the street. Tourism, like globalization, is not a new idea in Nicholas County—but there has been recent activity to develop tourism in conjunction with state and federal development initiatives like the Main Street Program, established to assist communities with revitalization efforts. For many years, I heard peo-ple in discussions about Carlisle development lament the fact that the deci-sion had been made to build the main two-lane road from Lexington and Paris, in the Bluegrass region, to Maysville, on the Ohio River, through the rural edge of the county instead of through the county seat of Carlisle. Then that development talk turned to gratitude for the placement of that same road, Route 68, because in being bypassed, the whole town square around the courthouse had been pretty much untouched, architecturally, for more than a century. That historic charm, instead of a beacon of backwardness, was reenvisioned by some as a valuable resource in the development of the tourism industry in Nicholas County.

By the mid-1990s, tourism had become the state's third largest industry after coal mining and automobile production. Kentucky seems to be on the way to a lot of places tourists go—the Smoky Mountains, the beach, Orlando, Florida—but it is not usually a final destination. An exception is the 2010 World Equestrian Games, held in the Bluegrass region of Kentucky. Culture and history have become part of the language of tourism promotion, and even though mountaintop removal is a key coal-mining strategy with economic and political heft, there is some talk in state-led development discourse of the clearcutting of forests and the removal of mountaintops as blighting the tourism potential in the eastern part of Kentucky. Keeping the "character" of small towns—with general stores instead of Walmarts—became of interest as local identity began to figure strongly in a statewide tourism development strategy. It was a key moment for state intervention as some small towns, like Sadieville (a small town of 300 near the Toyota plant in Scott County), faced decisions about whether to remain incorporated towns or be dissolved and let the county absorb them, which made it easier to administer services and give in to the suburban sprawl.

Governor Martha Layne Collins announced an economic development strategy emphasizing historic preservation in 1986, the Main

Cover image from brochure printed by Carlisle-Nicholas Co. Tourism, Inc., with the Kentucky Department of Travel

Street Program. She said that the revitalization of downtowns in small towns would make communities more attractive to industries choosing a new location. Those who have studied the effectiveness of the Main Street Program have found that it was most needed in towns that were very near larger cities (unlike Carlisle) because they were the most likely to lose local business to those urban centers and become indistinct as towns with the spread of suburbs (Smith 2007). Kentucky Governor Paul Patton (1995–2003) announced another program, Renaissance Kentucky, for downtown building restoration in small towns across the state.

There have been several attempts to brand Kentucky's tourism venture—one recent marketing slogan being "Kentucky's Unbridled Spirit," drawing on imagery from the horse industry—and even some self-mocking humor drawing on stereotypes of Kentucky. In 1990, for example, a state tourism spokesman, Jim Carroll, said he would speak to visitors from California on a "Third World in the U.S. Tour," although he said that many Kentuckians did not agree with the name Global Exchange had given its tour (perhaps because they were not interested in comparing the tremendous class disparities within the state to global North/South disparities, which was Global Exchange's emphasis). "We just hope we have enough time to put on our shoes and kick the pigs out of the yard before they get here," Carroll said (Swasy 1990). Being on the edge, Nicholas County both receives poverty tourists coming to see and work in Appalachia and sends its own groups on mission trips to help out in Appalachia.

Nicholas County's tourism development efforts have largely been led by women. Jo Lynn Garrett, in 2009, recalled having come back home to Carlisle in the 1980s, with a degree in interior design and coursework in architecture from the University of Kentucky, to work in her family's furniture business. She joined with others in the Nicholas County Historical Society, and a historical preservation consultant, Donna Neary, and got to work documenting 350 historical buildings in and around Carlisle. They built on research that Cammille Wells, a businesswoman, had done in 1980. Sherry Howard, a local archivist and genealogist, did historical research on the buildings and Jo Lynn Garrett worked on the architectural inventory. (You can see the architecture on Main Street, and take a virtual walking tour of buildings in Carlisle, on the homepage of Carlisle and Nicholas County, http://www.carlisle-nicholascounty.org.) Others working on the project with Jo Lynn Garrett, Donna Neary, and Sherry Howard put together a film and slide show that could be shown in local and state venues to promote historical preservation. Jo Lynn said that as she showed those images:

> People were amazed to see the little details—carriage stones, manhole covers where they used to put coal down the chutes . . . and some of the glass that adorns the buildings, you know, curved glass and little designs in it, the iron building fronts, [and] the flavor of the architecture, whether it was New Orleans architecture, Victorian . . . just a lot of little details.

She said that people watching her presentations who might live in town or work in those buildings every day said, "I didn't know that was there; I didn't know we had that."

In an interview with the *Carlisle Mercury* 22 years earlier about the project, Jo Lynn Garrett said:

> The Kentucky Heritage Council considers Carlisle to have one of the three best historic town squares in Kentucky. This is, for the most part, because the overall character is consistent. In other words, we don't have a McDonald's fast food restaurant sitting beside the Deposit Bank. The overall historical character is intact. (Mathes 1987:13)

So something that teenagers had complained about for years was reframed, in tourism development discourse, as a saving grace for the community. People started seeing old buildings as a resource, especially as individuals from out of town started moving in (often in retirement), buying those buildings, and investing in their restoration. "Outsiders" brought fresh perspective.

Carlisle received a Main Street grant of $5,000 (with a certificate presented by the governor) that inspired increasing local investment in tourism. In 1990, members of the Nicholas County Historical Society worked with the Department of the Interior and the Kentucky Heritage Council to get 305 buildings in Nicholas County declared eligible for the National Register of Historic Places. Gladys Shrout and Julie Metzger became co-chairs of Tourism, Inc., in Carlisle and began attending statewide tourism seminars and networking with the leaders of Kentucky tourism development and learning how to apply for state funds for tourism. Gladys Shrout, addressing community representatives at a meeting in the recently restored railroad depot, said this in 1990:

> Right now we have a big package in Carlisle we've never opened. It's filled with charm, beauty, and history. We have to find a way to open it. . . .
>
>   It is really impressive what we have to offer. Tourism is popular in a lot of towns. Our task is to devise a means to attract tourists. (Spradling 1990:1)

At this same time, all the clothing stores in the historic storefronts were closing down (with shoppers going to Walmart in neighboring towns), but the county was beginning to import people seeking land and history. A "Tourism Talk" column started appearing in the *Carlisle Mercury*. In "Tourism Talk," Nicholas Countians were reminded not to refer to Carlisle as "dead" or "in the boondocks" to strangers passing through:

> For too long Nicholas Countians have felt inferior to larger areas which offer shopping centers, a variety of restaurants and nightlife. The reality is that people who live in such places are looking for what we have to offer if only for a day or a few hours on a pretty afternoon. . . .
>
>   When they come they want to capture some of the serenity of life in a smaller town. What to a local person may seem "dead" or "in the boondocks" is to a traveler a treasure, a discovery, to be enjoyed. When you see visitors give them a friendly smile, take a moment to welcome them.

Let your pride show. Tell them of the beauty of the county. Tell them of the county's rich heritage which lives on today. Invite them to linger, to enjoy the area and to come again. (Tourism Talk 1990)

The Kentucky Heritage Council provided funds and the local National Guard unit provided labor to start renovating the Carlisle Jail as a tourism drop-in center. Tourism, Inc., leases the jail building from the Nicholas County Fiscal Court; the county has long since had to send anyone arrested to regional prisons. The brick jail, once famous in high school lore as the building a prisoner dug out of with a spoon, is now fully restored, and tourists can eat lunch there and find tourism literature on other places to visit in the county. You can even participate in online tourism in Carlisle and Nicholas County by visiting http://www.carlisle-nicholascounty.org and clicking on the tourism tab. Now, there is a tourism brochure that can be picked up at rest stops along the Interstates in Kentucky (see the brochure's cover on p. 84).

In addition to state investment, much of the capital investment for recent historical renovation, as part of tourism development, has come from those moving into the community with an interest in the architecture and history. The Garvin family, for example, has bought and restored several buildings on the courthouse square. Two local residents, in 2009 interviews I did with them, commented on the newcomers' efforts. They did not feel that there was a rift between those placed as insiders and outsiders participating in tourism projects. One said:

Our geography here is very unique. Our town does not have a U.S. highway. There's only one U.S. highway in the county, and it's miles from the town. There are no interstates in the county. Because of this, it's actually preserved a lot of our historical heritage that otherwise would have been lost. And I think people have come in who are aware of that and make us all proud of it, and that's an important part of the future of our county to be recognized—the heritage. . . . I'm sure the newcomers have helped the tax base of the county, since we've lost the industrial base.

Another local resident commented on the joint efforts of long-term residents and newcomers:

It's very exciting to me that the people who have moved here from other places have so many ideas for making a nicer place to live. Some of them have gotten involved with the Industrial Authority and the Chamber of Commerce, and they have some new and exciting ideas. But they're working with the people of the community so it's not separate. And the renovation of the Neal Building is very exciting, because it's an old building that's being turned into a community center and museum. And many of those people have helped with that, as well as people who have been here a long time.

Many local organizations (with long-term and new membership) have promoted tourism development in different ways. In 2001, the Rotary Club put up a roadside sign at the place where tourists would turn off the main two-lane road, U.S. 68, and drive the three miles into Carlisle. Here is a brief review of tourism efforts in the county over the last 15 years:

- There was a special passenger run of the (now commercial) train between Paris and Maysville, stopping at the renovated Carlisle Depot.
- Court Days (originally activities and markets on the courthouse square held when the circuit judge was holding session and people came in from the county to the courthouse) were revived by the Chamber of Commerce.
- The Carlisle Community Woman's Club designed a Nicholas County afghan, with local scenes, to help begin the celebration of the county's bicentennial in 1999. (That's when I organized the bicentennial oral history project, with the Historical Society, as one of many other local activities that year.)
- The Wesley Chapel Christian Methodist Episcopal Church, in partnership with other groups, began restoring the Henryville cemetery.
- A doll museum was opened on Main Street.
- There are reenactments at the Blue Licks historical Revolutionary War battlefield on which Daniel Boone's son Israel, and many others, died after the war was over but before word of peacetime got to Kentucky. Blue Licks Battlefield State Resort Park is on the border of Nicholas and Robertson Counties (historically both Nicholas County). Native American history is also featured in the park's museum.
- The last cabin Daniel Boone occupied in Kentucky is in Nicholas County, along with a number of other historic sites with varying degrees of preservation and public access.

Most of those working on tourism development have concentrated their efforts on the renovation of historical buildings for community use, hoping to build both community interest and attract tourists from out of town that way. But one person involved in local tourism efforts told me in 2009 that he hoped that natural resources as well as historical resources would be considered in tourism development:

> I would like to see the wonderful natural resources that we have in this county further appreciated and utilized. We have more wild land than any other inner or outer Bluegrass area. We have a stretch of almost wild river—the Licking River—which has wonderful recreational possibilities. I'd like to see our county develop in a way that would protect this. If we bring in one polluting factory, that's all gone. And I think it would be a bad deal, because I think in the long run, people are going to hunger for peaceful, beautiful, rural and natural surroundings. Ecotourism is a possibility. It's starting at the state park, with canoe trips. I think we should use what we have to our advantage, instead of trying to invent something new.

The Nicholas County Historical Society has worked with the Licking River Rural Economic Authority to develop a series of local heritage trails.

The historical society is restoring the Neal Building, long the site of Eugene and Powell Neal's Square Deal grocery store, as a museum and visitor's center. Joan Conley, a local journalist who was instrumental in turning the local committee formed to commemorate the nation's bicentennial in 1976 into a permanent organization called the Nicholas County Historical Society, edited the History of Nicholas County, which was recently republished.

Local and state tourism development discourses are linked, in all of these efforts. Carlisle–Nicholas County Tourism, Inc., and Chamber of Commerce have posted signs at the edges of the county saying (as you see in the frontispiece of this book) "Welcome to Nicholas County: Friendly, Fruitful, and Rich in History." As you drive on down Route 68 into Mason County, you'll see Mason County's sign featuring the words history, culture, and commerce. These county projects are connected to a larger state development discourse valorizing rural identity. As one Nicholas County official put it, as we talked in the 1980s about options for the community with the fall of tobacco echoing, as I had been told, in local cash registers: "I don't want to see Carlisle changed so that it's not Carlisle anymore." Of the three main development projects pursued in the county over the following two decades (textiles, Toyota, and tourism), he threw his hat in with tourism. It facilitates that kind of identity-based development.

Working the Edge: Joining Appalachia

Thinking back to Tom Hensley's proposal, one of the things he did—living along the river that divides a Bluegrass ADD county from a Buffalo Trace ADD county, and having relatives on both sides—was work for cross-county collaboration. Another Nicholas County farmer who was, similar to Tom Hensley, "placed" at the edge of several counties, with relatives in each of them, and who was also spending his own money to travel to Frankfort to try to get cross-county collaboration on industrial development going in the 1980s told me: "We're trying to get a spirit of inter-county cooperation because Kentucky is so diversified, they've had more or less county rivalry over the years." Like Tom, he was frustrated by the deaf ears he encountered. Around that time, a county official told me about the lack of city–county and county–county collaboration, "The politics of it are still too strong to overcome," and a factory worker said that anything like a city–county merger to help with development was "way on down in the future." A businesswoman who moved into Nicholas County from another state in the 1960s had this to say in the 1990s about her take on cross-county relations:

> I was amazed at the number of counties when I came to Kentucky. One town and one county. And of course a Kentuckian doesn't want to hear this, but first, it seems like Kentucky could progress more socially and maybe economically—all, if they had less counties and more people grouped together. . . . Everybody is like a different little country over the

border. This is not the way to get to socialize and get to know people and learn something new other than what you've been taught for a hundred years. I don't know if it will ever come about, but it's sad that every little county has the same bureaucracy to support and maintain. . . . It was just like two foreign countries, those county boundaries sealing us in or out.

The climate is much more favorable for cross-county cooperation now than it was 25 years ago. There are many possible practical reasons for this, including a change in some of the revenue streams for small municipalities from county-based to region-based; increased commuting across county lines for work; and the challenge of running community services (needing to engage federal and state guidelines in ever more complex ways) on such a small scale with government workers who mostly do something else for a living. Instead of seeing us languish at the edges of various development districts, Nicholas County officials started working those edges to bring in funding from more sources—funding that was very much needed. Nicholas County Judge-Executive Larry Tincher told me in 2009 that he had heard an argument one time between a farmer who said that Nicholas County could not survive without tobacco and a factory worker who said that Nicholas County could not survive without Jockey; then he said:

> Well, now we've lost both. And we're still moving forward. We may not be running as fast as we want to run, but we're still walking. So we're maintaining services without having to increase taxes on taxpayers, and that's a hard thing to do. . . . We've had to tighten our belt. We actually have not cut any funding to any programs that we provide funding to, but it would have probably made my job a lot easier, and my staff's job a lot easier, if we were in a time when we had funding that was available, to where we didn't have to worry about how we were going to come up with this. That just adds a little more stress, but we've got broad shoulders.

I asked him how the global economic crisis was being felt locally, and he said:

> It's affected everybody. And a lot of people don't understand that. It's a commonsense issue. I mean, out there, we've lost all the manufacturing jobs in the United States. . . . You've got people in high political office that say well, we're creating this many jobs, or that many jobs, but they're not the $15–20/hour jobs that people are used to. They're the $6 and $7 an hour job at a fast-food store, or at a Walmart, and that's the jobs that have been created. . . . And that's really put a hurt on us. We depend too much on foreign trade, on foreign countries to manufacture the goods that we buy in the United States. . . . The globalization issue cannot be good for us. It falls back to what I just said earlier about the manufacturing jobs. We have got to produce something. . . . We can't depend on all of our products being manufactured overseas. And that's not a knock on globalization or the world itself. . . . But when you look around your own communities, your own nation that needs help, we've got to be a world leader in showing people that we can produce something instead of depending so much on them.

Judge Tincher hoped that one route to development might be real estate development along the newly expanded Route 68 through the county, so that commuters from bigger towns might choose to settle in Nicholas County. He was working on getting grants for infrastructure, like road improvement, as a means to development.

As tobacco income fell and the plants closed, there were several public meetings convened by the Community Action Council to discuss increasing poverty and to inventory community (e.g., church and business) as well as local government resources available to address growing problems people in the county were having with getting by. As different futures were being imagined for the community through the official development discourses followed in the last section of this chapter, there were also subaltern (or not top-down) projects in which residents of Nicholas County were taking alternative economic development into their own hands. Yard sales grew tremendously through the 1980s and 1990s as a way to redistribute clothing, tools, and household goods and bring in some cash. At one point, they were so successful that the state tried to tax yard sales, but citizens held that off. Informal sector (or underground, untaxed) work grew in the county also. One form of that was the gradual extension of the already-existing kin swaps of farmwork, construction, and child care to incorporate more cash labor for more people (with unreported income). Another form of informal sector work was the growing underground trade in prescription medications like painkillers. That trade constitutes a large portion of the county's economy now, but even in the 1980s it was growing.

Just under 20 percent of Nicholas County residents (around 1,600) are on disability (a form of social security) benefits; formal sector employment often means losing those benefits, secure in regularity but not necessarily in providing an adequate household income. A common reason for being on disability is work-related injury, either in farming or factory work. Employment options for many Nicholas Countians involve some physical labor. It has not been easy to enter the information economy, for example, given the lack of access to educational and technological opportunities most residents have had. Thirty-seven percent of Nicholas Countians over 25 do not have a high school degree; 92.5 percent do not have a four-year college degree. That limits possibilities for finding other kinds of work once physical labor is not an option.

In 2004, over $18 million came directly into the county for retirement and disability benefits; a large percentage of the population, then, lives on a fixed income. As the cost of living increases along with unemployment within family networks, the kinds of informal-sector employment mentioned above might be seen as economically necessary in the absence of other ways to boost income to meet basic needs. In 2008, 17.4 percent of Nicholas Countians were reported by the U.S. Census as living below poverty level. Many Nicholas Countians are living on the edge economically, then, as well as figuratively in the development landscape and literally on the edge between lowlands and uplands. Development strategies have to take that into account.

In 2008, Nicholas County was incorporated into the Appalachian region by becoming a county served by the Appalachian Regional Commission (ARC). This took a lot of lobbying on the part of Judge Tincher, Bluegrass ADD representatives, and Kentucky legislators. Judge Tincher told me in an interview the next summer:

> Buffalo Trace also, the ADD district which Robertson County is in, worked to coincide with Bluegrass ADD to try to include us in the Appalachian region. It's a hard thing to get into, because it runs all the way from New York State to Georgia. And they only add a few counties, certain years. Some years, they don't add any. But for 9 years, the Bluegrass ADD took me to Washington, DC, knocking on the door trying to get into the ARC. So you know, knocking on the door paid off. But what it does—we've also lost . . . over 90% of our industrial workforce. And the Appalachian region is for, not poor people, but for poor communities that need assistance. And they don't provide everything that you need. But it is an avenue where maybe each year we could get possibly a grant that would help improve the lifestyle of our community. They work well with the schools, the hospitals. . . .

By saying here that the Appalachian label does not mean impoverished people, Judge Tincher was standing up to the same stereotype that Appalachian residents have had to fight in "othering" practices ranging from policy discourses to Hollywood movies and television shows that situate poverty within the Appalachian mountains, somehow corralled there as spatially and temporally distant from the rest of the nation. These stereotypes can be internalized, and Judge Tincher was asking Nicholas Countians not to see acknowledging Appalachian identity as owning the stereotype. There is a long tradition within Appalachian communities of rejecting stereotypes of poverty and ignorance and placing the region globally within the political economic context of extractive industries accountable for the challenging economic conditions that residents must negotiate actively and creatively on a daily basis. Appalachian news media like the *Mountain Eagle*, songwriters, storytellers, and documentary collectives like Appalshop counter stereotypes with political economic analyses and positive accounts of the cultural and environmental resources of the vast region. Judge Tincher went on to describe the technical details of mapping the language of the federal Appalachian Regional Commission onto the landscape of Nicholas County:

> There's differences in the ARC. There's distressed counties, there's at-risk counties, and then there's counties that are doing well. Nicholas County, unfortunately, is split. The northeastern half of our county is a distressed county, next to Robertson County. But the city of Carlisle, and the southwest portion of Nicholas County, is considered an at-risk county. Now, what that means, when you apply for a grant, if you're at risk, it's a 70/30 match. You have to put up 30% of whatever the grant total is. If you're a distressed county, you put up 20%. So there is a little difference, being distressed and at risk. And the projects that we're working on [assistance

for the hospital and a recycling program] are all in the at-risk category, they're not in the distressed category.

Judge Tincher, like many public service employees in the county, is also a tobacco farmer. He talked about the difference in soils across the county paralleling the "at risk" and "distressed" ARC labels. "Everybody has to live somewhere," he said, "and all land is not plush land. . . . But that doesn't mean the people are less important. Because everybody is important. God didn't make any nobodies." Like those in other counties participating in the ARC, Judge Tincher saw exciting possibilities for working together in development planning regionally rather than just at the scale of the county government. Working in multiple arenas on development is like crop diversification. Judge Tincher said that he could see the effects of the fall of tobacco's significance in the county: "Per capita, we were probably one of the biggest tobacco producers in the state. . . . It's changed a lot of people's lifestyle. . . . It's been a big blow. It really has." He knew other options needed to be explored.

With the tobacco buyout, land stopped coming with a tobacco base, which meant that the value of land went down. With the loss of payroll tax because of the factory closing, Carlisle and Nicholas County had to pursue new strategies for supporting local services, and federal grants were one of the sources to be pursued, through whatever regional agencies that might help. In the end, becoming part of the Appalachian Regional Commission (originally established by President John F. Kennedy in 1963 and made a federal agency in 1965) was a political decision made for Nicholas County by the U.S. Congress. The bill was introduced through the House of Representatives' Committee on Transportation and Infrastructure and was passed as one of the Appalachian Regional Development Act Amendments of 2008. Nicholas County is now part of a 23-million-person region that can serve as another forum for coming up with alternative "tobacco town futures." Although the Appalachian region is stereotypically associated with coal production, that industry is no longer the major job provider (partly because of mechanization in mountaintop removal mining); many other communities are also exploring service and tourism options. In 2010, Nicholas County received $46 million in road improvement funds, mostly to widen U.S. Route 68; those commuters and tourists may be coming to town after all. It is possible that being formally associated with Appalachia, a trans-state region with established cultural and ecological attractions, will increase Nicholas County's tourism possibilities.

Inclusion in the Appalachian Regional Commission is as close as the region comes to having a unified political identity, since it crosses so many state lines. That political identity has been used to forge networks that counter the stereotypes that were often fostered through War on Poverty imagery. Appalachia is a diverse cultural region, in part because of the centuries of multinationally controlled extractive industries that brought international labor forces to the mountains, but also because of Native American nations' ongoing contributions to regional politics and culture. The ARC is just one kind of network spanning the region. ARC activities are partnerships between federal, state, and county governments and area development districts. To learn more about the ARC, you can visit its website: http://www.arc.gov. Nicholas County's two identities, first as a tobacco town and then as an Appalachian community, have roots in the New Deal, since President Franklin D. Roosevelt's administration both set up the tobacco program to help stabilize Depression-era small farms and identified Appalachia as an "economically distressed" region.

Contrary to media portrayals of isolation, Appalachia has always been a region completely enmeshed in global political economies. Its early history involved colonial conquest and the displacement of Native American nations. There has also been an emphasis on capital extraction by international investors in the coal and lumber industries with a multinational workforce. In the twentieth century, Appalachia was featured in debates between Keynesian and neoliberal economists about the cause and alleviation of poverty. And now, the region's forests are significant in global climate discussions since it is the second most biologically diverse region on the planet, next to Amazonia. Through those lenses, Nicholas County might be viewed as indeed engaging globalization, at the edge of Appalachia.

In 2009, I asked several Nicholas Countians what they thought about being labeled as Appalachian. The *Carlisle Mercury* had run several headlines about becoming part of the ARC. Not everyone, however, can or does read the newspaper. One person I spoke with had heard of the ARC, and hoped some money could be obtained for improving the water system out in the county. Another said that he felt Nicholas Countians did more work and shopping in the Bluegrass than in the mountain region, just because it's easier to go downhill than uphill, and that not many people in the county would probably identify themselves as Appalachian. A retired service worker told me she thinks many Nicholas Countians are not aware of being part of the ARC.

When I asked Judge Tincher, who had worked so hard for the ARC designation, how people in the county were responding to it, he said:

> Some people take an understanding that if you become an Appalachian region, that it's nothing but bringing poor, poor people into your community, or it's poor, poor people. That's not the case. It's to help people. And that's what it's all about. Is it going to make a big difference overnight? No. But eventually, we're going to see benefits of it.

Commodifying Rurality

In both state and local development discourses, Nicholas Countians are finding that an increasingly marketable resource is rurality itself. The commodification of rurality (Kingsolver 1992b) can take a variety of forms, whether in marketing an untroublesome, hard-working labor force to potential industrial employers, or a bucolic landscape, neighborliness, simplicity, authenticity, and history ("placing" rural experience in an earlier time) to potential tourists and new residents caught up in dreams of urban flight. Some aspects of commodifying rurality are obviously problematic and can include marketing whiteness to those whose urban flight is connected with white flight, as well as the offer of lower wages linked to notions of a captive labor force without the education or ability to pursue other options. Nicholas County farmers have told me on a number of occasions that they take advantage of certain stereotypes of rurality, getting better prices for their tobacco or vegetables in urban markets because they are perceived as "earnest, hard-working rural people," and they play that up, talking about raising crops as a family and about being loyal and honest in their marketing relationships. Rurality is commodified in other ways, as it begins to be seen as a vanishing resource.

In Lexington, Kentucky, where there is rapid urban growth, a Purchase of Development Rights (PDR) program was started in 2000, and in Georgetown, where housing developments sprouted up on many farms within sight of the Toyota plant, PDR discussions were renewed in 2007. The American Farmland Trust keeps track of easements—basically, paying people not to develop their farmland—in 14 states. In the Bluegrass region of Kentucky, where farms—particularly horse farms—are key to tourism, concern has grown about losing that visual landscape to housing and industrial development. When the Paris Pike—a stretch of U.S. Route 68 between Lexington and Paris, Kentucky, that is famous for its views of fenced fields, old "wolf" trees standing in the pastures, and thoroughbreds—was widened in the last decade, stonemasonry was taught to workers (including some from Nicholas County) so that the trademark fieldstone fences could be rebuilt to retain an authentic viewscape for tourists. In Scott County, the rural setting valued by Toyota in the corporation's choice of location for the plant was being endangered by Toyota-related development.

> PDR programs enable property owners to sell the development rights to a non-developing body, while continuing to farm the land . . . the program will help farmers maintain their livelihood and keep the county's agricultural heritage alive. Scott is looking to closely imitate Fayette County, which has the only county-level PDR program in the state. (Ogawa 2007:1)

Out at the edge of the Bluegrass, Nicholas Countians have seen the commodification of rurality in several ways. Because Nicholas County is at the edge of two regions, sometimes "outsiders" buying property are picturing themselves in different landscapes. A local official told me in the 1980s, for example, that coal company executives were coming west to Nicholas County to buy a farm "in the Bluegrass," and "horse money" was moving east to find more affordable land in the hills. "Tobacco tourists" sometimes stop beside the road to photograph workers in the field; tobacco is a photogenic crop, with its bright green burley leaves, shading to brown as the plants dry on stakes in the fall fields. Tourists taking pictures of tobacco and cattle do not feel the chemical spray and do not realize the necessary role of the pet food factory they may pass on the road in processing the carcasses of live-stock not sold (for various reasons) for human consumption at the stock-yards. They see the picturesque side of farming, and it really sells—in locally made postcards and arts and crafts that are commodified as authentically rural by association with the landscape of their production. There are many ways in which the local landscape can fit into people's imaginations, but all of them probably involve imagining rurality.

Frank Mathias, a historian who grew up in Nicholas County, wrote a letter from his home in Ohio to the editor of the *Nicholas Countian and the Carlisle Mercury* on April 16, 2004, as the Jockey plant was closing down, to suggest that development plans take Nicholas County's agricultural landscape into account:

> Agriculture was our economic base for 150 years before Jockey was heard of, and it behooves us to investigate and act upon any possibilities offered by the modern science, art or business of agriculture.
>
> By agriculture I am thinking in addition to traditional Kentucky farming, and offer several ideas of Carlisle developing as a modern green space center for the study, use and recreation involved in arboretums, city gardens, tree programs and green-belts for hikers and bikers. Those things fit well into a longtime agricultural community.

Some people bought second homes in Nicholas County, at Lake Carnico, for example (constructed in the 1960s as a development project), for recreation and then—as a Nicholas Countian told me—"it's such a nice place to live that they've wound up moving here, and this becomes a permanent home." They then end up commuting to jobs in the city. There is also an increasing pattern of people choosing to move to Nicholas County because of its rurality and inexpensive housing costs, and then telecommuting (working from home via the Internet). The Federal Communications Commission, in part using 2009 stimulus funding, is working on expanding high-speed Internet service to rural areas, which will make this kind of arrangement even more common.

Two decades ago, as part of Kentucky's bicentennial celebration (as a state), the Kentucky Department of Agriculture and the Kentucky Heritage Council started the Historic Farms Program, under which several Nicholas County farms were registered. Centennial and Bicentennial Farms had to be in the same family for 100–200 years, in continuous operation as a farm, and still be producing at least $1,000 in agricultural products per year on at least 10 acres. Tom and Lida Hensley registered their farm as a Centennial Farm through documenting its continuous operation by her family, the Letchers, for 132 years.

Nicholas Countians were beginning to realize that tangible elements of the landscape, long taken for granted, were being commodified and sold out of the county. Jo Lynn Garrett (the person who worked so hard to put so many buildings in Carlisle on the National Register of Historic Places) told me in 2009, for example:

You see a lot of things that we still lose. We lose log cabins. I know of three log cabins that have been moved out of the county. . . . This is probably within the last four or five years. I hated to see that. It's just like a part of *our* history, our landscape, just taken away.

More commonly than log cabins, I see barns as a key symbol in the commodification of the rural landscape. On the Hensleys' farm, the barn itself was declared a Kentucky Heritage building; Lida's ancestors had fastened it together with wooden pegs (Hensley 1992:3). On the outskirts of Lexington, people started buying barns and converting them to houses. The Hughes family, who did that in Nicholas County, was profiled in the Lexington newspaper. In Kentucky, it is tobacco barns especially that are symbolic capital associated with rurality:

> Tobacco barns, more than any other feature, mark the Kentucky landscape. Whether new and well-maintained, or old beyond memory and listing like ships in a storm, these structures are Kentucky icons, no less than grain elevators on the Kansas plains or skyscrapers in Manhattan. (Stull 2000:153)

In the photo below, you see Loretta Mann looking out of the doorway of her tobacco barn. The Mail Pouch tobacco sign carries symbolic capital as well:

> Some people are just thrilled to spot a rickety barn still emblazoned with a Mail Pouch Tobacco sign. . . . "They're symbols of endurance and hope for the future and a connectedness to the past and all the people that have made a living off the land. . . . When I see a barn, it gives me a feeling that the farm will persevere and go on." (Suzi Shoemaker, quoted in Copley 1999:K3)

Loretta Mann and her tobacco barn (photo by author)

In 2005, the "Clothesline of Quilts in Appalachia" project came to Kentucky. Volunteers, including some professional artists, started painting a single, colorful eight-foot by eight-foot quilt square on the side of a barn that could be seen from the road as part of a project encouraging tourism in Appalachia. There are several tobacco barns with quilt squares on them in Nicholas County. The project cleverly unites, in the commodification of rurality, the symbolic value of both barns and traditional arts and crafts in association with farming and Appalachia. Arts and crafts production is another development project that has taken off in eastern Kentucky, including in Nicholas County. Sometimes, like the quilt project, barns become part of the art. When Brenda Emmons made this punched-tin painting of Loretta Mann's tobacco barn that now hangs in my room as I write this book, for example, she framed it with the oak wood from tobacco sticks, used to hang tobacco plants in the barn.

Although many Nicholas Countians have taken their crafts skills for granted (and there is widespread sewing skill, for example, because of experience in the garment industry), some have marketed their crafts production widely, and rural or Appalachian identity adds to the value and perceived authenticity of the items. There is a Kentucky Craft Marketing Program set up to facilitate that development strategy. That program, Berea College, and many other organizations worked together to open the Kentucky Artisan Center at Berea to feature and market the work of Kentucky craftspeople.

Punched-tin painting of Loretta Mann's tobacco barn by Brenda Emmons (photo by author)

The visibility that the Kentucky Artisan Center and other tourist sites give to local artisans increases the value of work by those who might have seen their crafts production as a hobby before. Several Nicholas County artisans market their work widely: Loretta Mann is a weaver, and tourists have been coming to her log cabin home in a river valley for decades to buy her work. Sue Rule is an outstanding quilter who was commissioned by Cincinnati artist Terrie Mangat to quilt a number of her fabric artworks. Sue Rule's stitches—all made on her Saltwell farm in Nicholas County—can now be seen, if you look closely, in the Chase Manhattan Bank in New York City, in the Alfred P. Murrah Federal Building in Oklahoma, and in a traveling exhibit that started in Los Angeles and went around the world. John Sibert developed a reputation as a woodworking craftsman and sold items from his home; Carolyn Bowles took wood all the way from milling it to woodworking to painted crafts items that she began selling in California through her sister's contacts. There are many such stories.

Nicholas County now has an Arts and Cultural Association (formed through a grant from the Kentucky Arts Council), and artists Regina Barnes, Larry Mitchell, and Cate Wagoner formed the Courthouse Square Arts Guild (see http://www.csag.info). The Guild promotes the work of a number of artists in the community; it has a space on Main Street for exhibits, classes, and sales. Both of these organizations have sponsored arts programs and contests to encourage local children in arts education and production. Artwork and crafts are also featured at the county fair and at local and regional festivals. Crafts, long practiced in rural households, are no longer just being sold at yard sales and given as family gifts (perhaps not having been valued, by many, as highly as "store-bought" presents because of both widespread artisan skills and capitalist ideology emphasizing cash values). Arts and crafts are shaping up to be a strong "tobacco town future" scenario related to tourism.

Developing Agricultural Alternatives

Although a few people, like Tom Hensley, had been thinking about this long before the tobacco buyout, the search began in earnest—backed by necessary capitalization—to find crops and markets that might be feasible as alternatives to tobacco. The Community Farm Alliance, a diverse group of small farmers and local food movement supporters across Kentucky, was instrumental in lobbying for the Master Settlement Agreement Phase II funds to be used to support growers who wanted to shift from tobacco to other crops. Putting in the infrastructure required to try alternatives—from grapes to goats—cost too much for most small farmers, so the investment of Phase II funds in buildings, fencing, field structures, soil preparation, training, and other necessities was key to keeping people on their farms through the transition from the tobacco program.

In 1988, an article in the *Carlisle Mercury* warned that the transition from tobacco to vegetables, for example, would not be simple: "Kentucky burley growers experimenting with new crops are like unemployed factory workers retraining for a new line of work, agriculture experts say" (Mathes 1988b). The Carlisle businessman who said to me, about Tom Hensley's proposal, "It'll have to be a whole new generation that *wants* to try something different as they're starting out," turned out to be right. A survey of tobacco farmers in 1995 found "that younger and more educated farmers were more eager to supplement tobacco income with other ventures and were more concerned about the long-term uncertainties of tobacco agriculture" (Collins 1995:A1).

That generational shift had to be crafted consciously in high schools across Kentucky, where vocational agriculture classes, often also sponsoring the Future Farmers of America school chapters, long taught young people how to grow tobacco not just through textbooks but through hands-on experience. Estep and Johnson (1999:A1, A8) reported that 23 public school districts, including Nicholas County, across Kentucky owned tobacco bases (marketing quotas) ranging from several hundred to almost 10,000 pounds. The school districts either leased these tobacco allotments out for additional income, had agricultural students raising and selling the crop, or both. When they interviewed a Nicholas County official, he said that selling the base would not be popular. The school still has a tobacco barn on the hill next to the elementary school that was used by high school students to house their crop.

Vocational agriculture classes in many school districts like ours confronted dealing with the tobacco buyout directly and adding new skill sets into the educational mix. In the Montgomery County High School, one county over from Nicholas, the students in vocational agriculture started working with lambs instead of tobacco as their hands-on project, learning to shear and show them at the Future Farmers of America Market Lamb Show at the Kentucky State Fair. Sheep were very common in the area a century ago and are making a comeback, along with spinning and weaving wool. In 2006, the Nicholas County High School agricultural students grew tomatoes and peppers as a joint venture with a local minister who makes and markets Poppie's Salsa.

Younger farmers were in the minority as Kentuckians went through the transition from the tobacco program. The largest number of full-time farmers was the over-65 group; only a thousand full-time farmers in Kentucky were under 25 (Associated Press 2001:C3). Many of those young farmers making a living solely from the farm were using the Internet to find markets and had their crops and livestock data computerized. There was definitely a generation gap in the search for agricultural alternatives, and that might partly explain the tremendous controversy over hemp as a viable alternative crop in Kentucky. Although hemp had been plentiful in Kentucky fields during the nineteenth century, as I have mentioned, and again as a war-effort crop during World War II, in the late twentieth century it was associated with illegal marijuana use rather than rope making, and it is not unusual to see law enforcement helicopters flying over Nicholas County farms to find hidden marijuana crops for the underground drug market; those crops found are destroyed.

Those who advocated hemp as an alternative crop to tobacco argued that the plant grown for fiber did not have the same properties as the cultivars used for marijuana production and that it did not make sense to import hemp fiber from other countries when it could be grown in Kentucky and contribute to the local economy. One farmer said that trying to get high smoking industrial hemp would be like trying to get drunk on nonalcoholic beer. Those who wanted to keep hemp-growing illegal argued that it would be too difficult to tell the hemp crops, if legalized, from illegally grown marijuana, since they were basically the same plant. Although some argued that a hemp industry would generate more money in Kentucky than 10 Toyota plants, a governor's task force said the legal obstacles were too difficult to overcome, and university test farms steered clear of research on the controversial crop.

The showdown came when an elementary teacher invited Woody Harrelson, an actor advocating the hemp industry as a way for U.S. farmers to continue farming, to talk to her class as she presented both sides of the issue. After that talk, Harrelson was later arrested in Kentucky for symbolically planting four industrial hemp seeds and the teacher was investigated by the school board. Harrelson went free, but the African American teacher who invited him to speak, Donna Cockrel, was investigated by her school board over the issue and later fired. (She sued.) The argument is still going on about domestic production of industrial hemp. The Kentucky Industrial Hemp Association imported hemp meal, since it was illegal to grow hemp in the U.S., and farmers started testing it as feed for everything from catfish to cattle. One native Nicholas Countian, three-time gubernatorial hopeful Gatewood Galbraith, has actually advocated replacing tobacco with a quota system for farmers growing legalized marijuana in Kentucky. "I just couldn't really figure out why no one else seemed willing to discuss it," he said about his unsuccessful election platform (Galbraith 2004:96).

The CFA has been an effective force in helping farmers figure out alternative crops and markets to replace tobacco on small farms. It has received financial support from Farm Aid, since its founding in 1985, and from subscriptions to *CFA News* sent all over the state and outside Kentucky, to people like me following its efforts. As the Kentucky legislature debated how to distribute settlement and buyout funds, the CFA was right there with its Model Marketing Plan, worked out with details on (1) direct marketing of diverse agricultural products, from packing houses to farmers markets and contracts with food services in state schools, hospitals, and prisons; (2) farm stands, community-supported agriculture subscriptions, and agritourism; (3) regional beef marketing and processing networks instead of out-of-state processing; and (4) education and market development for farmers transitioning from tobacco. The CFA had not only mobilized the research necessary to work out this detailed plan, but members also attended the hearings to ask that the Kentucky Agricultural Development Board (established to distribute the settlement funds) meet the needs of small farmers with low incomes as well as those with large-scale agricultural operations. In May 2000, the *CFA News* headline read "CFA Victorious!" as it reported that the testimony of Community Farm Alliance members and the organization's suggestions had made a difference in shaping House Bill 611, the legislation that set up the structure for distributing tobacco settlement funds.

There was minimal CFA membership in Nicholas County, but Buddy Switzer, a farmer from the next county who belonged to the CFA with his wife Kim, wrote a letter to the editor of the *Nicholas Countian* on September 8, 2000, explaining the recently passed legislation:

> During the 2000 session of the General Assembly, legislators made history by passing legislation that gives Kentucky farm families and rural communities the ability to develop comprehensive plans that strengthen rural farm economies. House Bill 611 created local Agricultural Development Councils to facilitate the planning process and a state Agricultural Development Board to fund local, regional, and statewide programs identified in county plans.

He went on to outline the steps county residents needed to take to inventory and address needs in exploring alternatives to tobacco:

> A county might identify a mobile processing unit as a need in order to develop a market for pasture poultry or they may identify a need for a certified community kitchen in order to make jams and jellies from locally grown fruit. . . . Local councils must not look at the process as complete until meeting the goals and vision set out by community residents.

This process worked unevenly in tobacco-dependent counties; in Nicholas County, planning went on through the networks farmers tended to already trust, like the USDA agricultural extension office, instead of through mounting a grassroots planning campaign, but Kentucky invested more settlement money in small-scale agricultural alternatives than many states did, and farmers took advantage of those funds to diversify. The CFA's efforts to set the tobacco transition in global context—communicating with U.S. Congress members as well as state legislators about the local effects of transnational free trade policies, for example, and sponsoring social justice tours for small farmers who came from Latin America to compare experiences—were not conversations that many Nicholas Countians participated in, but some did, and people could keep an eye on the growth of local agricultural alternatives like those profiled in the last chapter of this book.

Tobacco production did not stop with the buyout, and as noted in the last chapter, there are still fields of tobacco in Nicholas County in 2010, with new arrangements for direct marketing to tobacco companies. Some University of Kentucky research groups and others long associated with tobacco production did not cease to work on tobacco with the settlement agreement and buyout but did shift focus. There has been research on genetically engineering the tobacco plant to produce insulin and other needed pharmaceuticals, like drugs used to treat AIDS, cancer, and malaria. One group investigated folk medicinal lore about tobacco relieving wasp stings in the field. Amish farmers started planting genetically engineered tobacco, claimed to be nicotine-free, for cigarette production. Most Kentucky burley production, however, has continued to be the traditional variety sold to companies like Philip Morris.

In 1989, I sat with a retired factory worker on a cold winter evening in her family room. She shifted the lever to pull up the footrest on her chair and told me she did not see a future in tobacco for local farmers, but that it would be hard to make the transition:

> I think we should have the alternative crops, but how it's going to work, I don't know. . . . I mean we're just so set in our ways and everything. . . . I think the biggest thing with tobacco and all is education. . . . I think if we get people educated enough to the problem, that that would solve a lot of it. I think our main key is going to be education.

With the buyout, the necessary education about alternatives to tobacco came from many directions, from the local extension agent, Mike Phillips, to the examples farmers could see around them—often in other counties, on a larger scale—as the settlement checks started coming and people could retrain and retool to try out some alternatives. Here is a quick overview of what people tried in eastern Kentucky.

Some Kentuckians increased soybean and corn production, often for feed, but growing grain on a large enough scale to make it worthwhile was not feasible on hilly farms. Hay grows fine on hillsides, though, and the proximity to horse farms made growing alfalfa hay for thoroughbreds (on a small scale, contracting with particular horse farms) a feasible alternative for Nicholas County farmers.

The poultry and pork production Tom Hensley had envisioned on a large scale did not work out, in part because of the requirements for water and for wastewater processing that could not be met and in part because many Kentuckians rejected the idea of "factory farms" for chicken and hog production like those in North Carolina. Furthermore, poultry houses require a lot of startup money, and the Kentucky hills get cold enough that a lot of money would have to be spent on heating the poultry houses. There was also bad press generated by a large-scale poultry operation investigated for labor violations related to employees who were children and undocumented immigrants (sometimes both). The state passed regulations limiting the size of hog operations because of citizens' concerns about waste from the farms in already-polluted waterways. On a smaller scale, sheep production increased (as already mentioned) and some farmers started raising goats and marketing them for meat.

In Nicholas County, cattle production was already providing much of the income on tobacco farms, so most of the settlement-fund investment was made in strengthening beef cattle production. Phase I funds were used in Nicholas County to give 213 farmers assistance through projects facilitated through the agricultural extension office on agricultural diversification; fencing improvement, forage, hay, and grain storage improvement; cattle genetics and cattle handling (with education and certification programs); dairy improvement; and water enhancement. The local Agricultural Development Board (with farmer and citizen participation) received a $312,000 grant for fencing improvement. One farmer told me that farming in his part of Nicholas County was like farming in Scotland—cattle could roam the hills, but growing any kind of row crops was out of the question. By 2005, cattle production had passed up tobacco as the major earner on farms in Nicholas County. There are some concerns about ant-trust violations and pricing with major packing houses (local beef processing has been largely squeezed out by IBP, Cargill, and ConAgra), but most beef cattle continue to be sold through stockyards in other counties to be processed in other states.

A few explorations of alternatives to tobacco involved looking toward the natural resources of the hills themselves. Kentucky State University got a large grant from the U.S. Department of Agriculture in 1995 to study the commercial possibilities of growing pawpaws—trees, found in Appalachian woodlands, that have a mushy fruit like a banana. Selective logging, and the construction of new regional lumber mills, became more common. Keeping a walnut tree, for example, to sell at a time when a farmer is short of cash is kind of like keeping savings on the hoof with cattle. Christmas tree production was tried in several places. Some people tried to cultivate ginseng, which is usually dug up in mountain woodlands and is valued for traditional medicinal purposes, but found that growing it as a crop was more time-consuming than growing tobacco.

My parents, Wendell and Virginia Kingsolver, have participated in two kinds of protests during their 65-year relationship: Civil Rights marches and actions to save woodlands and watersheds. (I joke that I was a green diaper baby.) As environmentalists with forests on some of their hillier farmland in Nicholas County, they have been investigating with the Kentucky Land Trust the possibility of local farmers being compensated for carbon offset credits. (That is a trade in which companies or individuals wanting to reduce their carbon footprints pay someone somewhere not to cut trees in the hope of mediating the damage to the atmosphere of, say, riding in an airplane.) In order to register to sell carbon credits, though, a farmer with woodlands has to pay a forester to inventory the woods and certify them, and then re-inspect them periodically. That kind of investment is difficult for small farmers; larger-scale organization would be necessary for that to work. It is a thought, though, for how Nicholas County farmers might make income from what they see as the steepest, unproductive hillsides grown up in trees.

Although water issues present a challenge for aquaculture, there are farmers in eastern Kentucky now raising catfish, trout, shrimp, yellow perch, and walleye for use in restaurants and households. Some farmers used buy-out money to get into commercial earthworm production. Beekeepers got assistance with settlement money, and that, in turn, helped growers of crops needing pollination. Some farmers turned to species that were seen as more exotic on Kentucky hillsides, like llamas, ostriches, and rheas (large flightless birds from South America used for their meat, like ostriches). Donnie Myers, a rhea producer in Robertson County, said:

> With tobacco you make a living, but you struggle day to day to make that living. . . . I can see birds making us a living that we could never have dreamed of. There's just no comparison between birds and tobacco. . . . If we sell enough chicks before I plant tobacco, I'll lease it out . . . and I won't fool with tobacco again. (Bortz 1993)

In 1997, The First Kentucky Ostrich Abbatoir (slaughterhouse) Company opened to process the birds grown on individual farms.

Some farmers used settlement money to plant grapes; wineries had been common on the landscape 200 years ago and started making a comeback. Vineyards were planted with hopes of also attracting tourists, and that has worked out well in some locations already having other reasons to be a tourist destination, like a scenic river district or the horse farm region of the Bluegrass. Individual and part-time farmers looking to diversify their crops, but not become large-scale growers, planted grapes to sell to wineries.

Vegetable production has turned out to be a very successful alternative to tobacco production. This is still labor-intensive, but with the right timing and well-established marketing plans, it can work. As I have mentioned earlier in this book, tomatoes, peppers, and cucumbers had been promoted through agricultural extension projects decades ago as routes to farm diversification, but the catch was marketing, which is the problem Tom Hensley was working on with his plan. Today, both the production and the distribution have been worked out in eastern Kentucky. Sometimes this is through producer cooperatives, which the CFA has taken a lead in organizing; sometimes it is through direct sales in farmers' markets or roadside stands (which save fuel costs for the farmer). In some cases, vegetables are marketed through contracts with large corporate buyers, and sometimes those contracts are on the smallest scale, as "shares" bought by individual households in community-supported agriculture. All of those things are happening in Nicholas County, and I will give examples in chapter 5.

The road has not been easy. There was a vegetable cooperative that went under, early in these efforts, in part (again) because of labor infractions with undocumented workers. Droughts have hit vegetable production hard in some years. And there was a berry glut one year that made prices drop. Farmers who are able to talk directly with buyers at farmers' markets and farm stands tell me that they are able to change the species and varieties of fruits and vegetables they plant every year to fit with what people want to eat (or preserve for later use); that process has been useful for them.

Post-buyout agricultural marketing has been well documented by a number of social scientists. Mark Swanson (2001) followed the search for alternatives to tobacco, and the difficulty with finding any alternative crop that would be as lucrative, in another Kentucky county. Taro Futamura (2007) has written about the way place identity was commodified through Kentucky Pride labeling and local food festivals. Nicholas County has long had an annual Blackberry Festival, and many other communities in the region do, also. Fairs and farmers' markets have drawn together several different development projects in the region: tourism, arts and crafts, and alternative agricultural production. Marketing efforts have been helped by the growth in the local food movement across the United States (see Norberg-Hodge, Merrifield, and Gorelick 2002; Kingsolver, Hopp, and Kingsolver 2008), which was strong, in places, in the 1970s during the "energy crisis" and was renewed again in the twenty-first century with concerns about climate, energy sources, and economic justice. Food advertised as "local" has increased value now in much the same way that rurality has been commodified. Farmers work that into the mix, along with global strategies like marketing organic tobacco to the European Union via computer, or selling blackberry jelly online.

I cannot talk with Tom Hensley, who died a few years ago, about his thoughts on the current diversification of agriculture and increased efforts to cooperate regionally in development planning, but I imagine he would say there is still not enough connective thinking going on. What I do see happening in development, that he promoted, is more valuing of local skills, knowledge, and places in talk of development instead of the absolute dominance of the strategy promoted in the illustration on p. 66 of *attracting* capital investment and industry to *bring* development. Whether because of increased agency or the view that state-led development is not going to be the answer, more Nicholas Countians are finding diverse, small-scale ways to keep a livelihood going, sometimes connecting with skills already there but not thought about that much at all—certainly not as development strategies—like sorghum-making or painting old pieces of barn siding decoratively. One skill required for establishing one's own marketing networks that most people in Nicholas County have is living in a small town (discussed in the next chapter), which has also long been seen by many, at least jokingly, as more of a liability than an asset. With the recent economic downturn, the changes in manufacturing jobs and the tobacco program are certainly felt keenly, but many Nicholas Countians are also noticing the positive side of living in a rural community.

Questions for Students

1. In Nicholas County, there is the annual Blackberry Festival. In Irmo, South Carolina, there is the Okra Strut every summer. Are there food-related festivals where you live? If so, how is that related to the way people think about place and identity (Futamura 2007) and what do you know about how the festival is related to historical and current agricultural production?

2. Do you think manufacturing jobs have been coming to or leaving your region? Why? What is the major source of employment in your area? Do you know whether the ownership is local, national, international, or some mix of those?

3. Duncan and Duncan (1985:3) noted that "protecting water would pay off in immediate economic benefits to residents and can be a significant factor in the future growth and development of rural Kentucky." What do you know about your water supply? Where does it come from? Are there any major pollutants in your water supply, and how is water quality monitored? In the twenty-first century, the privatization of water is a major global issue, and there have been major social conflicts over water ownership (cf. Shiva 2002, Olivera and Lewis 2008). Who owns/controls your water supply, and is that ownership regional, national, or transnational?

4. How do you think of social and economic class in relation to tourism? What are being marketed as tourism attractions in your region, by whom, for whom? How does context matter in the commodification of history? For example, how might the same object be priced very differently if it is sitting in a cluster of objects on a tobacco wagon at a roadside yard sale or if it is labeled as an antique at a boutique?

5. How much do you know about the local forms of government where you live? Do you have anything similar to Kentucky's county system? What kinds of services are local governments providing, and how do they fund those services? How much competition or collaboration is there between local governments in your region? What are some examples?

6. Compare my definition of development at the beginning of this chapter with the various development projects discussed throughout the chapter. Does everyone seem to have a voice in negotiating development, or only some people? Do you see differences in who might and might not benefit from the various development projects? What do you think about the concept of "development" itself?

7. Jane Collins (2003:70), in *Threads: Gender, Labor, and Power in the Global Apparel Industry*, has written about paternalist social relations in southern textile mills:

> The factory and the community that surrounded it were portrayed as a "family" with shared interests. The owner, however, was always the one who determined what those interests were. Paternalism operated by providing nonwage goods and services, maintaining an ideology of beneficence, and cultivating deferential relations between workers and bosses. Some have argued that through such means it transformed power relationships into moral obligations—a system of mutual responsibilities, duties, and ultimately even rights.

How would you compare the patron-owned (or locally owned and managed) factories with multinationally owned factories, from the perspective of the Nicholas Countians whose views are represented in this chapter? What advantages and disadvantages to each form of ownership have been expressed?

8. Pem Buck (2001:183) has argued that local elites in Kentucky, however inclined they were to help their communities, have had little choice but to "operate within the constraints on them by the needs of capital and international capital." She argues that those constraints have led to even greater disparities, as nonunionized, low-wage, and high-risk industries were enticed by elites to come to Kentucky. "Local business leaders advertised the virtues of their workers, touting particularly their work ethic and their willingness to work for little because they grew their own food" (Buck 2001:183). What have you read here that supports or contests this view that development strategies have increased economic disparities in Ken-

tucky? What kinds of development options do you hear people talking about in your own community?

9. In this chapter you have read arguments made at the local and state levels for buying products made in Kentucky, or in the United States. You have also read about both the positive response to the Toyota assembly plant being built in Kentucky and the anti-Japanese sentiment (sometimes associated with World War II imagery like "Tokyo Rose") that came up in public discussions at the time it was built. Dana Frank, in her book *Buy American: The Untold Story of Economic Nationalism* (1999), follows a number of moments in U.S. history when "buy American" campaigns have been emphasized. She notes that economic nationalism has sometimes gone hand in hand with racist, or anti-immigrant, impulses arising from fear of foreign workers and capital, and that it has sometimes been used to emphasize economic justice in preventing jobs from following the lowest wages and worst working conditions around the globe. How would you situate "buy American" and "buy local" campaigns within the larger context of transnational conditions for workers?

10. Anthropologist Mary Anglin (2002:14–15) has written: "No longer can Appalachia be simply regarded as a land of poverty or a problem to be solved with the right combination of wisdom and progress but must instead be understood as the locus of interventionist discourses with ulterior motives: missionary, entrepreneurial, literary, academic, and otherwise." What image do you have of Appalachia? Why? In what ways has Appalachia served as an "other" in discourses of identity and development in the United States, and how has that furthered stereotyping? What processes link your region to Appalachia (if you don't live there yourself)? Anglin (2002), Batteau (1983), Billings, Norman, and Ledford (1999), Blessing (2007), Eller (2008), Foster (1988), Gaventa (1980), Stewart (1996), Turner and Cabbell (1985), and Weinbaum (2004) have all shown in their writing how traditional images of poverty and powerlessness in Appalachia can be understood very differently by seeing the Appalachian region in global political economic context. What can you learn by thinking about Appalachia as a *global* region?

Chapter 4

How to Live
in a Small Town

*O*n the 1930s, the local Future Farmers of America came up with a slogan for Carlisle, the "little town with a big heart," and it has stuck. The sign you see in the photograph below was put up by the Carlisle Rotary Club in 2002, out by U.S. Route 68 at the turnoff toward Carlisle (which passersby would not otherwise know was there). There have been various versions of the sign over the years, and I remember watching a slow battle unfold, from the school bus window, as I rode into Carlisle from out in the county, past one of the "little town with the big heart" signs. Jesters or vandals, depending on your perspective, kept crossing out "heart" and writing "mouth," and if the sign got restored to its original saying, they would come again and write "the

Carlisle welcome sign (photo by author)

little town with the big mouth." Rumors are certainly part of small-town life, as this chapter describes, but that was not the kind of first impression Carlisle promoters had in mind for tourists. Neither was the much more sinister "KKK" someone spray painted on the back of the sign pictured on the previous page just after it was erected. Since that graffiti was seen by those leaving town, whether it was a comment on racism within or beyond the community was ambiguous. No matter what statement is made in a small town, there is always back talk, sometimes made verbally and sometimes silently. In all, given the amount of work people do as volunteers to help each other out and keep the community going, "the little town with the big heart" seems an appropriate label for Carlisle.

I did not think about it while I was growing up in Carlisle, but after returning and thinking about it as an anthropologist for 25 years, I realized that living in a small town requires a set of skills, and that those skills are a resource that people can draw on, especially in hard times. My husband, Mark Whitaker, who is also an anthropologist, suggested I name this chapter "how to live in a small town," not because I think I am good at it (I am not) but because I kept telling him that was what I was learning from people: living in a small town takes a skill set. Mark and I were married over 20 years ago in a field on my parents' farm by my philosophy professor from Memphis, Michael McLain, who had gone out with my father to find the judge-executive on his tractor to get a signature on our marriage license. Mark's relatives, who drove down from New York State for our wedding, fit right into Carlisle because they had small-town skills from where they had grown up in Pleasant Valley, New York. They set their chairs out in the street and talked, and found Eddie's restaurant when they wanted coffee. They took a table next to the regulars who had met at the same time for years. (Those regulars bought their table when the restaurant closed down to take across the street and keep the daily conversation going.)

If you have never lived in a small town, you may not know what I mean by it taking skills. Think about having a Facebook page with thousands of friends and never being able to "unfriend" any of them—it takes a lot of energy and political skill to maintain that many relationships over a lifetime. Living in a small town is not a passive activity, unless you just happen to reside there and do not participate in community life. Rural life has often been stereotyped in relation to urban life, like modernity's undeveloped/ developed dichotomy, as a deficient experience, lacking in something. Instead of being somewhere people just end up, many residents choose to stay, or move back, to small towns because of their positive assets.

Jo Lynn Garrett, for example, grew up in Carlisle and moved back after she finished her university degree in Lexington. She had a place in the family business, but she also had decided it was a place she wanted to live. In 1987, soon after her return to town, she was interviewed for a story in the *Carlisle Mercury* about why she came back. "There is a special feeling in Carlisle," Ms. Garrett had explained:

I realized Mom and Dad [Mr. and Mrs. Paul Garrett] started out from scratch, and built one of the finest furniture businesses in Kentucky. . . . They have quality service and a lot of satisfied customers.

Those are the people I grew up with. Good ole sweet faces who know who you are and what you're all about. I'd rather be with these people than any on earth. (Duncan 1987c:4)

Twenty-two years later, Jo Lynn Garrett talked with me in an interview about the skills of small-town living:

I think there's a lot of people that still live here from my [high school] class and a lot of them work here. . . . I know there's not that much job opportunity, but I think that a lot of people find ways to [live here] because they want to be here. . . . They've always lived in a small community, they know small community ways and the way you live in a small community, so they stay here; that's where they want to be.

Of course, staying is not always a choice, given that it takes some resources to move away, but young adults who commute to school or work elsewhere often continue live in Nicholas County because of the economic resources like land owned by relatives that a trailer can be put on, and social resources like free child care and extended kin and friendship networks unavailable in urban areas. A number of people, like Jo Lynn Garrett, have chosen to move back to Carlisle, or to move to Nicholas County from other places. A number of us have also left, and I will get to that later in this chapter, but here I want to focus on the skills and work required to keep a small town going.

If I were giving advice in this chapter on how to live in a small town (which, of course, Nicholas Countians will find ironic since I no longer live there), I might say: (1) Listen to stories about past events and the places in which they occurred, since those are often guideposts in current social life. You need to learn the back story, as well as the landscape. (2) Do not expect everything to work exactly by the written rules; justice may be a little flexible and decisions made more at a community than an individual level. (3) Go to some school events, even if you do not have children—that's where a lot of community life is centered. (4) Before you register to vote, find out whether all local elections take place in the primaries; party politics may not correspond to your expectations. (5) Never say anything about anyone that you would not want their relatives to hear—you may be speaking with one of them. (6) Subscribe to the local newspaper, and read *all* of it. (7) Do not expect anyone to occupy just one role in town—your mail carrier may also be your mayor. (8) If someone invites you to dinner, ask if he or she means a noon or an evening meal. (9) If you are invited to go fishing, say yes, even if you are a vegetarian—that is a great time to hear those stories back in #1.

Every small town is different, which is why this chapter is *not* really a how-to guide. But in the following sections, I will give an overview of examples of, and perspectives on, small-town life in Carlisle and Nicholas County:

the role of memory; belonging (insider/outsider issues, and incorporating diversity); neighboring; networks, for better or worse; civic participation; the role of the newspaper; economic life; demographic shifts toward an aging population; class; churches; schools; community events; and small-town global encounters. Some of these issues have been touched on in earlier chapters, particularly in the discussion of "tobacco town" life.

Many towns and cities across the United States are having to figure out ways to keep community services going as public funding is withdrawn from them due to budget crises. One of the things that can be learned from following small-town life closely is how people have long worked together—across class and other lines—to provide public services, through creative use of multiple resources including volunteer labor, in a constantly challenging environment. If a community hospital loses its funding and closes its doors, for example, residents still need emergency care, and in some small communities volunteer fire departments have taken on EMS training to provide the immediate attention local residents, including them, may need unexpectedly. This is the kind of problem solving with which residents of small towns like Carlisle have long been familiar, and this chapter documents the work of sustaining community life.

It is important to note again here, as I did in the introduction, that I am writing from a particular vantage point. It is, in Nicholas County terms, an elite perspective, as are many of the development plans discussed in the previous chapter (given that fewer than 10 percent of adults over 25 in the county have four-year college degrees—that is, institutional training that facilitates grant seeking, etc.). My intention here is not to romanticize small-town life. Many have written about small towns as disappearing (see Ellis 1995), and sometimes they are romanticized as the history and heart of America while at the same time being looked down on as places that encourage a fear of outsiders and change. For example, Sam Roberts' (1995:E2) syndicated article "The Mythical Appeal of Small Towns," describing small-town residents as less healthy, more prone to domestic violence, and more likely to be anti-immigrant than city dwellers, was published in the *Lexington Herald-Leader*, illustrated by a photo of Carlisle's downtown. I ask that we look a little more deeply at what can be learned from those who live in small towns—who develop long-term relationship skills with particular places and with not a handful but with hundreds and hundreds of people over a lifetime, and who rely on those relationships as a noncash resource. In economic hard times, it is those less measurable aspects of living in a small town that some people have come to value more and move to rural areas to find. There are rewards as well as hardship to be found in small-town life.

A woman who chose to move to Carlisle from an urban area in the 1950s said, for example, in 2009:

> Well, it was hard to get used to having no anonymity when I came to a small town . . . but there are so many rewards. There are so many good people here that care about each other. They know about each other's

business pretty well—not so much as used to be, because people are busier, and have other things to do; the gossip mill is not nearly what it was earlier. But people care for one another, and if some catastrophe happens, everybody comes, brings food, and supports the family. People even put in crops for a man who breaks his leg or something. So that sort of thing is wonderful in a small community. People still care about one another and support each other in all kinds of ways. Extended families are something that is available here, for keeping children and all when other people are working. That happens here.

Bank managers and others in larger towns and cities say they like to hire Carlisle workers because of their "small-town values." "As a citizen of a special place, albeit one with acknowledged warts, a member of a small community is considered a good person—virtuous, loyal, trustworthy, and altruistic. Community serves as a metaphor for their intimately connected lives" (Salamon 2003:3). That metaphor can be used to economic advantage. The commodification of rurality described in the previous chapter does not just mean value-added for vegetables at farmers' markets, but in some cases those stereotypes of loyalty and honesty work in the favor of employees commuting from small towns.

Community is made from the telling and retelling of stories about who we are, where we are, how we are or are not connected, and what has happened in the past or might happen in the future. A newcomer navigating social relationships might have difficulty, unless and until some of those stories are learned, understanding how particular events—like the rivalry between the city and county high schools before they were consolidated and the city school was knocked down, or a fatal accident that tragically linked two families for life—might be the third partner in a current conversation, or the deciding factor in a community political decision. The social, historical, and physical terrain all need to be learned to live in a small town. As Tuan (1977:183–184) says:

> Abstract knowledge *about* a place can be acquired in short order if one is diligent. . . . But the "feel" of a place takes longer to acquire. It is made up of experiences, mostly fleeting and undramatic, repeated day after day and over the span of years. It is a unique blend of sights, sounds, and smells, a unique harmony of natural and artificial rhythms such as times of sunrise and sunset, of work and play. The feel of a place is registered in one's muscles and bones. . . . Knowing a place, in the above senses, clearly takes time. Building up that sense of place involves memory, too.

There is one piece of land at the outskirts of Carlisle on the main road that many of us see in different ways, most of them connected to the global in some way. Right now, a gas station and store stand on it, with trucks bringing fuel in, the price of which is somehow connected to the war in Iraq and the oil spill in the Gulf of Mexico. When I was in elementary school, my friend Kim and I worked together on a project to build a mountainous landscape out of corn starch on cardboard outside her home in the trailer park that occupied that same piece of ground. She and her sister and her mother were living there to be near her father's Nicholas County relatives while he went for long stints to work on the construction of the Alaskan oil pipeline. When my grandfather and others in his generation looked at that trailer park, they saw in their mind's eye the tobacco warehouse that stood there once, having been built on top of a site they associated with fun. That same flat place had been where people put a skating rink when it was cold, or where the circus unloaded from the railway across the road to entertain Nicholas Countians for a brief while, or Chatauqua speakers came through to inspire, inflame, and entertain them. All this illustrates that there are not *too* many flat places in Carlisle, and the importance of rail and truck transportation in connecting Nicholas County with other places, but I bring it up also to explain that any of those images may be in the mind's eye of local speakers as they give directions or pause for reflection in the phantom landscape connecting topography and memory.

The tourism brochure on Carlisle, the cover illustration of which is shown on p. 84 in the previous chapter, says, "Welcome to Carlisle, where people smile and say hello and time moves slow." Time may *seem* to move slowly sometimes because a moment can be thickly populated with the work of maintaining small-town relationships, an investment and duty related to people coming to each other's aid when needed. A church lay leader recently laughed as he described not being able to eat his meal because there were so many people to say hello to as everyone passed by his table to get their Sunday dinner at the restaurant on the courthouse square; he may have seemed to be eating slowly, but it was because he was busy—"good busy," as people might say in Nicholas County.

Incorporating Diversity

In the 1980s, I was talking with Cordi, a factory worker, about insider and outsider status, and how belonging is negotiated in Nicholas County. She said, "Some people get pegged as outsiders, and some people are taken right in." I have seen that happen, too, and I think it is more a matter of whether they work on (or already have) the skill set for living in a small town than a matter of happenstance. Sometimes, though, it is a matter of "knowing the codes"—finding access to the way word actually gets around, for example, rather than expecting it to be posted publicly and officially, even if that is the law. A neighbor who did not grow up in Carlisle once complained to me that "they don't let outsiders *know*" about changes in policy, when she found that the rules had changed for using her bank account. I have heard the same thing about some jobs being much harder for "outsiders" to find out about than "insiders."

Because many small-town residents can be "placed" as either insiders or outsiders, or both, in specific contexts, it is not possible to figure out insider or outsider status by place of birth. Someone born in Nicholas County might be deemed an "outsider" because his or her family migrated to the area from farther up in the mountains four generations before, and someone else born in a different country might immediately become an insider, as Cordi said. Dr. Osias Villaflor and his wife Ruby Villaflor were born in the Philippines, for example, lived in New York and West Virginia, and moved to Nicholas County in 1982. Ruby Villaflor told a *Carlisle Mercury* reporter in 1991:

> Carlisle is our home . . . we found a warm reception in Carlisle. Then we knew, Osias and I, that we would live the rest of our lives here among these people. Our homeland seems so far away now, we feel we have always lived here. (Shepherd 1991:8)

Dr. and Mrs. Villaflor became involved in community networks quickly through both the medical practice and community service.

On the other hand, Sarah, a young person who grew up in Carlisle and tried to move back as an adult with her husband, who was from a neighboring county, found that it was difficult to "reintegrate" into the community. She said:

> I really wasn't an outsider, but I had been gone. . . . Because I really wasn't engaged much in activity, I always had the impression that I didn't show the right amount of respect. That when I didn't serve the ties to Carlisle when I was in college, [people felt that] I had basically turned up my nose at the whole community. . . . You've got to pay your dues.

Sarah described the political and social importance of socializing at sporting events in Carlisle, for example. She said that working outside of Carlisle made it harder for people to maintain the level of activity required to maintain insider status:

> Those people who are leaving the community to work . . . to some extent you're torn, because you really are in two worlds. I think there is a survival tool—because I was in two worlds—you have to either say, well, I'm either all the way in or all the way out.

Not putting time into community events consistently since high school, Sarah felt, made her more of an outsider. She described getting the same question I got when I moved back to do my fieldwork: "You got out of here—why would you come back?" Many of us who have shifted between insider and outsider status return "home" for key life events, as I did when I got married in Nicholas County. Sometimes people just come home "to find out about things," catching up on local gossip, as a professional who had moved away decades before still does. He said he felt left out, with the community going on about its business in his absence.

Things do not stand still in a small town, even though it may seem to others that things move slowly. Surprisingly, it is sometimes not "insider" but "outsider" pressure for things not to change. In the 1980s, a local government official told me, "Some people moved here because it's a sleepy little village and they don't want to mess that up." So newcomers from urban areas might be more resistant to development plans than long-term residents are because of the image of small-town life that initially attracted them to move to Carlisle.

Sometimes in small towns, insider/outsider can take on the sinister overtones of racism, with its potential for structural and physical violence. "Belonging" or "not belonging" can have multiple layers of meaning, for example inclusion in local, racialized, ethnic, or national communities. Those seen as not "belonging" may be "othered," or valued differently—usually less. An important question to ask in communities like Carlisle with a majority white population is whether the historical decrease in minority residents through outmigration is due to local experiences of "othering," to following opportunities elsewhere, or both. As people are being "placed" in Nicholas County, individual and kin identities may be emphasized over ethnic, national, or racialized identities. That carries the problematic potential of treating an individual—because he or she is known, and can be "placed" in local networks—as "exceptional," or different from others in a generally feared or discriminated-against group.

Because whites are the dominant group in numbers and/or power, "whiteness" (and the privilege it affords) is seldom discussed as an identity in U.S. contexts (see Hartigan 1999). In Nicholas County, salient distinctions of identity one might hear discussed include nationality, e.g., Mexican; religious community, e.g., Amish; or racialization, e.g., African American or white. Racialization is a term Omi and Winant (1994) use to discuss the process by which power gets attached to arbitrary physical characteristics. It is important to note that "race" is a cultural construction, since it varies so much around the world (from being defined by height in China to wealth in Central Africa), even though most people in the United States talk about it as a biological identity, with skin color as a marker. If race is mentioned in Nicholas County contexts, it is often discussed in relation to African Americans, or black identity, and is spatially associated with Henryville, on the edge of Carlisle, since that is traditionally where most African Americans have lived in the county. It is also possible to hear whiteness discussed in Nicholas County, but seldom in dominant public discourse.

Interestingly, Henryville stood as a free black town in Nicholas County before the establishment of Carlisle. Residents had moved there from surrounding counties, according to local African American historians. Lottie O'Bannon (1976:79) observed that, as in many other U.S. communities, "Because of segregation, Henryville became independent in the areas of business, churches, fraternal organizations, education, and social life." In the early twentieth century, there were grocery stores, a second-hand shop, barber shops, restaurants, a rooming house, and lodge halls for the United Brothers of Friendship, the Sisters of the Mysterious Ten, the Odd Fellows and Household of Ruth Lodge, and Masonic and Eastern Star orders. Two doctors practiced in Henryville. There was the Booker T. Washington School, until the Nicholas County schools were integrated and consolidated. Henryville had a slaughterhouse, serving farmers in the region. Two churches—the Wesley Chapel CME Church and the High Street Christian Church and a number of bands anchored community social life, along with the lodges. Henryville had a Volunteer Fire Department, and residents combined resources to run a water line from Carlisle (O'Bannon 1976).

Mary Ann Moore went to work during the Depression, when she was 12. She could not yet cook, so the white family she boarded with gave her $1.75 a week to keep their children, and then raised that to $3 a week after she learned how to cook. She said a lot of white households in the region were set up that way—they had a black "babysitter, cook, and housekeeper." Sometimes the child working for board in a Carlisle household was from a white rural family, as mentioned previously; class, gender, and racialization all played a part in constructing a domestic workforce.

When she was an adult, and ran her own business, Mary Ann Moore decided who she would work for and who she would not, and she drew very clear lines around her professional life; she had had enough of the family metaphor in her early workplace. She spoke up when she saw injustice, and she equated racism with ignorance. She had felt the hot breath of that ignorance early in her life when a car full of KKK members from another county tried to scare her, but she had walked away. She told me in the 1980s, after many of Henryville's residents had moved away, there were "not but a few of us here to protest," so what she saw as situations needing to be addressed, like unfair property deals on Henryville land that had been owned through oral deeds for generations, went mostly unchallenged. She and I were at a funeral in Lexington one time, talking with an old friend of hers from Carlisle, and her friend said, "I like to go visit, but I could never live there again—and there's not many to visit."

Like Mary Ann's friend, many in Carlisle have "voted with their feet" about small-town life. The absence of those who have left, and the silences left in community life by where they would have been, says a lot about how diversity is *not* incorporated into small-town life. Silences like this can be problematic for everyone. For example, if sexual preference is never discussed publicly (except as a slur on the playground), then stereotypes can persist, with broad-reaching negative effects. Beliefs like "only gays get AIDS" or "that's a problem in cities, not rural areas," coupled with the silence about HIV/AIDS in many rural communities, has led to the most rapidly rising rates of HIV/AIDS among rural heterosexual teenagers.

There is a sort of "don't ask, don't tell" policy in many small towns like Carlisle about sexual preference that emphasizes individual identity over a larger lesbian, gay, bisexual or transgender (LGBT) group identity. Young people have often left town to find larger communities in which a broader range of identities and opinions are circulating in the public sphere. However, it is not always necessary to leave town and go to a city to establish a public gay or lesbian identity. Mary Gray interviewed young people who identified as LGBT in rural Kentucky communities and found that young rural LGBT teenagers in Kentucky, rather than using the Internet to "escape" small-town life, used new media "to expand their experience of local belonging" (2009:15); they incorporated social media and other resources available on the Internet into the types of public space they already navigated in everyday life. As with any personal disclosure on the Internet, social media must be used carefully, but individuals who may feel isolated for various reasons can find much-needed information on the Internet about larger communities with shared interests or identities.

Diverse perspectives represented in community conversations can increase everyone's lifelong learning opportunities and strengthen the range of resources to be tapped for community problem solving. Children in Carlisle, however, as is the case with children in other communities that have one dominant ethnic or religious perspective (e.g., European American or Mexican American, or Christian, Hindu, Jewish or Muslim), may have little direct exposure to people holding different perspectives on historical and current events, for example. One may have to work harder to find opportunities for interactions that include perspectives very different from one's own outlook on the world.

There are many reasons why people have chosen to leave Carlisle and never come back, with losses to the community and to themselves. One reason people have given for leaving town is to obtain a college education, which sometimes means people have to find jobs elsewhere. That education may be seen by some as a liability, as when a friend in Carlisle once told me, "Your problem is, you have been educated beyond a belief in absolutes." Anthropologists are known to be interested in areas of cultural contestation that tend to be silenced in community life, and to learn by moving between social contexts, but many other Nicholas Countians have done this as well.

Mary Ann Moore's son, James Richard Bean, moved back to Carlisle from Maryland toward the end of Mary Ann's life, to help care for her and to work on redeveloping Henryville, which was inhabited at that point by a number of elderly people who could not keep their places up very well without the younger generation to lend a hand. James Richard Bean rebuilt his mother's house and started a community revitalization project in Henryville. He and others restored abandoned property and cut weeds in the cemetery and in other lots. James Richard said:

> Henryville is not Henryville any more. It used to be all black, right? Now you look in here right now. We have around 25 black people in Carlisle who live up in this place around Henryville. . . . The whites have come in because the place looks better. . . . They are investing their money in Henryville now because it's a beautiful sight. But at the time, these old houses and everything, weeds and everything, they didn't want to come into deserted [areas]. Now this area is becoming part of Carlisle. Like it always has been. They see it all as one. It's not "this is a black area here, segregated," no.

In 2004, Sharnetta O'Bannon, an African American Nicholas Countian, was crowned queen of the Blackberry Festival, an event at the core of Carlisle community life; this would seem to support James Richard's view that Carlisle was now viewed "all as one," not as having separate black and white events and spaces, as it once did.

I asked James Richard if Henryville would be included in the tourism development efforts in Carlisle and Nicholas County. He said:

> It *will* be. It's got to be a part. And especially if I have anything to do with it because if you look into the history of Nicholas County, this was the first settlement here before the whites even got here. The blacks had the first settlement. That has got to be told. . . . It has a good historical place here in black history and blacks have contributed [to the community].

At tourism centers in Kentucky, you can now pick up a Multicultural Tourism Guide, and there is a growing tourism focus on African American history in the state, including maps of the Underground Railroad, on which there was a stop in Nicholas County. If you take Route 68 on from Carlisle toward the Ohio River, you will come to Maysville, Kentucky, the site of the new National Underground Railroad Museum. So it would be very possible for Nicholas County to feature its African American history as part of the tourism development plan, in coordination with efforts already underway in the region.

James Richard Bean continued our conversation about Henryville, saying:

> We had a lot of very professional people here, see, and what happened is no jobs here for the blacks, so they did the next thing. The closest city was Cincinnati, Ohio, where they had Armco Steel, these factories, so one group of families would leave to go up there and . . . there were other younger groups, because older people would stay.
>
> Because they were already rooted. And a lot of people used to come from Ohio back home on holidays. There used to be a crowd of people, but once the older people died off, they had no reason to come back. There was no work here anymore. So that's why everything started deteriorating, see? You've got to cultivate it and replenish something for it to keep on growing, right? This right here was not replenished. But I hope that I can do something to replenish it. It will grow back, but Henryville is not going to be Henryville any more. It is going to be Henryville, but it is a part of Carlisle. . . . It always was part of the city, never was in the county. And it will grow back just like any other city, once you've got houses, once you put roads in, once it becomes a suburb like it is supposed to be. . . .
>
> Everything is coming together. When I left from Carlisle going into the service, this was such a good stepping stone because all this race riot and everything, we didn't have it here. We did not have it here. It was a different way of living. We could go anywhere we wanted. I never, I have never seen yet, a black toilet or a black water fountain, in Carlisle or anywhere. I haven't seen any. Definitely not here. We rode the Greyhound bus, we never did sit on the back of no bus, you know what I'm talking about? And this was a good stepping stone for me, because I knew there

were good people, and we socialized. See, the reason why some people don't get along, they never socialized. . . . And people sit back, shy in fear of certain things they don't understand, until they get to know it. And that's how the world is going to be. . . . You've got so much interracial marriage now, mixed kids, so how are you going to be against this or that now? . . . The world's going to get better, it's going to get better. And now the opportunity opens up for everybody to be.

James Richard Bean told me that his mother, Mary Ann Moore, used to ask him whether he missed being in Maryland after he moved back to Carlisle. He said he had told her:

I didn't mind coming back home. I said, I live in the suburbs, Mom. I'm living the same way I did in Maryland, in DC. You know, it doesn't have the excitement, it doesn't have all that, but I'm living the same way, see? And I love being back home. This is the best thing that ever happened to me, you know.

He said that he and his wife liked knowing all of his children's teachers, and the fact that the teachers communicated with them and knew that there was family unity supporting what was happening at school—that communication, he said, was easier to maintain where everybody knows each other.

That communication at school was also important to Rose Marie Farah, who had lived in Atlanta, Georgia, before coming to Carlisle to marry Licha Farah, in 1968. In a bicentennial oral history interview in 1999, she explained to me that they had met through letter writing. Licha Farah had come from Lebanon to marry the daughter of a Lebanese American storeowner in Carlisle, Christine Abraham; after he became a widower, he reached out to a broader network and met Rose Marie, whose parents had immigrated from Lebanon and settled in a small town in North Carolina. Very soon after Rose Marie and Licha married, they sponsored his sister and her husband and children to immigrate to Nicholas County and helped them get established on a farm with a dairy. She said:

And so here we started. . . . I put five kids in Headstart that summer, and tried to learn my Arabic a little better and tried to teach the Headstart teachers a few things to tell them how to handle the kids, and we got them going and they made great strides in school. . . . In time, we brought other members of the family over. . . . So I said I had my own refugee center . . . at one time we had 24 children, and 23 of them graduated from college.

I want to say that Carlisle was good for us, and good for all these families because small towns sometimes aren't familiar with foreigners and cannot accept someone that is different. . . . We are Catholic, and . . . even though we are in a new age, smaller towns are sometimes slower at accepting Catholics sometimes, you know. But when I came here, I was so amazed at the wonderful spirit among the churches here, and the ministers. It's ecumenical. We have so many occasions during the year to worship at each other's churches. And that's been a wonderful thing. . . .

And all the ones that came from Lebanon felt the same way. Where Lebanon is such a problem with this religion and that religion and they don't get along, [here] they don't look at your religion first, or judge you on anything like that.

Rose Marie Farah reflected on the recent immigration of workers from Latin American nations to Nicholas County to work on farms, mostly in tobacco. She said that it was probably hard for the men who came alone to work and send money back to their families, as her grandfather had done. Rose Marie said, "He came at a time in the early 1900s as a peddler, and some farmers were afraid to let him sleep in their barns." Of the growing Latino community, she said:

So many of them come for so many months and then go back. . . . I think there are more and more coming and bringing families, because they have quite a community: they have actually a Mexican mass at night, and the Mexican ministries you know, up there in Fayette County, and I think that's wonderful. So I believe [the Latino community] is getting to be a little more active, you know, full blown. And I think it's nice.

A Spanish-speaking ministry was started in the twenty-first century by Sister Dorothy Bondi at the Shrine of Our Lady of Guadalupe, which had been in Nicholas County (changed, at some point, from St. John's) long before there was a Latino community in Carlisle to appreciate the connection with the Shrine of Our Lady of Guadalupe, Patroness of the Americas, in Mexico City. Lidia, a recent immigrant from Mexico, made this statement, which was translated for the Ursuline Sisters' Multicultural Rural Outreach newsletter:

We have lived in the United States now for two years, and for us, it has been very good. Learning the language has been difficult, but . . . we have work here, so economically our life is much better.

We are hoping this year to celebrate the feast of Our Lady of Guadalupe together with the Anglo community, and to continue to share our traditions and learn about their traditions, too.

Youth groups from Cleveland come to Nicholas County each summer to work with the multicultural rural outreach program, to learn about both Appalachia and the experiences of new immigrants mostly from San Luis Potosí, Veracruz, and Chiapas, Mexico. The Cleveland volunteers represent another dimension of insider/outsider in Carlisle. They mainly work on housing projects in the county, helping to fix up the sometimes makeshift residences (in retrofitted barns, for example) for Latin American migrant workers on individual farms. Since there are no migrant labor camps in the region, the 200 or so seasonal, mostly male workers live in very isolated conditions. Sister Dorothy described people walking for hours from the farms where they worked in the county to get to town for a business transaction or to go to mass. She said the teenagers from Cleveland were surprised that they were meeting people of around their own age who had already been working on their own and living in another country.

A white farmer who has been hiring white teenagers from a local church group to work in the fields with Mexican workers on H2A visas said something similar to me about the Carlisle teenagers being impressed by the Latino workers they had gotten to know. The language barrier, however, along with whatever "othering" may be going on, has meant that those Latinos who have settled in Nicholas County permanently have been incorporated less quickly than newcomers of other identities, except through the church community. There are much larger Latino communities, with Spanish-language newspapers, health and legal services, and Latino-owned businesses, in more urban areas in nearby counties, such as Paris and Lexington, Kentucky. New immigrants from Latin America who may have made the journey to Nicholas County through paying a *coyote* (a labor contractor transporting undocumented immigrants across the U.S.–Mexican border), and have later returned to the region with legal immigrant status, have tended to settle in those more urban communities.

Sister Dorothy, who translates for recent Latin American immigrants in schools and prisons over a several-county area, says that where there are larger Latino communities than in Nicholas County, there tend to be more overt experiences of anti-immigrant discrimination. It is difficult to tell whether there is less discrimination in Nicholas County than in counties with larger populations of recent immigrants from Latin American nations or whether there is less *reporting* of discrimination. The familial model often used in hiring migrant workers, like the patron management model in factories discussed in the previous chapter, can serve to silence critiques workers may have of labor conditions—especially when citizenship status may further hinder speaking up. This is the flipside to consider regarding narratives in this chapter about positive relations between Latino workers and Anglo employers.

Regionally, there have been some extremely exploitative working and living conditions reported for Latino workers, especially those with citizenship in other nations who came to the United States without official visas. Ben Figueres, president of the Lexington Hispanic Association, told the Urban County Council, "We are the new slaves in Lexington" (Honeycutt 1998:A1). Berthina Cervantes, a social worker, went to a farm in the Bluegrass region in 1992 and found 35 men living in a house without electricity or water. "These were people with legal papers who were living in Texas and working in a factory," Cervantes said. "They left their jobs and came here and found everything they were promised was a lie" (Rios 1992:A14).

Unacceptable housing conditions have often been discussed by workers, but they are seldom reported because of fear of deportation and/or loss of promised wages. Undocumented Latino workers can be targeted for robbery because false identification papers make opening bank accounts difficult (necessitating carrying or hiding large amounts of cash); those robberies often go unreported as well.

The connection between central Kentucky tobacco farms and human trafficking (by coyotes, or some other labor contractors), not often highlighted, burst into the public sphere in 1999 when 13 people died in an over-packed van that crashed in New Mexico on its way to the Bluegrass region. There has been little oversight of conditions of contracting relations in rural Kentucky, but advocacy networks have been growing. In 1998, the Lexington Hispanic Association asked the Burley Tobacco Growers Cooperative Board for $53,000 toward migrant services, given the growing number of tobacco farmers hiring migrant workers from Latin America; the Cooperative did not immediately act on that request. One barrier to formal legal and social services has been undercounting in the census figures, since those numbers are often collected in the spring before seasonal agricultural workers arrive in Kentucky.

In 2001, *La Voz*, a free Spanish-language newspaper, was started by Alejandro Gomez for circulation in Lexington to Latinos living in the larger region.

> "Finally, our community will have a paper to call their own, a place where they can find out about resources available to them, read about issues of importance to them and see their faces and their language," said Gomez. (Brim 2001:B1)

The *Lexington Herald-Leader* also added pages in Spanish. Roberto Arroyo, the owner of a *tiendita*, or small store, specifically for Spanish-speaking customers, explained in an article in Spanish profiling Latino-oriented businesses:

> "No pueden entrar a Kroger y preguntar cómo se puede conseguir una licencia de conducer. . . . Nosotros servimos como centro informativo." (Batcheldor 2000:13)

> You can't go into a Kroger store and ask how to get a driver's license. We serve as an information center. (Author's translation)

Nicholas Countians formed a Migrant Resource Coalition in the 1990s, initiated by the Cooperative Extension Service, and long-term residents who were most likely to need Spanish-language skills—workers in the schools, health care, social services, business and agriculture—started taking the Spanish-language classes offered by Sister Dorothy in Carlisle. She also taught English to new immigrants who were exclusive Spanish speakers. The use of Latin American immigrant labor in tobacco peaked in the late 1990s. As tobacco production decreased, so did the demand for migrant farmworkers. In the 1990s, though, tobacco was going strong and there was a hotline through the Employment Services Migrant Program that either migrant workers or farmers needing tobacco labor could call to find each other. Trucks with signs advertising $10/hour jobs in tobacco (in Spanish and English) were patrolling the streets in towns around the region. Some local officials, farmers, and business owners told me in interviews that they felt the reason immigrant labor was in such high demand was that so many local workers were now drawing social security (disability) benefits, which they risked losing if they took on the kind of temporary work that tobacco production cycles required. Tobacco was not the only industry employing new immigrant labor, and Latin

Americans were not the only new immigrant workforce in Kentucky; in 2001, Russian and Ukrainian miners were being recruited for work in coal mines.

I asked Sister Dorothy why she chose to come to Nicholas County to begin her multicultural ministry. She said:

> I grew up in Cleveland, and where I lived you could walk to seven Catholic churches and Catholic schools, but each one was a different ethnic group. So in the summer, each ethnic group had their own festival, and food, and music and stuff, and we went to all of them. So I think very early on, I developed a love for different ethnic celebrations and backgrounds. And I just loved it. All of those different nationalities sharing their backgrounds so proudly.

She had planned to go to El Salvador, but a colleague convinced her that there was just as much need for her services in central Kentucky, and so she came to live in Carlisle and started driving around the rural county roads and meeting migrant workers on tobacco farms. Where there were families with children, she started serving as an interpreter of both language and culture with the school system as needed and organizing ecumenical soccer games to get Nicholas Countians together across the language barrier.

When I asked Sister Dorothy about how she felt new immigrants from Latin America had been received, along with her own work, by long-term residents of Carlisle, she said:

> Right here, they're wonderful. Right here in Carlisle. Because they're not so overwhelmed. In Lexington, and in Paris, it might be a little different. [She has translated for Latinos in schools and prisons in all three contexts.] Here, the church has been so open to them and they know them, and have parties with them for the kids and everything. That's why I really wanted to work here. It was just a very open kind of atmosphere.

I decided early in this project not to interview the Latin American immigrants themselves (even though that would mean mediated representation in this narrative), because of the way I am "placed" in Nicholas County. Both undocumented immigrants and those on H2A visas are under "the gaze" of the state and their direct employer already, without me adding to that vulnerability by entering the mix as someone who might be close friends with the farmer on whose land they live and work. In many ways, I am associated with the power structure of the county even as I try to describe it, and that presented an ethical quandary; I wanted to make sure that those I interviewed in Nicholas County would feel completely free to say no. Much of my work as an anthropologist of the U.S. has focused on anti-immigration legislation (see Kingsolver 2010), based on interviews in Spanish and English from California to South Carolina. My future research will cross county lines and involve learning much more with and about Latinos in Appalachian Kentucky.

Another group of new immigrants that tends to be less fully incorporated into small-town life is the growing group of Amish farmers buying land, sometimes in extended family groups, and now establishing construction businesses and a local store. I have already explained that the local school system is where much socializing as well as socialization takes place in small-town life. Since the Amish families educate their own children and do not use the public schools, they are not incorporated into the community via that route. The most interaction long-term residents and Amish newcomers have with each other is at the Southern States Cooperative agricultural store, the grocery store, buying eggs directly from Amish farmers, and in construction work (where sometimes Latino and Amish workers are together on a job). This is a community that I think will continue to grow in the county, as I will discuss in the next chapter; the Latino community has shrunk from around 500 to 200 seasonal workers, or fewer, but as James Richard Bean talked about in Henryville, there are several mixed families of Latino newcomers and long-term Nicholas Countians, and there is a permanent Latino cultural contribution to the local fabric of community life.

Networks, for Better or Worse, and the Role of Media

In Nicholas County, *neighbor* is a verb: people have sat up night after night with elderly or ill people who were not their relatives, because they did not have anyone else and wanted to be in their own homes; volunteers have pulled neighbors from burning buildings and cars. Sometimes, as factory shifts have gone to overtime and neighboring networks have been overtaxed, people have been exhausted, and some have said that neighboring is really breaking down in the county. Kin networks involve a lot of unpaid caretaking labor, like neighboring does, and sometimes people balk at the sheer amount of work it takes to maintain those networks. Most of this caretaking work is done by women. Alleen, who was caring for her parents and several other relatives, said to me one day during a brief respite she was taking in her front-porch swing, "I'm tired of being a single woman with married responsibilities." Gloria, who was older than Alleen, said in exasperation to a group of other women at a community event, "I married my husband, not his whole family."

Funerals are an occasion for intensive neighboring, as people come together to help a family heal, but they can also be a time for either clearing the air or sealing different accounts of past events. One person told me that the only person who could be completely honest and not worry about the talk would be a person on his or her deathbed. But talk, and its consequences, can outlive particular individuals. Some kinds of talk can be seen as a form of social control, and that includes descriptions of the town and its history, as Charles Gates (a Carlisle native) said in an interview:

> See, people around here are very peculiar. If they don't like you, they don't want to be buried in the same cemetery with you. I don't know what meaning that has, but. . . . It's cause for friction in a lot of families,

and the friction's still there. It's not forgotten. But it's a part of the history, too. It's a part we don't need to get more of. . . .

See, in this county we have a tendency that if you're not from a certain family, you don't mean nothing. And you're treated that way through society. It's society itself here that's not what I'd call conducive to good living. And it was hard for me to adapt to this when I came back here from the military. I'm retired military, so I was away 20 years. I came back here and ran into things I never knew existed when I was young. Well, I just never had an interest to even *know* they existed. I've always felt that history was a very important thing, and history is always something that could be rewrote. Nothing is final in history.

James S. Brown (1988:62), in his book *Beech Creek: A Study of a Kentucky Mountain Neighborhood*, wrote, "relationships of the past, far from being dead and unimportant, were significant in understanding even the latest local occurrences." That is what Charles Gates was also saying, and what I could see in the way elderly women in Carlisle would keep their police scanners on in the 1980s, following official versions of current events as they unfolded, and then keep a backchannel of gossip going that filled in the history and context of those events. Talk can be like waves washing over themselves in Carlisle.

I once played music for a revival in which the sermon was called, "Forgive Our Cows' Tongues." Like cows' tongues, there is a rough edge to talk in a small town. Talk can seem to have a life of its own. Mary Ann Moore called me up one morning and said, "I have some talk. It jumped on me last night." Rumors are visceral members of the community, and sometimes people act preventively, as in the case of a woman who wrote a letter to the editor of the *Carlisle Mercury* recently to say to those who might want to gossip about her, she was not drunk or high on drugs when she had her car wreck and it was no one's business but hers.

The newspaper editor himself took a proactive stance with this 1988 headline: "Devil worship rumors called unfounded." Once talk gets going, it is hard to stop it, and it can have lasting and negative effects. A public official told me in the 1980s:

That's what makes it bad, in small towns. Now if you worked in Lexington, and you have a hundred people that don't like you, well, the percentage is not going to bother you. You know, who cares? In Lexington, it's a big enough place. Nobody knows anybody, so you just do your daily work. But if you've got five people in Carlisle that don't like you and may be trying to get back at you in some way, then you've got a problem. That's why, you know, it's better to listen to people. I've found that most people in town here, if you just listen to them, you'll come along good. I haven't had any problems with anybody.

One Nicholas County couple had moved to another state for a while, and then moved back to Carlisle. The wife said, as we heard a car pass by her screen door, "Anonymity is worth a whole lot, too. Because, let's face it, in Carlisle everybody knows everybody. It was kind of nice not to know what was going on down the street." She remembered the advice her husband, who was from Carlisle, had told her when she first moved to the town: "Don't go out and talk about anybody, because you don't know—if you're sitting there badmouthing somebody—that you aren't talking to a brother or a cousin or whatever."

Negative talk within Carlisle is one thing, but if it gets outside Carlisle, people tend to band together to combat stereotypes of rural life. In 2008, there was an event in Carlisle that was picked up by CNN. A trailer fell apart while being hauled (with occupants) from one site to another because of an eviction, blocking Route 68 for nine hours. The sheriff, observing that the trailer was not roadworthy in the first place but trying to help the occupants, finally had to have the pieces pushed down the hill to get it off the road, and the trailer owner (unhurt) was very angry. The national news story played up the rural poverty angle (which led to a California billionaire donating a new trailer to the woman who had lost her home) and invoked comparisons with the sheriff of Mayberry RFD, on the *Andy Griffith Show.* A Nicholas County High School journalism class did an analysis and critique of the news story and the way it stereotyped rurality, discussed how they would have written it without those stereotypes and exaggerations, and wrote a letter to the editor of the *Lexington Herald-Leader* about it. I was told that the Carlisle diaspora (young people who left Carlisle to live in other places) started a social media thread about the whole event, one person writing, "There is nothing stranger than seeing U.S. 68 on my television on CNN."

Dr. Frank Mathias, a historian in Ohio who grew up in Carlisle, recalled in his memoir *The GI Generation:* "Few people, things, or events escaped some form of happy or cruel publicity in Carlisle, whether through gossip, sermons, or editorials" (Mathias 2000:11). Sometimes that publicity, embedded in kin and non-kin social networks, has had very practical consequences, sometimes positive, as in the new trailer provided to the person featured in the national news story, and sometimes negative, as in business lost by a local store from which a person with a large kin network had been fired.

In Carlisle, businesses might be thought of as more network-related than in urban contexts. Accounts might be carried for long stretches of time until residents' tobacco checks, or other checks, come in and bills can be paid. A person who had to close a repair business because of competition with Walmart (where the new item was so cheap it could be replaced instead of repaired) kept up the repair business out of his home, and some people just kept showing up as they had when he had a storefront. Local businesses went together on an advertisement in 1989 in the *Carlisle Mercury* that said "Don't gamble away your community's future." The text went on to say:

> You're betting against the future of your community and the happiness of your family every time you spend your money out of town.
>
> When we buy from those who buy from us . . . either our labor or our products, we're getting full value for the money we have worked so hard to earn.

> The stakes are high when you gamble with your community's business district. Your best bet is shopping in your hometown stores. (*Carlisle Mercury*, September 14, 1989:8)

Of the family-owned businesses in Carlisle, the stores that sold large items that would be hard to haul home to towns farther away and stores that were needed in emergencies, like local pharmacies, stayed open; stores that sold portable items, like clothing, were the first to close. A dollar store opened at the edge of town that is locally dubbed "the Carlisle mall." It sells items of all sizes, but the main reason for its success is probably its access to the supply chain of a multisited corporation, keeping prices lower.

A lot of the talk that happens in social networks in Nicholas County has to do with subsistence—where the first corn is coming on, when squirrel or deer season starts, who has the best yard sales, where the best fishing holes are—and that talk crosses class lines. Many Nicholas Countians, because there are woods, ponds, and gardens accessible through most social networks—whether one lives in the town or in the county—continue to participate in some noncash subsistence activities, like gathering berries for a pie, picking greens, or fishing for enough of a mess for a Sunday fish fry, along with cash activities. Some people, known for particular skills, sell things from their home, like cakes for special occasions.

Some talk, as Charles Gates indicated, has to do with class, which (as in dominant U.S. culture) is another topic not directly talked about very much. Instead, it will come out in sideways comments, on physical labor being real work and paperwork not being work, for example. There are some practical consequences of class divisions being deemphasized in most direct talk in a small town. One is the difficulty of union organizing across the lines of what may be seen as kin and other loyalty networks. As Shaunna Scott (1995:121) observed in her work on mining in Harlan County: "The ideology of community emphasized the experiential, historical, and structural common ground between the local elite and the working class. It did not, however, articulate the equally important differences and conflicts between the classes." Another consequence of not talking about class, or socioeconomic differences, is the masking of need. "Poverty may be considered an even more dire issue in rural communities because of how well it is hidden. . . . Additionally, the rural poor often receive little benefits from the federal government" (Edmonson 2003:25).

In Nicholas County, poverty is not confined visibly in stereotyped ways, as in housing projects (where there is actually a range of incomes); it is possible to be quite isolated on the landscape and for people not to want to speak up to let relatives know they do not have enough food to eat or money to pay the utility bills. People who experience poverty may find it difficult to access federal public assistance for reasons of literacy, transportation, or not wanting a relative working in a public assistance office to know about their economic situation. Neighboring only goes so far, and there is hidden need and rural homelessness. Janet Fitchen (1981), who worked to address rural poverty, said the planning discussions of local elites seldom include input from those experiencing extreme poverty, whose perspectives are an often untapped resource in problem solving in small towns.

As I will discuss in the next chapter, the biggest silence in the local planning process—as is the case across the rural United States—is about the economic and social role of the underground drug trade, and that needs to be taken into account in discussions of possible futures for the community. Breaking that silence, and organizing a community-wide conversation that acknowledges economic realities, would take all the skills I have been talking about in small-town life, and then some—including media support.

A Nicholas Countian summarized the role of the local newspaper for me once by saying, "The *Mercury* is the Bible of Carlisle." There have been several newspapers over the small town's history (the *Rat Terrier* in the 1800s was an early one), sometimes two at once, with either local or regional owners, but the most consistent newspaper has been the *Mercury*. There has been a *Carlisle Mercury* since 1867, and it has won over 300 state and national awards for its journalism. Many local young people, including my older brother and sister, have apprenticed there over the years and learned how small-town news is produced. The strong, discrete identities of small communities around the county, in addition to Carlisle, may be read in copies of the *Mercury* through time in the columns. A 1932 page of the *Carlisle Mercury* featured a larger number of local columns—from Headquarters, Scrub Grass, Walnut Grove, Miranda, Blue Licks, Sugar Creek, Taylor's Creek, Barefoot, Deavers, Little Rock, Ell Creek, Stringtown, Saltwell, Barterville, Jackstown (written by my great-grandmother, who mentioned a weekend visit from her daughter and son-in-law, Louise and Roy Kingsolver, and their son Wendell, my father— they talked of going back to Lexington with plenty of food from the farm during the Depression; many other visitors were probably similarly provisioned from "home"), Oakland Mills, Stony Creek, Maple Grove, and Ellisville.

A single page in a 1952 copy of the *Carlisle Mercury* features a smaller number of social columns called "Milltown," "Bald Hill," "Crayton," "Jackstown" (still written by my great-grandmother), "Saltwell," "Oakland Mills," "Upper Licks," and "Colored Notes;" that last column, written by Aurelia Hamilton, discussed visits from residents of Cincinnati, Chicago, and Detroit to their parents in Carlisle. This exemplifies what James Richard Bean said about industrialization and African American migration from Nicholas County. Almost 60 years later, those community columns in the *Carlisle Mercury* have given way to more regional stories from other counties. This probably reflects both changing social networks and changing ownership of the newspaper. Another weekly newspaper (with local ownership), the *Carlisle Courier*, started up in 2010.

Editing a small-town newspaper is a challenging job. As Lynd and Lynd (1965:374) in their study of a small town in the 1930s pointed out, local newspapers are caught between the pressures of community expectations, local advertisers, and sometimes external owners unfamiliar with small-town life.

One of the editors of the *Carlisle Mercury* once told me that the role of a local newspaper is to reduce controversy, not stir it up. Mediating gossip, rather than feeding it, is another goal as frequent editorials over the years have stressed. On October 4, 1990, for example, Hank Bond, the editor of the *Carlisle Mercury*, published this editorial:

> There is nothing easy about running a newspaper.
> From the advertising staff to the editorial staff, everyone works as hard as possible to present the best possible product for all our readership.
> For some reason, the newspaper has continued to be the target of continuing criticism. . . . We do not enjoy working every week with a cynical outlook, and won't. . . .
> There is no way to cover every event or news item. The priority is set by what will serve our readers best in our opinion, and that's the way it is going to remain. It is not based on the desire to run down or for that matter promote another person or business. . . .
> What this newspaper will do, is to present as much news as we can, not from the grapevine. Gossip is for those who want to talk on street corners or on the telephone. Gossip does damage, every time.
> We want to present the news in a factual, efficient manner, not produce yellow journalistic news, that creates controversy not really there, or facts which we cannot substantiate. . . . It is our obligation as a newspaper to perform in this manner. . . .

Stephen Scalf, the editor of the new *Carlisle Courier*, faced some of the same dilemmas the other editor mentioned. He had been sent an allegation against a business in a letter to the editor that he thought would be better framed as an opinion than as fact, and better addressed through the legal system than through the local newspaper. He wrote in an editorial published in the *Carlisle Courier* on May 26, 2010:

> I was hoping to make it through my first month as editor before having to face tough decisions about what to put in the paper. That didn't happen. . . .
> Opinions belong in the Letters to the Editor; accusations should be sent into the paper as leads to be investigated for a news story. We will let you know the results of our investigation and our decision on whether or not to run the story.

I have thought a lot over the years, as my subscriptions to newspapers from Nicholas County have followed me around, about the difference between large-scale newspapers that often do carry stories heavy with conflict and the cohesive role of small-town newspapers in featuring what is seen as locally significant, whether good news or sad: individual and group accomplishments; upcoming community and church events; soldiers killed and soldiers coming home; obituaries with photos; unidentified photos that only close kin and friends would recognize with captions like "Lordy, Lordy, look who's 40!"; news of crop diseases; school news; car accidents, fires, and rescues; receipt of funding for local infrastructure; historical photos with a call for collective memories of individuals or events; publication of the county budget, in full; nursing home news; the extensive court news, with every arrest, lawsuit, and change of property; and stories that you just about have to be rural to get excited about—someone finding a nine-pound mushroom, a poodle-shaped potato, or a twin tomato. Like the man who went home "to find out what's going on," many of us in the Nicholas County diaspora try to stay connected through reading the local newspaper.

Civic Participation

As I was interviewing a middle-aged Nicholas Countian in the 1980s, she said, "If you were to just talk to young people, pretty much the consensus is that there is just not much here, there is not much of a future here. What work is local, doesn't pay very well." A young adult at that time told me:

> It's *scary*—this is my *home*—but when I look around, I don't see young people coming back here. There's not much for them to come back *to*, I can't blame them, but I see all the *old* people we've got to support, and I wonder how we'll do it.

Others commented on how few young people were taking their place in community leadership. I started thinking about this as the problem of the invisible young people and decided to see if they were really disappearing from the county. I followed three Nicholas County High School classes (1973, 1978, and 1983) from their reunion data and found that over half of the young adults from each class were still living in the county in 1988 (often on their parents' property, to keep expenses down), but of that majority, many were commuting hours each day to jobs in other counties. You might as well be invisible in small-town life if you leave town before dawn and get back after sunset, catching up on chores on the weekend instead of going to community events. That solved part of the mystery of the missing young people, but at that time, at least a third of each class was living and working outside Nicholas County, and that number was growing. Based on 2000 U.S. Census figures, the county's median age was around 40, and the 2009 estimate of residents over 65 was about 15 percent, a little higher than the state figures.

Nursing homes have become more formalized in Nicholas County, as it has become more difficult to count on family and neighboring networks to provide complete care for the elderly and as long-term health care became a possibility through Medicaid.

> During these past 20 years Kentucky nursing homes have evolved from a cottage industry to an integral part of the Commonwealth's health care delivery system. . . . Kentucky must start preparing for a dramatic increase in the elderly population and a plan to meet their health care needs. (*Carlisle Mercury* 1988:1, 6)

The nursing home and hospital joined in one facility out by the Jockey plant at the end of the 1970s. There is a public health clinic next to it, which provides low-income health care, vaccinations, home health, and wellness programs. An apartment complex for low-income residents over age 55 is administered through the Community Action Council and connects residents with home health and Nicholas County Senior Citizens Center services. The latter provides elderly people still living in their homes with a place to go for programs and meals. The community infrastructure has enlarged to fill the gaps growing in local caregiving networks. A Nicholas Countian I was interviewing about the future of the county in the 1980s cocked her head, thought a minute, and said, "If people like small-town life, we'll have to work for it."

It is a lot of work to maintain community, and there are a number of people in Nicholas County who have dedicated their careers to that project. Health care provides a significant number of jobs in Nicholas County, along with elected government positions (most of which come with good salaries for the area, and benefits); the biggest employer, since the factory has left, is probably the school system. Not all of the employees live in Nicholas County, but many of them do. There are a number of paid and unpaid residents contributing to civic life—the *visible* counterpart to "those invisible young people." Despite talk of dwindling numbers, there is still a remarkable number of Nicholas County adults of all ages contributing their time and resources to community outreach through various civic organizations.

Here are some examples of that civic engagement. In the 1930s, Dr. Charles Mathers set up the Mathers Fund to provide school clothes for children who needed them; that fund is still going strong, with local donations, and has been utilized by many families. The Rotary Club has also quietly assisted many families in economic need. The volunteers in the Health Care Auxiliary have raised money for equipment for the hospital for over 30 years and provide volunteer assistance to patients. (My mother, Virginia Kingsolver, has worked with the Auxiliary, the Girl Scouts, and several other civic organizations in Carlisle.) Civic groups are sometimes gendered, like the Homemakers and the Women's Club, and tend to move through community life as a generational cohort (a "junior" version forming eventually with a new cohort, which is usually welcomed by an aging cohort tired of carrying the bulk of volunteer or organizational work). The Carlisle Community Woman's Club raised money in 1986 to give toward the Jaws of Life, which the Nicholas County Fire Department has used to rescue many people from cars crushed in accidents. The volunteer fire department and members of the National Guard have provided many volunteer hours in collective service projects as well as vital emergency services. Some families are dedicated to public service; Frankie Hughes, for example, served as mayor of Carlisle and all three of his sons have been volunteer firemen. Without the work of volunteer firefighters and emergency medical workers teamed with hospital staff and paid emergency workers in the region, many community members would not have survived accidents and other health crises. An important small-town skill is keeping community services going, through social networks, since full-time specialized services are often not available.

In 2004, many organizations joined together to raise $53,000 (almost twice the median household income in the county) for the American Cancer Society in a Relay for Life. Volunteers across all age groups have also joined together in county cleanup campaigns. In 2006, Caring Hearts—a nonprofit organization working to provide much-needed services for disabled individuals in the county—formed with local volunteers. In 2008, the Nicholas County Community Action Council, providing social services in the county, received a grant to assist those in the community who were homeless, mentally ill, or having problems with substance abuse. Since small towns traditionally have not acknowledged or addressed these three problems, these services are an important contribution. Another problem not talked about much in rural Kentucky (the state with the highest incidence in the nation) is domestic violence. Nicholas County's three Masonic lodges worked together in 2001 to provide 911 cell phones to survivors of domestic violence to help prevent repeated incidents of violence.

It is possible to see some class divisions as Nicholas Countians separate into "those helping" and "those helped," but these are crisscrossed by the many ways of being "placed" in relation to one another in community life. In the volunteer services mentioned above, for example, people work together across any such divisions and benefit across the board as well. The global neoliberal tendency for public services to be privatized might be thought of as having been anticipated in small-town life, since government assistance networks had never fully penetrated rural areas in the first place.

Some issues in civic life, though, *have* brought about huge rifts among Nicholas Countians in the past three decades. One was the wet/dry vote over making alcohol sales legal again, after being a "dry" county since Prohibition. There were petitions, community meetings, the formation of organizations on both sides of the issue, and passionate speeches. A speaker for Citizens for a Better Community, urging fellow voters to keep the county dry, said, "We are trying to keep the little town with the big heart from becoming the little town with the broken heart." When the vote came, Nicholas Countians decided 2-to-1 to legalize the sale of alcohol, making the county "wet." There was backtalk (as there always is) that the eight inches of snow made it harder for many elderly people supporting the "dry county" position to get to the polls to vote.

Another highly charged community issue was the passage of the occupational-payroll tax by the members of the fiscal court. There was a lot of public contestation about the tax, but at a public meeting a representative from the Bluegrass Area Development District explained the need for it in neoliberal policy terms: "Apparently under the new federalism of the Reagan administration in Washington, the trend has been to push the programs and responsibility for funding programs back to local government" (Bond 1987:1). A member of local government told me that a portion of federal and state money used to be distributed back to counties through "revenue sharing," and when that stopped, "that left us in a world of hurt" because the county government had to come up with some way of generating income to make up for public monies lost. The payroll tax was unpopular, and even *more* contested (all the way to the Kentucky Supreme Court) was the decision by the City of Carlisle to annex the county schools into the city (which did not require moving the city/county line very far) in order to impose a payroll tax on Nicholas County's largest employer. This eventually happened; the money was used to address the city's deficit, but it then had to be compensated for in the school system's budget. These local tensions were very much related to national and international economic policies.

The most recent community rift, over the local government's decision to move the Blackberry Festival to the fairgrounds at the edge of town from the courthouse square in Carlisle, had an impact on the local elections—with that being given by many as a reason for voting the judge-executive out of office—but that outcome may also have been influenced by national politics, given the anti-incumbent fervor of the 2010 electoral season. A Nicholas Countian once told me:

> *Everything's* politics in Kentucky. The power structure starts at the court-house, and works on out, and—in many instances—the politics comes ahead of the betterment of the constituency's interests.

Most actors in the official political arena in Nicholas County are male. There are what Karen Brodkin Sacks (1988), an anthropologist, has called "centerwomen"—women whose authority derives from community trust and informal rather than formal leadership—in Nicholas County (like those working for tourism development). Few women have been elected to public office, though. One woman, a community leader herself, told me that she would not vote for a woman, "not if she had *wings*. I think women have problems with authority." This may have been related to patriarchal kin, political, and Christian ideologies; I never quite figured it out. In 1988, the first woman—Juanita Smith—was elected a Nicholas County Magistrate. The magistrates make up the fiscal court. A farmer once answered, when I asked what it took to win an election in the county: "Family. Friendship. What they have done for people." It seems that women *do* have what it takes to get elected to public office.

City and county interests have sometimes been played against each other in the neoliberal policy era, as with the dispute over annexing the county schools into the city, but increasingly, there is a move to work across city/county lines, and county/county lines, given the difficulty of funding solutions to problems on a very small governmental scale. Penny Miller (1994:293), writing on Kentucky politics, observed: "Alongside the compulsion of Kentucky citizens to decentralize and fragment their government, there are tendencies—both in Kentucky's political culture and its institutions—toward combination and centralization. Centripetal forces . . . may be more important in the future." In 2009, the newly formed Carlisle–Nicholas County Chamber of Commerce convened a meeting of representatives of a number of the civic organizations listed above to work toward the formation of a Civic Council to better coordinate local planning.

Flexible Justice

Ten years after we had finished high school, one of my classmates was being arrested frequently, and another classmate was the jailer. On the night of our class reunion that summer on someone's farm, those roles were suspended; being placed as classmates took precedence. In this social context, justice was flexible. I am not suggesting that you move to a small town in order to pursue a life of crime—there is competent law enforcement in Nicholas County. It is just that the slippage that is there in the national legal system (like the way class plays into prosecution) is more *obvious* on a small-town scale. Some people refer to "the 150 who can't get arrested" in Carlisle, for example, to talk about local politics. A state trooper once complained that people knew things they were not saying about an investigation. There is definitely an insider/outsider code when it comes to matters of justice. As I was growing up everyone knew, for example, to stay out of the way of the 100-year-old man when his car waggled its way all over the road into town. He only went to town on certain days, at the same time of day. We also knew to stay off the rural roads late on Saturday nights when boys would play chicken in their cars. Neither the teenagers nor the centenarian were likely to be pulled over; the danger was to out-of-towners who did not know about these local road hazards. There is, then, some flexibility in the application of the law in a small town. In suburban developments in which people tend not to know each other, there is usually a proliferation of written rules to keep the peace (Perin 1988). In a small town, ambiguity is not only tolerated more readily, it is sometimes a necessity.

Court is held in the Nicholas County Courthouse by a circuit judge who also holds court in other counties, in rotation. Cases regarding public intoxication, theft, and divorce, for example, are handled in circuit court. But if someone is arrested for murder, a local grand jury has to decide if there is enough evidence to send the case to trial (in another county). Because of deeply intertwined social networks, perhaps some fear of reprisal, and a communal sense of justice sometimes trumping trust in court decisions, I have been told that it can be hard to get a grand jury to send a case out of the county for prosecution. Some cases deemed by folk justice to be clearly self-defense, as in a case of extreme domestic violence, may not have found their way to trial. The frightening side of flexible justice, of course, is why we need a justice system in the first place. Because of fear, silence, and unchallenged power, it is possible that a murderer, rapist, or bully could go uncharged and be seen every day in a small town by survivors of violence, or their relatives. That is why collaborative outsider and insider perspectives work best in law enforcement, as they do in social science. Here, I am explaining the thickness of relatedness as it plays out in a small town, but if that becomes a person's nightmare, he or she needs to have recourse to a larger network in which the legal system takes precedence over social networks.

In 1994, a man escaped from the jailer, jumped out a second-floor window of the Nicholas County courthouse, and disappeared. A month later, he called the jailer at his home at 2:00 AM, and told him where to come pick him up. The jailer and his wife got in their car and rode out to rendezvous with the escapee, who quietly climbed into the car and apologized to the jailer's wife for having run away from her husband at the courthouse. There is a kind of economy of trust in this story (the knowledge that the prisoner would not represent a threat, for example) based on the prisoner and the jailer (a different pair than my classmates) having known each other for 15 years. This time, he went to jail in another county. In 1997, the Carlisle Police put a reminder in the local newspaper, "If you don't want your vehicle stolen, don't leave your keys in it." Three cars, all with the keys in the ignition, had been stolen in one night. Sometimes both expectations and trust have to be adjusted a bit in small-town life.

This is not a Mayberry RFD story. There are many contexts around the world in which different frameworks (social, legal, and religious, for example) overlap with some flexibility between them, with neither taking complete precedence all the time. But there have been increasingly global encounters in law enforcement, as in other dimensions of Nicholas County life. Some local illegal activity is related to much larger political economic contexts, both in the economic need that may propel it and in the circulation of items in the underground market. Farmers, for example, have had to be more vigilant in guarding supplies of ammonia (used as a fertilizer), copper, and their livestock. In 2009, three people were arrested for cattle rustling in Nicholas County, selling the stolen cattle for $1,200 a head outside a stockyard in another county. Local residents have been arrested for illegal trade in food stamps, alcohol, and marijuana. In 1996, state police arrested 25 people in a single day's raid in Nicholas County for drug trafficking, mostly in marijuana, after a long investigation. In a more high-tech crime, a Carlisle couple was arrested for allegedly creating counterfeit $20 bills with a computer in 2007.

The biggest illegal trade, by far, in Nicholas County—and across rural America—is in prescription pain medication. Brian Canupp, who served as assistant county attorney in Nicholas County and now practices law in neighboring Bourbon County, described to me how the trade works in rural Kentucky:

> The market for prescription drugs is vastly different now than it was 10 years ago. When I started practice, pills were there, cocaine use was fairly substantial, and crack use, in particular, was a real problem. Marijuana has always been a drug of choice, and alcohol. But now the move is to prescription drugs, and that makes a lot of sense in terms of so many people who reside in Nicholas County and are now dependent on assistance, be it social security benefits, AFDC, WIC, those sorts of programs. There's not really a strength of economy.

I asked whether the number of people living below the poverty line was increasing in the county. He said yes, and continued:

> With the use of prescription drugs, there's really not the stigma of street drugs. There wasn't. And four people could pool together in an automobile, share gas costs, share room costs, drive to Florida (where, supposedly, the legislature has passed laws to change the pill mills), but to visit four or five doctors in Florida, visit a doctor in Georgia, a doctor in Tennessee (basically come up I-75), and be able to stay in a drunken stupor or a medicated stupor for 30 days until it was time to get back in the car and go do it again. But they would make money on the deal, because the trip sponsor would split the pills with them.

"Would the trip sponsor largely be out of the county?" I asked.

> No, there have been several in the county. But the network that exists, or existed, has been a multicounty operation. . . . There were loose associations among dealers. If one dealer got low, he could call another and say, you know, I need to get re-upped, basically a pill loan. I don't know of cash changing hands. Generally, it was a credit kind of thing. So then the dealer who was short, when he sent his next crew down, would try to find another person to go, so he would have his regular inventory, plus what was needed to pay off the loan. I know there have been several dealers who are now out of business.

Brian described a recent collaboration between several law enforcement units that resulted in the arrest and conviction of at least 10 dealers. He said that federal prisons actually had more options for rehabilitation services than the local prison system.

In 2009, according to a wire report, a doctor in northern Kentucky pleaded guilty to distributing prescription drugs illegally, having collected over half a million dollars selling oxycodone, hydrocodone, and other pain medications. He was part of a ring in which recruiters got fake patients to come into his office for fake prescriptions, and then the recruiters would take the fake prescriptions to pharmacies and split the drugs with the people posing as patients and sell the rest. A year later, a doctor in Florida who had been writing fake prescriptions for many of the illegal drug rings in eastern Kentucky was arrested (Estep 2010). As with the larger drug war in North America, arresting the small-scale dealers and drug users without arresting those who have more far-reaching accountability (like these prescribing doctors) does not eliminate the problem.

Meanwhile, there is the question of why addiction to pain medication and the economic need to sell pills is so widespread in Nicholas County. Maybe sometimes flexible justice means opening up the lens for a broader view of the interconnected issues, including the political economic context. Like antitobacco education, antidrug education is starting earlier and earlier with children in the county. Some dealers who have been arrested in Nicholas County have been high school students.

Sites of Socialization

Where do young Nicholas Countians get socialized (or learn who they are and how to be citizens)? In addition to social networks already discussed, this often happens through churches, schools, and community events.

As I have already mentioned, Nicholas County's religious diversity is not represented by practitioners of the major world religions (e.g., Buddhism, Christianity, Hinduism, Islam, and Judaism) but by varieties of Christianity: Catholic and Protestant congregations. I have learned, in both Kentucky and South Carolina, that in this kind of dominant religious landscape, the inhabitants are often socialized to see Methodism, Lutheranism, Catholicism, and Presbyterianism, for example, as different religions rather than different forms of Christianity, a single faith. In the local context, this level of distinction makes sense; in global context, those distinctions would be more collapsed. In the 1980s, I counted over 150 Protestant Christian churches in Nicholas County, between formal church buildings, storefront churches, and congregations that met in homes. Not everyone attends a church, by any means, but most people come into contact with several within their social networks.

Churches take on a lot of work in civic space, offering American Sign Language classes, Spanish classes, and adult literacy training, for example. They also serve as a home base for out-migrants in many ways, individually for life events like weddings and funerals, but also collectively, as in the Wesley Chapel CME Church's "Old Landmark Day," or annual Homecoming day. Carol Greenhouse (1986) has said that people in small southeastern U.S. towns dominated by Christian churches often learn about authority and conflict resolution or avoidance through their socialization in church. In Nicholas County, if there is a dispute within a church, people usually just start another one.

Another dominant civic venue in small towns is the public school system. Arthur Vidich and Joseph Bensman (1958:171) observed 50 years ago in their study of a rural community:

> In contrast to the village and town boards, the school board is faced with making important decisions on issues which have far-reaching consequences in the community at large. Politically it is the area in which most community issues, interest, activities and discussion are present.

That may still hold true, since the public school is the touchstone of many people's concern for the future, as it is embodied in their children. Influential decision making is not all top-down in the school system, though; it also happens between the children themselves, as they learn how to "place" each other in terms of various locally salient categories of identity (e.g., county/city or Assembly of God/Presbyterian).

The Nicholas County public schools are children's portal of equal access to global information and technologies, and they are the key site for addressing the divided experiences of literacy in the county. (Estimates range from 25 to almost 50 percent functional adult literacy in Nicholas County; functional is an ambiguous word, and all of these figures are projections rather than precise numbers.) I have known many dedicated teachers in that school system, and because of the size of the school and community, it has not been uncommon for everyone in a generation or two in Nicholas County to have studied the same subject under the same teacher (with only a few quirky results, like all those adults who had one elementary teacher tending to confuse left and right because of her mirror-image teaching technique). The current teaching staff brings diverse experiences and interests to the students, and students like the recent immigrants from Latin America bring their experiences, as well. Community members have worked with school staff to provide extracurricular opportunities for students in athletics, academic bowls, science fairs, band, theater, and other experiences that take them beyond the borders of Nicholas County.

Community events are a site for socialization into small-town life, as well. The Blackberry Festival, around the Fourth of July every year, used to have a dog show. Children from all over the county would bring our dogs, and every one of them would get a ribbon, with the judge making up new categories on the spot until they had all been doled out. Instead of entitlement, all I can think of about that event is that it taught graciousness—from "shortest tail" to "most lopsided ears," everybody got included somehow. When I think about it, we were educated as rural children not only by the school system, but by the agricultural extension service and 4-H program, too. Many of us wrote our way through Soil Conservation Service essay contests, learned how to make posters and give speeches and demonstrations in 4-H, and see a project through from beginning to end (which fosters research skills). With the current emphasis on cultural and linguistic diversity in 4-H programming (the Cooperative Extension Service's National Center for Diversity has been located at Kentucky State University) and migrant services in the public schools, it is increasingly possible for children whose parents may identify as farmers and farmworkers to interact in 4-H and other regional student organizations.

Many of the skills of rural life that I have mentioned in this book are taught through 4-H as well as through socialization at home. The annual Nicholas County Fair, also sponsored through the Cooperative Extension Service, has all kinds of events to enter, from pageants to tractor pulls. There is a hall in which items can be entered for judging under numbered categories, for example: Horticulture Items, #93, Broccoli, largest head; Canning, #153, tomatoes in juice. One year my brother Rob, who grew up to be a biologist, was indignant to find his carefully preserved hognose snake, in its Mason jar, set by the judges among the canned vegetables. There had been hundreds of entry categories, but none for pickled snake. The tomatoes won.

There are many other events in which facets of community identity are performed: the Lions Club Horse Show, family reunions, parades, community prayer services (to pray for rain, for example, in times of drought), and special events that link local and national identity, as in the September 11 observance in which a Nicholas County family talked about their experience visiting Ground Zero in New York City. As throughout much of the rest of the nation, anthrax preparedness drills and other national security measures were rehearsed in local contexts. These are moments of socialization into a dominant national narrative. Contestation might be expressed by not attending public events, or through silence, but it would not be likely for one to hear a public debate of the U.S. policy in Iraq and Afghanistan at a 9/11 prayer service in Carlisle.

That lack of public counterpoint can be problematic, and some residents may leave because of it. I do not want to lend support, on the other hand, to comfortable notions of small towns as being small-minded about the world. No size of community has a monopoly on either discrimination or tolerance. Living in different regions of the United States has taught me that the stereotypes of where tolerance and intolerance may be found are misleading, and even dangerous. Wendy Brown (2006) has pointed out that the term "tolerance" can itself be silencing of diversity because it re-inscribes a norm. A student from an urban context in California once told me that she was tired of other students expecting her to be representative of a category of racialized identity that they placed her in visually, instead of seeing her as an individual. She might have a better chance of being known as an individual in a small town like Carlisle. However, the problem of exceptionalism (in which someone might be known as an individual rather than as a stereotype, without the stereotype itself necessarily being discarded), raised previously, begs the question of how major changes in majority/minority numbers and relations might challenge the welcoming reputation of Carlisle and other small towns with similar demographics. In Murfreesboro, Tennessee, in 2010, for example, there is national attention to widespread local resistance to the construction of a much larger complex for the existing unobtrusive Islamic Center of Murfreesboro. A spokesperson for the Islamic Center, Camie Ayash, said:

> It's still a little mind-boggling. It seems like the community is very accepting of us as individuals; when I take my kids to school, I don't run into any prejudice because I cover my hair, but the concept of Islam overall makes people nervous because of 9/11. (Kauffman 2010)

In the political landscape of the United States, small towns are often characterized as reinforcing dominant cultural and religious national narratives. Although I have participated, in this chapter, in some formulaic descriptions of small towns, such views need to be examined critically. There are small towns in New Mexico that have been predominantly Spanish-speaking for centuries, for example; small towns have different histories, including the global economic histories that may explain why they are situated on the landscape as they are. Diversity may have a different salience in a small town. Living on a farm and living in town may be a major distinction in high school social life, for example, as Foley (1990) observed. But the work that people do together in small towns—across whatever differences they may have—to sustain community services under challenging conditions could be instructive for those facing similar challenges at different scales.

Global Encounters

Besides using the Internet, how are Nicholas Countians engaging the global? As James Richard Bean and Charles Gates relayed earlier in this chapter, serving in the military gave them each a different perspective on Nicholas County: a basis for international comparison. Others have had military or National Guard experience, or have traveled to Japan for training as Toyota employees, or have taken missionary trips to Jamaica or Russia, or have migrated from other countries to Nicholas County. The high school has been a major site for global engagement in Nicholas County. Students participated in the Schools for Schools program, raising money in 2008 for construction of schools in Uganda and learning about the experiences of long-term war and displacement that have shaped the lives of people their own age in Uganda. One group of 20 students and 10 adults went on a trip to the United Kingdom. The Carlisle Rotary Club has hosted study groups from Argentina and India and has sponsored exchange students from Thailand, Japan, Russia, Germany, Sweden, and France. In 2010, exchange students from Norway, Germany, South Korea, and Switzerland were living with families in Nicholas County and attending the high school. Several Nicholas Countians have adopted children from the People's Republic of China and coordinate Chinese language and cultural instruction together. Sometimes people just pass through Nicholas County on longer treks: a woman walking across the country, for example, and a cowboy riding around the world to raise money for the National Cancer Society were profiled in the local newspaper, of course.

There is a way in which living in a small town socializes a person into a "mental distance" from urban centers, which can persist even if one is commuting to work there every day. I think that is *not* because small towns are somehow backward, or in another time, but because of the difference between being thickly or thinly related to a place through social networks (which, as you have read, take a lot of work and skill to maintain) and everyday experiences over time in a single landscape. The skills of living in a small town are one of the resources Nicholas Countians have for imagining "tobacco town futures."

Questions for Students

1. What kinds of experiences can shape your sense of place? If you are studying in a college or university, have you gone to a different place for your education from the one you grew up in? If so, what is it like to go "home" now? Do you feel, or do people expect you to be, different? How has your perspective changed? If you are living where you grew up, do you still spend time with people you knew in high

school? What changes do you notice in your cohort, or age group, as you get older and make your own decisions about where you want to live?

2. There are many ways to construct "home" and "family." As an anthropologist, I see that as an active and intentional process set within larger political economic relationships that may constrain or facilitate people living near or far from what they consider to be home and family. If someone asked you who your family is, and where "home" is, what would you say? Would your answer change depending on who asked you? What examples can you think of that illustrate the way home and family are constructed culturally?

3. Reciprocity refers to the give-and-take of resources (whether material or social support) among kin and/or social networks. Generalized reciprocity means that assistance comes to people as they need it most, without any tally being kept of who has helped whom, and how much that might have cost. Balanced reciprocity refers to the exchange of gifts or services of approximately the same value between the same exchange partners, as when some people in the United States give each other holiday gifts (and are embarrassed or cease the exchange if the gifts are not roughly equal in value). What kinds of reciprocity networks are you involved in? "Embedded in the networks that link people loosely or closely are social resources used to organize and mobilize for activities on behalf of the community" (Salamon 2003:17). Sometimes in a large enough group, people feel like if they do not help out, others will. Small towns cannot afford to work like that; as Salamon points out, if enough people move in to enjoy the benefits of small-town life without contributing to the work it takes to keep a small town going, then the generalized reciprocity breaks down. How much do you participate in your civic community, however you define it?

4. Agnes Aamodt (1981) has written about the dilemmas of being an "insider" in a social science research context, since the researcher is expected to fulfill established social roles, and it is difficult to participate in new community roles or networks. How might this chapter be different if it had been written by someone else, not already familiar with the community? How would you design a comparative research project to study life in a small town and in a city? Who would you want to talk with, and what questions would you ask?

5. There has been a lot written about "community" in the United States. Some define communities by elements of place, shared interests, and social interaction (see Poplin 1979:8–9); communities can also be online, where members may never meet in person. What do *you* think constitutes a community, and why?

6. Kitchell, Hannan, and Kempton (2000:104) describe the way that stories are used to construct individual and group identity and to socialize new members of a group: "It is through stories that citizens within the figured world paint the picture of that reality for newcomers." Think about how you have entered a new context— a new school, organization, or community, for example. How were stories used to tell you about the identity of that group or place, and how did those stories include or exclude you? How do you use stories in the construction of individual and group identity? If you are studying social science, how might you think of theory as storytelling, and everyone as a theorist? "I see theory as the stories we tell ourselves to make sense of life and to determine where we are as we navigate social space" (Kingsolver 2001:4). How might you think of the stories Nicholas Countians tell about social life as social theory?

Chapter 5

Tobacco Town Futures

As I have been looking through my notes to complete this book, I realized that the 17-year cicadas have emerged *twice* in Nicholas County during my research there. It is time to sum up what I have learned from listening for 25 years to people talk about the possible futures of a tobacco town and to see how these reflections intersect with those of others, including the young people whose essays in the postscript start the conversation on the *next* quarter century or more of global encounters in Nicholas County.

Looking at past imaginings of the future and comparing them with what has happened can be useful, as can situating our current experiences and understandings of globalization within historical context. Kentucky farmers who organized a century ago against tobacco monopolies for setting the prices in their direct-buying relationships with local growers (and then profiting from global sales) might not be surprised to see that arrangement prevalent today—what they might find surprising is that there was anything else in between.

In the late twentieth century, the year 2000 seemed a magical date that catalyzed conversations about the future of many dimensions of human experience, including agriculture. In 1985, and again in 1989, there were stories in the *Carlisle Mercury* predicting that there would be fewer farmers, all using computers, tending genetically engineered crops and livestock. Farm-grown fish were predicted to be much more prevalent in 2000 because of overfishing and offshore pollution (Moffet 1985: 9)—a sobering prediction, given the 2010 Gulf oil spill. Tobacco would be growing still, but producing genetically engineered pharmaceuticals; sheep engineered to produce rich wool and lean meat were imagined grazing in Nicholas County fields. Ginseng and mushroom production were predicted to be up, and small dairies down, given the expected entrance into the market of a bovine growth hormone that would increase dairy production for high-tech operations and knock everyone out of the business (which just about happened). There were warnings in both articles that without more education and diversification, small farmers could become low-paid workers in a mostly mechanized world of satellite-controlled agriculture.

It is interesting to see how we imagined the future in the past, like digging up time capsules buried on the lawns of courthouses across the country.

My parents and others in their generation have told me that they hold onto things—twine, old machine parts, scraps of cloth—because of being Depression-era children and never quite trusting that the bottom will not fall out of the economy again. They believe they might need to be resourceful in a noncash economy, as they had watched their parents be. Farming skills are one of the things they have held onto, and passed on. In the current economic downturn, many younger people have started listening more to that generation to make sure that noncash subsistence skills are not thrown overboard in the race to growth-oriented development and cash returns on investments. Investing in local agricultural economies can have a variety of motivations—from a fear of terrorists threatening the food supply or of genetically modified foods to an interest in having more face-to-face than face-to-faceless transactions. That desire for "reenchantment," as Max Weber (1958) called it in his description of the alienation he saw growing with industrial capitalism, may be new for some, but in Nicholas County (as described in the last chapter), the knowledge and skills required for community engagement and mixing cash and noncash activities are old hat, at least for older residents.

In a program called Food for Thought in four Kentucky counties around Cumberland College, high school students planted a garden and delivered produce to senior citizens in exchange for their stories about rural life, which the students published (Stamper 1998). Intergenerational conversations and education, facilitated by extensive social networks in rural areas, but weakened by the outmigration of young people for employment, constitute a resource for understanding globalization. As Mary Jo Maynes, Jennifer Pierce, and Barbara Laslett (2008: 44) have noted, "beyond the time frame of the individual life course, narrators usually refer to a range of other temporal and historical frames—familial, institutional, and national—when they tell their 'own' stories." By asking people in Nicholas County to explicitly comment on globalization in interviews and oral histories over the last 25 years, I have tried to learn from explanations of the future that were situated in both historical and global context.

Any discussion of Nicholas County has to take into account the fact that the global economy turned a while ago from being based on gold bars (always a source of pride for Kentuckians, since the U.S. supply was kept at Fort Knox, in our state) to being based on debt—the buying and selling of the promise of future payments on consumer credit cards, farm loans, and home mortgages, kind of like trading in hog belly futures. As the mortgage crisis rippled through economies around the world, the fragility of that system was exposed, but Nicholas Countians still owe payments on that debt, so cash is definitely a necessity.

Discussions of the county's future *also* have to take into account the fact that there are only so many ways to raise cash in times of rising unemployment, and one of them is dealing illegally in drugs. As Sister Dorothy said, in 2010:

> I think our biggest problem is drugs. I think it's the root of all problems here. . . . There are drug sales going on in our parking lot, even in the day. Kids gather. They're not in school. They drop out. . . . And they're going to Florida to get prescriptions. And there's monthly runs, with vans, back and forth to Florida. . . . It's gonna be the downfall of this town unless somebody really takes the bull by the horns. A big, big problem.

There are separate conversations going on in the county about—for example—the development of tourism and local agricultural markets, the aging of the population, illiteracy rates, and the drug economy. Looking at how all of these are connected in terms of global encounters can be useful. In earlier chapters, I have talked about how global free trade agreements, for example, have caused the shift in the textile industry from the southeastern United States to other countries—often, now, China or Bangladesh; how "buying locally" can itself be branded within larger neoliberal economic markets, along with the commodification of rurality (that can problematically graft honesty and loyalty onto whiteness, already valorized); and how shifting rural demographics, and individual drug busts, can be understood within larger political economic contexts. One of the major questions about the future of small-scale farming in Nicholas County has to do with a national policy issue: health care. Since most farming households have needed to have at least one member in an off-farm job with health care benefits, it will be interesting to see whether health care indeed becomes more affordable and more universally available (as promised in association with recent national legislation), and whether that will enable farming households to stay on the farm, if they want, even with the loss of off-farm employment.

Another national policy that may affect Nicholas County's economic and social terrain, as I have mentioned, is the introduction of reliable broadband Internet availability. This would mean more college graduates might stay home and telecommute, but it might also mean an influx of low-wage service work, like call centers. Low-wage employers are going to seek out the workforce in rural Kentucky, as has happened in the past, because of the lack of unionization and, frankly, other employment options, but this time Nicholas Countians could find themselves competing with workers in India and losing out because of low literacy rates. Literacy, and education, as many people have told me in conversations over the years, are key to Nicholas County's economic future.

It does not do much good to talk about planting grapes as an alternative to tobacco, or anything else that requires investment, without being realistic about the economic resources people have readily available and the debts they already have. As one Carlisle resident put it in the 1980s, as she rocked on her embroidered chair and I could hear her clock tick, "It all comes back to the dollar . . . the dollar is going to take us all." People in Nicholas County need to make a viable living, and according to a document signed by representatives of the United States and 47 other governments in 1948, they also have a right to one. Article 25 of the United Nations Universal Declaration of Human Rights says (in the gendered terms of its day):

Everyone has the right to a standard of living adequate for the health and well-being of himself and his family, including food, clothing, housing and medical care and necessary social services, and the right to security in the event of unemployment, sickness, disability, widowhood, old age or other lack of livelihood in circumstances beyond his control.

I imagine most Nicholas Countians would agree that if there are more employment opportunities in the region, they need to provide not just any wage, but a living wage—which means that a full-time worker should not have to choose between paying for housing, utilities, food, or medical care; compensation, even if the employer claims to be strapped because of the global economy, ought to be enough to live on. As some would say, one could just stay *home* to starve. Researchers at The Pennsylvania State University have put together a website (http://www.livingwage.geog.psu.edu) on which you can look up what exactly a living wage would be in different occupations in Nicholas County, and compare that to other U.S. communities. I recommend doing that.

Succinctly, what I have learned from this project about what will be important in imagining and enacting "tobacco town futures" is: (1) literacy and education are going to be important, as is acknowledging the skills and resources already in place in the community, rather than devaluing them; (2) more inclusive consideration of Nicholas Countians' identities (including, for example, those working illegally in the prescription drug market), skills, needs, and spokespeople is vital, if tough to pull off; and (3) it is going to be important, in the next decade, to hang onto enough local ownership of land. As Bernard Nietschmann (1974) has documented for communities on the coast of Nicaragua, as boom and bust cycles come and go, it is always possible to return to subsistence resources and a less cash-focused, more community-based economy *until* the next boom becomes the subsistence resources themselves, and then there's nothing to fall back on when the bust comes.

There will be, as Nicholas Countians' words on the pages of this book predict, an increase in people from other regions, even other nations, buying land in Nicholas County, both because it is inexpensive relative to their cost of living in other contexts and because they are looking to purchase rurality itself. As Carlisle residents have pointed out to me, newcomers' capital and new ideas (most of them, anyway) will be welcomed. But, in the closest I will come to a cautionary note in this conclusion, enough land will have to remain both affordable and in the hands of long-term local residents to (1) sustain the very sense of rural community that newcomers are investing in, and (2) sustain the residents—of all incomes—themselves (or ourselves, if I ever move back). As pointed out in the introduction, local communities may themselves be on the landscape because of global economic patterns (like the capitalist development that spread homesteads across the county and sent hogsheads of tobacco down the river to New Orleans), and those patterns shift.

One of the advantages to letting this book project mature (or cure, to use a tobacco metaphor) for a couple of decades is that if I had written it when I was younger, I would have expected it to make unique observations. Now I am glad to see connections with others' work, since we are all mentored and "placed" in communities, including communities of thought, and this book is itself about various kinds and levels of relatedness. Here are some of the other writers with whose work my conclusions resonate. Anna Tsing (2005), in *Friction: An Ethnography of Global Connection*, talks about the friction between modernization discourses and plans (like state-led development), and the plans and actions of local communities (sometimes seen as backward and in need of development) as a productive friction—with creative contestation of plans hatched within a global capitalist context (like the clear-cutting of forests) that might end up having disastrous local consequences. This is akin to Nicholas Countians "working the edge" in development. Ruth Levitas (1993), in "The Future of Thinking about the Future," provides a useful reminder about the planning process:

> The solution, however, is not to call for more and better utopias, more and better images and maps of possible futures. These will follow when we have better analyses of the present which identify possible points of intervention, paths and agents of change. (Levitas 1993: 265)

Samuel Collins (2008:125) believes that the very aspect of neoliberal capitalist development that spurs seeking ever more diverse markets will lead to its no longer being a dominant force on the landscape, given that those diverse markets (like the centralized production of automobiles vs. the farm stands through which Kentucky Pride vegetables are sold) will themselves encourage a range of ways to organize production, distribution, and consumption.

Some authors have looked at very similar situations to the one I am talking about in this "tobacco town" in other places. Jane Adams (1994), in *The Transformation of Rural Life: Southern Illinois, 1890–1990*, for example, describes the way residents of rural communities there in the 1940s and 1950s (the same period of industrial boosterism described here in chapter 3) hoped to have it both ways, planning economic development that they hoped would "enable the people of southern Illinois communities to share the benefits of new technologies while simultaneously enriching the quality of community and family life and broadening the numbers of people who had access to democratic forms of government and civic participation" (Adams 1994: 245).

Looking at rural Canadian communities, Jennifer Sumner (2005) emphasized civic participation as both a goal and a resource in rural development, also, suggesting that we might consider "sustainable globalization" strategies in which rural communities network with one another. One such possibility in Nicholas County, for example, would be for local artisans to sell their work through an online site maintained by a group of rural community craft producers, involving members of those communities in the associated shipping, packing, and computer jobs—collaborating between communities along the lines Tom Hensley envisioned for agriculture, but from an even greater distance. Thinking beyond county lines to acknowledge belonging in the larger Appalachian region is a step in that direction, since there are such efforts underway.

Another writer whose ideas could be considered to be in conversation with my abovementioned conclusions lives in Nicholas County. As part of this book project, I sponsored an essay contest for seventh, eighth, and ninth graders in the Nicholas County schools, as I have mentioned. It was called the Roy and Louise Kingsolver Essay Contest on the Future of Nicholas County (in honor of my grandparents, who valued both local farm life and education). The question put to young writers was: "Given the importance of farming, especially tobacco, in Nicholas County's history, what do you imagine the county's future will be like?" The winners were given savings bonds and were promised the publication of their essays in this book (see the postscript for the three winning essays from each grade, chosen by a school/community committee). Students were also told that the winning essays would be published in the local newspaper, and that all entrants would be acknowledged at the Nicholas County Fair. I first advertised the contest in the summer of 2009, through the *Carlisle Mercury*, thinking that young people would have more time to write something optional like this in the summertime. No one entered the contest. Given the role of the schools in community life, explained in the previous chapter, you would think I would have known better than to go it alone. During the 2009–2010 school year, the Nicholas County Schools took on the promotion of the essay contest. Not only did teachers encourage students to write essays (and nearly 50 did), but they also organized a panel discussion at the school to help the students think about the issues. Representatives from the farming, government, and business communities were invited to address the young people. One of those speakers, Ed Taylor (a Carlisle business owner who moved to Nicholas County as an adult and has been a strong participant in civic life), published his remarks in the *Carlisle Mercury* as a letter to the editor on February 24, 2010:

> As you think about a future for the county, you might want to consider these thoughts.
>
> 1. Things could stay pretty much as they are. This is unlikely. People with money are already moving in. The county is scenically attractive and land is relatively inexpensive. These people bring with them interest in arts, education, different foods, and entertainment. They can go to Lexington or other places to pursue their interests but eventually pressure to fill these needs locally will emerge. Culture and values in the county are slowly changing.
>
> 2. With inflation, cost of services will increase. Taxes or prices will have to be increased or services reduced. The number of service employees could be reduced by merging services with adjoining counties or even by merging county governments. Nicholas County could cease to exist or get bigger!
>
> 3. We might attract new industry manufacturers to the County. This is the dream of current city and county governments. However, State Economic Development people have told us that this is unlikely. Every county is trying to do this and, like Nicholas County, most lack the infrastructure and suitable employee base to support a modern manufacturer.

4. We can work to attract visitors to the county. We already have an impressive welcome center, several significant historical sites, a genealogy library, a doll and toy museum, several restaurants and some marketable events such as the Blackberry Festival and Saturday in Carlisle. However, we have limited overnight accommodations and a weak, uncoordinated marketing effort.

5. We have a relatively strong farming community in the county but its economic impact is limited by the lack of secondary or value-added processes. Most of what's raised is shipped out of county for warehousing and distribution, auctioning, slaughter and butchering, or consumer product manufacturing. All of these functions represent jobs in some other county rather than in ours. I hope these thoughts will help you imagine a future for Nicholas County and, more importantly, think about how we will get to that future. Will it just happen, or are there things we can do to make it happen?

—Ed Taylor, Carlisle, KY

Tom Hensley had written to the editor of the *Carlisle Mercury* 25 years ago with some of the same rallying points; the conversation about the future of the community is a continuous one, although community identity, history, and possible futures are imagined differently along the way.

Several of the possibilities discussed by Ed Taylor—new residents, light industry (which could mean vertical integration in the agricultural sector), and tourism—might be facilitated by the expansion of Route 68, as Judge-Executive Larry Tincher and James Richard Bean told me in 2009 they hoped would happen. Judge Tincher said:

What I would like to see in Nicholas County, I'd like to see us expand a little bit as—actually, and I hate to use this term—as a bedroom community. Because most of the jobs that are being created are in the larger cities. And people have gotten to the point now that they're more comfortable driving two hours to work and raising their children in a smaller community, in a smaller atmosphere, than having to fight the big-city rat race. And personally, I think that's a good thing. I think everybody needs an opportunity to grow up in a small community if they can. . . . And I think we're going to see more subdivisions. . . . We need some more utilities and services to provide for people. . . . We need some kind of wastewater treatment plant on U.S. 68 that would service that area, plus maybe a subdivision and possibly an industrial park. And industrial park's a dirty word in this day and time, because there are so many of them sitting empty.

Judge Tincher's imagining of Nicholas County as a haven from the rat race echoes Stephen Hagan's comment, in the Orkney Islands across the Atlantic, that

the islands will become more attractive locations as people begin to realise that peace, tranquility and safety are much more desirable than the rat race "doon sooth." Our young people will flock back to their roots and enjoy the new opportunities afforded them and people will recognise that Orkney is the best place to live. (Peebles and Watts 2009: 46)

This is a *global* rural discourse, then. Back in Carlisle, Judge Tincher explained how U.S. 68, "one of the oldest federal highways in the United States," sits at the junction of three major through-corridors:

> If we could get that thing upgraded, that's going to increase the traffic flow, and that also gives the people in Ohio and the Maysville area an opportunity to travel south. . . . It would increase the possibilities for industry, it would increase the possibility for people to travel south, and spend money. If you've got a good road to drive on, that helps.

The funding for that expansion of U.S. 68 was approved in 2010. James Richard Bean expressed hopes similar to Judge Tincher's for suburban development and tourist services (like restaurants) along U.S. 68 once it was widened. He said:

> That is the hub of the wagon wheel, it's the center part, and if you can look within 30–35 minutes, you can go to Maysville, or Morehead, Georgetown, Mt. Sterling, Winchester, Lexington, Frankfort—so these are all the big cities and we are right in the center. They are going to commute, once the road [is widened].

This has happened in other areas, and it is certainly possible in Nicholas County, since newcomers are buying property in the county and commuting to urban jobs even *before* the road construction project.

Daniel Kemmis (1990) might suggest that new development along Route 68 be more coordinated between the urban and rural communities involved in networks of residence and employment:

> As rural life is threatened more and more severely by international markets, by technological dislocations and corporate domination, it may be time for a reassessment of the relationship between cities and their rural environs. It may well be that neither towns nor farms can thrive in the way they would prefer until they turn their attention more directly to each other, realizing that they are mutually complementary parts of the enterprise of inhabiting a particular place. (Kemmis 1990: 124)

Some combination of suburban development, light agricultural processing and manufacturing industry, service work, and small farms marketing to local, regional, and global buyers will probably be in Nicholas County's future. Since this book is called *Tobacco Town Futures*, though, I will end this chapter with a few examples of what is happening now on farms that were traditional tobacco farms, representing some future directions.

Loretta Mann

Loretta Mann lives in a log house that is over 200 years old. She likes that history, and she likes sitting on her porch—when she has a minute—and

Loretta Mann with
her loom (photo
by author)

looking up at the steep hillside across the road. Early one morning she saw a coyote run down that hill, but she is more likely to see deer, crossing to the river on the backside of her cabin, by the railroad track. Her tobacco patch is in hay now, and someone else comes to mow it. In 1983, she learned, from an older woman, how to weave rag rugs on a loom. She loved it. In 1810, there were over 300 active looms in Nicholas County; 200 years later, Loretta Mann is one of the few to keep the shuttle going, and people come from all over, she says, to buy the rugs that she stacks in a couple of rooms of her home. With someone cutting strips for her, she can weave several rugs a day.

With all the sewing skills in the county (from work at the garment factory) already, and the growing support for local artisans through the Courthouse Square Art Guild, there is a possibility of stronger fiber arts, and arts and crafts, production in the county (especially now that there are some sheep again), which would go along with the tourism scenario.

Mike Phillips

Having come to be the Nicholas County Agricultural Extension Agent in 1977 and stayed, Mike Phillips has probably been the person who has spoken with the most tobacco farmers in the county before, during, and after the transition in the tobacco program. He has had the opportunity, now, to work with three generations in 4-H programs, seeing some children become parents and then grandparents and stay in farming. In 1987, he told me that although the one big check for tobacco made it look like it was carrying farms economically, he could see in the ledger details that, for most small farmers, cattle production was actually carrying tobacco (as a calf was sold here to pay for extra labor, and there for a piece of machinery). I asked him then if he saw vegetables as possible alternative crops to tobacco, with a local processing plant. He said that might work in the future, especially using the nitrogen-freezing process, since vegetables that did not look perfect for the farmers' market buyers could be cut into pieces, frozen, and shipped to restaurants and other markets. But, he said, there were not yet enough vegetable growers in the county to support a freezing plant. That same year, he was asked by the *Carlisle Mercury* editor—for a story—whether the family farm was dying. (He has heard that question a number of times by now, I imagine.) He said the terrain and capitalization possibilities limited farmers' options, but that there was plenty of grass as a resource for cattle. Mike has told me that he has never tried to steer a farmer toward a particular alternative but to present options for the size farm the household has.

Over the years, as I have talked with Mike Phillips, he has seen beef cattle production as the most solid route for farmers phasing out of tobacco, and a lot of the settlement money was used for improvements for cattle (fencing, barns, forage, and livestock management training for the farmers). There have been a few bumps in the road with cattle—fear of mad cow disease rippled through the market, and then the economic recession. Mike told me in 2009 that beef prices have been low because consumers, with less money to spend, have been buying cheaper cuts of beef. At the time of slaughter, something has to be done with the more expensive cuts, so they are being ground into hamburger, too, just to sell the meat. That makes the return lower, so farmers are getting less for cattle as they sell them to the slaughterhouses.

He has seen the farmers in the county age—"the average age of the farmer is probably 60 to 63"—and decrease in number. "As older farmers retire, neighboring farmers tend to buy up those farms. . . . We are probably averaging 185 acres per farm, where probably 20 years ago that number would have been 75 or 80." The number of farmworkers from Latin America on H2A visas has gone down, he said, because cattle and hay take less labor than tobacco, and there was not enough work to keep temporary workers employed full-time; most are living in other counties, he said, and then come into the county for part-time farmwork when it is needed. The population that is increasing in the county, Mike said, is the Amish community. He said

Road sign
in Nicholas
County
(photo by
author)

that from two families four or five years before, Amish families had bought nine more farms and there was a community of 70 or 80 Amish residents in the county in 2009. I asked him how they were integrating into the farm population that had been in the county for generations. He replied:

> It's kind of amazing, really, that they have been really well received. I think today's producers look at them and remember how they did it 42 years ago and they can still relate to that, and are intrigued by it. There has been an overall acceptance of the blending of the cultures.

Mike said that some of the Amish farmers attended the classes he offered in the agricultural extension service office. Farmers can learn a lot from each other's techniques. He also said that more people (who were not Amish) were coming into his office to ask what they could do on farms they had bought— by finding them on the Internet, mostly—for a lot less money than they would have paid in the regions from which they had moved to Nicholas County. "Many times all they have is a piece of land," he said, "and they don't have the expertise, in many instances, of real management from an agricultural perspective."

One of the possible future crops for Nicholas County, Mike Phillips told me in 2009, might be growing switchgrass for fuel. Switchgrass was being grown on five acres experimentally that summer, and was going to be burned along with coal in a coal-burning power plant. He said that the idea would be to work up to a 20 percent switchgrass/80 percent coal mix. One challenge would be storage facilities, since the switchgrass would have to be kept dry to be the most effective fuel, but if that could be worked out by using existing facilities people already have for cattle forage, the county might be able to produce the 60,000 pounds of switchgrass that one power plant could use. Mike said Nicholas County would probably be the last county to get out of tobacco production altogether, but that might be one way to go.

Betty Gates Poe

Betty Gates Poe lives on a farm with her husband and son. She explained, in a 2009 interview, that she was the farmer and her husband commutes to a factory job. "We are totally opposite . . . you know, where it's normally, he's doing the farmwork and she's doing the factory. . . . There used to be some women that just farmed." She and I went through the Nicholas County schools together in the same class. One of our other classmates raises her own tobacco crop, but as Betty said, not too many women are individual farmers any more. Mostly, their farmwork is absorbed into the household labor and the man gets called the farmer. Betty said that she had seen women get paid less in the fields for doing more work. When she has hired people to help out with her tobacco crop, she said, "I don't care who they are, what color they are or what gender they are, when they step in my field to work, and they work, they get the same pay that anybody else would get, or they don't come into my field."

Betty Gates Poe had gone off and gotten a university degree, like I had, and had lived and worked in Colorado and Georgia, and then moved back to Nicholas County, where she had family. She said:

> You know, people can't understand why you come back, but it is the love of the culture, the love of the people, you know. . . . You can enjoy life more if you are comfortable with what you are doing and where you are. . . . I understand the people here a lot better, you know. If you have had a friend for 20 years, you are a lucky person. . . . They don't tell you in school that if you get to 40 and have 5 true friends, then you have been a very lucky person in your life. Money can't buy that. . . . It depends on what you cherish more. If you cherish more of the money and the high life than you do being able to go next door and sit down with a friend and have a pop, then that's where, you know, the benefits for a bigger town come in. It's harder here, but you have faith that if your neighbor next door dies, your friends next door will come over and help. . . . This is a nosy little town, but that's an advantage, too, you know. . . . That is what makes communities, to me.
>
> We have neighbors out there; some of them don't have the land to grow a garden. Oh, well, you know, I'll pick green beans and let you break them and then we will split them in half; how's that? It is just a little bit of their time and they benefit from it, and the world doesn't do that anymore.

> I put out 300 tomato plants. I know I'm gonna sell part of them at the farmer's market. I know I'm gonna give part of them to my friends to eat. I'm gonna can part of them, because I do have this canning business. I have a customer that comes out of Lexington and buys them, tomato juice and whole tomatoes every year. You know, he wants three or four cases a year. Our family eats them. If my neighbors need some while I'm growing and I just have some on the ground, they get them. There's people out here that need tomatoes to put up. Towards the end of the year, when the farmer's market starts dying down, everybody starts getting tomatoes. . . . I'd rather they come and pick than let them rot on the ground. I'm not looking to make a fortune. What I do is for me, right here.

Betty and another farmer went in 50/50 to plant raspberries. She could sell them at the farmer's market for $4.50 a pint (less than she had seen them sold for in the grocery store). She tried going to a vegetable warehouse that had been established in another county as a place for growers and buyers to do business, like the tobacco warehouses. But the buyer said he couldn't pay over $2 a pint, and that would have been all her profit, right there. The buyers did not even know what her pattypan squash were, she said, even if they were squash buyers, and they would tell her they did not look like squash. At the farmer's market in Nicholas County, she can talk about what they are with the customer directly, and how to cook them, too.

Betty said that people go back into survival mode in Nicholas County in hard times—slaughtering their own meat, canning, and so forth. She said in a big city they might say you should not be killing deer, "but they don't understand that is a part of our survival down here." She went on:

> You know, like I said, everything's gone down to money, money; what are they going to do if the economy completely busts? Nobody's got any money. They're going to have to learn like they did back years ago. They're going to have to know, well that neighbor has milk cows, we can trade them milk, you know, for corn. Of course, that is against the internal revenue laws because it's called horse trading.

Nicholas Countians have had some tax troubles over bartering; I guess when the tax on yard sales did not get off the ground, the enforcement of rules on bartering got stronger.

As we talked about the economy and the future of the county, Betty said:

> I would like to see something in here that would benefit some of those that need jobs besides a Dairy Queen or a Shell [station] at minimum wage. But if you do that, then you're also gonna lose part of that hometown experience.

She said that most of the people she knew with jobs in other towns drove to those jobs and lived in Nicholas County because they did not want to live where they worked.

Betty said her son had plans that would take him out of Nicholas County, but she hoped he would still have some connection to the land:

I would love for my son to be able to live on his farm that he was raised on, not necessarily to make a living off it, but to enjoy it. . . . He can bring [his family] home to the family farm and, you know, they can see nature, they can understand a little bit more about where things in the world come from, and where they've been. That is one of our main problems. We like to look forward in this country, but we don't like to remember what happens behind us. And we have to remember that in order to move forward with a more secure life.

Jim and Kathy Caswell

Jim and Kathy Caswell are farming land his father, also a farmer, bought in the 1950s. They have other relatives helping out, including some of their children and nieces, but they are at the center of the farm, with their own division of labor. "He grows it; I sell it," Kathy says. She has sold produce at the farmer's market in Carlisle for some time, and has recently opened a Kentucky Farm Bureau certified roadside market, on their farm. It is advertised on an Internet site that lists other Kentucky roadside markets.

In the 1980s, there was talk of possibly shifting to tomato production as tobacco seemed more and more like it would be phased out. Tobacco setters, agricultural researchers said, could be used to set tomatoes, saving equipment costs. It did not sound likely, for so many reasons, that our "tobacco town" would become a "tomato town," and it has not, overall, but 25 years later, the Caswells are showing that tomato production, on a large enough scale, can be a viable alternative to tobacco.

In 1987, Jim and Kathy Caswell were honored by the R. J. Reynolds Tobacco Company as being one of 48 farm families in Kentucky demonstrating strong agricultural leadership. At that time, they were raising 45 acres of tobacco and feeding steers over the winter for market. Kathy was a schoolteacher, Jim had come back to Nicholas County to farm after getting science degrees at the University of Kentucky, and they had just had their first child.

Seven years later, a reporter stopped Jim Caswell in his field, as he was hoeing his tobacco, to ask what he thought about the future of tobacco. He said, "I've raised tobacco since I was out of college and before that, I helped my dad. If someone asked me ten years ago, I'd say I'd be a tobacco farmer, not a cattle farmer who does tobacco on the side" (Stone 1994:1). He probably would not have predicted then that in 15 more years, he would be a tomato and cattle farmer.

When I asked Jim in 2009 about the transition from tobacco, he said:

Well from my perspective, that's probably one of the best things that ever happened to me, next to my wife and kids. You grew up in Nicholas County, you thought all you had to do . . . was grow a crop of tobacco and have a few cows and you could get by. That was a very easy way to go, and from my perspective, anyway, it just wasn't very challenging. But it was secure, and we had a big enough farm that as long as we kept doing it, we had plenty of income, no problem. But once that was threatened, it made people start thinking out of the box. I started out 11 years ago. I grew a few peppers, and before I knew it I was growing tomatoes, and before I knew it, I was growing 20-some acres of tomatoes, and it just evolved. The more we got our share of the market for that, it's become a pretty good enterprise. We've only got 15 acres of vegetables, but instead of selling more wholesale, we take it to the end, you know. We have more say in what's going to the market. We still have wholesale, we have retail, and we have farmers' market, but . . . we have more control of it.

They grow, wash, and pack their tomatoes (in boxes with the Kentucky Pride label) and sell to several wholesale companies that distribute them to fresh produce sections of grocery stores. "Everything's fresh market," Jim said. "We don't do anything processed. Everything is what you are going to eat." He said the corn and a lot of the other vegetables were for Kathy to sell at the farmer's market. "We're loving it. It's a lot of fun. It's good. But our big money, still, is our wholesale business. We ship out tractor trailer loads of tomatoes." Jim explained to me how he was able to get ripe tomatoes before anyone else, through careful management of the crop:

> That's from using some technology of plastic triple irrigation. Going out in the middle of the night—that's not technology—and spraying water on top of it to keep the frost from killing it. We have red tomatoes by the end of June. That's the top dollar. Even on your wholesale, we are getting up to $15 a box, which is pretty good, because they've still got to take it and resell it. We were raising 100 acres of tobacco, and that took everything you did. But once you start thinking, well, what can I do besides tobacco, that's when we were able to find other markets.

He and his partner in the tomato business flew to Florida, Texas, and California to study the tomato industry and find markets for their crop in Nicholas County. "We still raise tobacco, too. I didn't raise it for two years," Jim said, "and you kind of miss that income and for your labor, you've gotta have something to keep them busy." He hires H2A workers—the same men come to Nicholas County from Mexico every year, and one year-round worker with a family who lives in a house across the road from the Caswells' house. Jim learned Spanish, and that is the language they use as they work together.

Jim explained what it was like for him to make the shift from tobacco to tomatoes:

> We had to just almost rebuild our infrastructure here on the farm. Growing tobacco is not a challenge, if you grew up around it. Everybody and their brother around down here knows how to grow tobacco. But as far as growing vegetables. . . . It's been a challenge for me.

He then said, "I'm very happy with what I do." He enjoys the challenge of figuring out how best to grow the tomato crop and how to grow new vegetables that Kathy wants to sell at the farm stand, doing a lot of online research. He said:

> We've actually downsized. We've got less land than we used to do, but that was more me trying to slow down a little bit and farm more intensively and more diversified on smaller acreage.

Jim and Kathy sold the farm they had lived on for 18 years to an Amish family. "They built all those new buildings and everything," he said. "It's pretty neat." He buys most of his vegetable-growing supplies from Amish vendors in another part of the state.

Jim grows the tomatoes in rows in open fields, on plastic, with the water and other inputs regulated very closely. Jim uses computers to track all of his livestock, crops, and marketing closely:

> With any kind of farming, you can't control the weather, but with tobacco you didn't have to worry about the market. All you had to do was back up, dump your stuff, and go home. With vegetables, especially if you are selling it yourself, you may do everything just right and if you

Jim Caswell in one of his tomato fields (photo by author)

don't get it sold, you've lost it. You know, it's totally different than raising tobacco. . . . With vegetables, unless you've done your homework, you know, and got your market before you plant your seeds, you're not guaranteed anything. . . . There's nothing like working for yourself, but there's nothing as stressful as working for yourself, either.

When we were talking about globalization, Jim said:

Well, if I didn't have the global situation, I couldn't be selling tobacco right now. Nobody would be selling tobacco right now. I mean, vegetables are more local. That's one thing about what we are doing. I mean, that's the whole movement of why I'm in it.

And that is something the Caswells have in common with the farming family in the next, and final, example.

Three Springs Farm:
David Wagoner and Arwen Donahue

David Wagoner and Arwen Donahue bought their farm, a little over 100 acres, from his cousin; the Wagoner family had had descendants in Nicholas County for two centuries. David grew up in Lexington and earned a degree in landscape architecture at the University of Kentucky. He then lived out of the state until he and Arwen decided to buy the farm in Nicholas County and moved to Kentucky to live there in 1997. They started Three Springs Farm as a community-supported agriculture venture, and their daughter, Phoebe, is a partner on the farm. David has worked part-time as a landscape designer but has moved more and more into full-time farming. Arwen does many things on the farm she co-owns and sells her farm-related art through the Courthouse Square Art Guild and on their website. They have viewed Three Springs Farm as more of a community venture and sustainable ecosystem than a traditional family farm.

In 1999, the *Carlisle Mercury* profiled their plans for Community Supported Agriculture (CSA) on Three Springs Farm with the announcement: "The new wave of gardening has arrived at Nicholas County" (Jordan 1999: 1). David and Arwen were in the process of getting their land certified as an organic farm, and were accepting subscriptions from community members for 32 weekly CSA shares in a season at a cost of $13.30 per week ($425/year, at the beginning of the season). They planned to supply, over the growing season, 40 kinds of vegetables, along with flowers and herbs. Shares were purchased within a several-city region, and Arwen and David prepared to start stocking the 1/2-bushel baskets for delivery.

Three Springs Farm is now the longest-running CSA in central Kentucky. David and Arwen have been active members of the Community Farm Alliance, and David was one of the CFA farmers who lobbied in Frankfort, successfully, for HB 611, the legislation that made Kentucky's use of tobacco settlement funds the most accountable both to diverse local communities and to agricultural diversification. David Wagoner said, in the legislative hearing, "learning from other farmers has been critical for us" in the startup of Community Supported Agriculture (Vice 2000:7).

David Wagoner and Arwen Donahue have worked on community-building not only through delivering baskets of produce, but also through sending a hand-lettered and illustrated newsletter to their CSA subscribers, to let them know what was happening on the farm, and through their website (http://www.threespringsfarmcsa.com). You can learn more about what David and Arwen are doing on Three Springs Farms by visiting that website, which is how some of their apprentices have heard about the farm. They have come from all over the United States to spend a season on Three Springs Farm in Nicholas County learning about organic farming, dairying (working with their herd of Nubian goats), and beekeeping. Now that Phoebe is in school, David and Arwen are getting even more networked locally, starting a community garden at the school that involves Phoebe's class. "I hope it can grow to include all grade levels, including the high school," David said; he envisioned it as "providing outdoor learning, and produce for the school cafeterias. We will need a lot of support from the school and volunteers to make this happen, but we've made a start." Other students at the school definitely know about the project, because David Wagoner's name showed up in several of the essays submitted to the Roy and Louise Essay Contest on the Future of Nicholas County.

This book will end with the essays from that contest, in the postscript. Since it is *their* future, I think young Nicholas Countians should have the last word.

Postscript

Student Essays on the Future of Nicholas County

$\mathcal{H}$ere are the essays by the winners of the Roy and Louise Kingsolver Essay Contest on the Future of Nicholas County, by grade.

Winners of the 2010 Roy and Louise Kingsolver Essay Contest on the Future of Nicholas County. Front row (left to right): Finn Brutsman, Arris Stacy, Ethan Smith, Beth McCord, Ben Duncan. Back row (left to right): Kaitlyn Wells, Ashley Garcia, Katie Myers, Jamie Berry (photo by Amanda Switzer)

Seventh-Grade Students

Jamie Berry
How I See the Future of Nicholas County

Nicholas County is a small county in the state of Kentucky. Within Nicholas County there is a small town called Carlisle. Carlisle offered many jobs in the past. Most of those jobs are not available today, but there are still many jobs in Carlisle. Nicholas County once had a successful Jockey plant that shut down after many years of business. Many people relied on the Jockey plant to support their families. My mom once worked at Jockey, and when it closed, my family was struggling to get more jobs that paid enough to support our family. Many other families were also going through the same situation, and there just weren't enough jobs for everyone. Once Jockey shut down, many people began farming tobacco. Now, two-thirds of the people in the county rely on farming tobacco to support their families.

Today, the population of Nicholas County is about 6,000. With so many people and so few jobs, many people are forced to work out of town. My dad and brother in-law have to pay up to fifty dollars a week on gas just to support my family. Like many other people, my family cannot find any jobs close to home. Nicholas County has good resources that might encourage new business to move here. For example, now that Jockey is out of business, we have an empty building that is being wasted. The building is large, therefore a manufacturing business would have enough space to move in there. Then people like my dad and brother in-law could get jobs closer to home and save money on gas. That would save Nicholas County residents enough money to be able to buy groceries every week. My opinion on this problem is that we should bring new business here, and rely less on tobacco farming.

Although Nicholas County has a great farming industry, most of the farmers grow only tobacco. The residents that farm tobacco earn enough money to support their families, but if they diversify and grow vegetables, they can earn more money and support their families better. Some people in my family grow tobacco and make just enough to pay bills and get a limited supply of food. I have already told you that many people in Nicholas County farm tobacco, but there are other jobs in Nicholas County as well. Some of these include IGA, Dollar General, and Family Dollar. My sister is working at the hospital as of right now, and she is being well paid. However, the hospital does not offer many job openings, so many people cannot get a job there. In the future, I think the stores will expand and more people can find jobs.

I have identified many problems with the economy of Nicholas County. I think the biggest problem with our economy is that the farmers only grow tobacco, and many people spend more money on gas than is necessary, just to get to work. If the farmers diversify and grow more crops, and if we can encourage new businesses to move here, I think the economy of Nicholas County will get better, and be successful.

Ben Duncan
The Future of Nicholas County in My Eyes

Nicholas County and Carlisle have always been dependent on the farming of crops, tobacco in particular. But up until recently they had always had the stockyards and Jockey to help hold up the economy. But now there are no stockyards or Jockey, and we need to find new ways to improve the economy in the future. I think in the future we will still have to farm tobacco, but we should diversify farming and find new businesses to come to Carlisle to support the people that live here.

Part of the reason tobacco farming has been on a slow decline is because there used to be a quota system in Kentucky. Quota means share, so that means that each tobacco farmer in Kentucky that raised tobacco got their share of money for their crop, no matter what. The quota system came into play in the 50s or 60s, but in 2004, they stopped using the quota system. Now tobacco farmers just get so much per pound of tobacco they bring in and tobacco farmers have to have contracts with the distributing companies instead of an open market.

Statistics show that we are going to have to diversify farming. In 2000, there was seven million dollars worth of tobacco sold, and in 2009, there was only three million dollars worth of tobacco sold. This shows that to keep farmers afloat, in my opinion, we will have to diversify farming and grow more vegetables and fruits. We could grow more corn and green beans to sell to local stores. We need to find the right kind of soil for the right kind of fruit.

To get more industries attracted to Carlisle, we have to find things that are attractive to businesses, like Blue Licks or Lake Carnico. I love having all the lakes and parks and farms in this town and county that make it so beautiful. I love the open countryside behind my house, and maybe that will be attractive to businesses and business owners. Another way we could get businesses attracted to Carlisle is if we could raise the population. It is hard to do, but we have attractive stuff like I mentioned earlier, and people might be attracted to a small town.

The only problem with Nicholas County is a drug problem, but other than that, we are mostly peaceful. We can stop this drug problem with the proper law enforcement. Another problem is that we have limited space in town, but we have plenty of space in the county area. We definitely need to get more jobs in what space we have, because we have 6,800 people in Nicholas County, and only 4,500 of those people are adults. Only one-third (1,500) of those people are employed.

People can make a living off farming, but not just farming. My dad farms and works at Lee-Lynn Machining Inc., and my mom works as a teacher and does an after-school program for extra money. They work two jobs just to keep my family afloat and have money left over. You can't make a living off of just farming in an economic downturn. The economic downturn is stopping us from expanding manufacturing and working more hours. Businesses don't have the money to pay their workers or pay other businesses to help them with their jobs, so they have to lay people off and stop reaching out to other businesses for lack of money. But if we could get more jobs, we'd probably have more people or vice-versa. I think in the future we'll have to expand manufacturing and diversify farming.

Beth McCord
How I See the Future of Nicholas County

Nicholas County, Kentucky is a small farming community in northeast Kentucky. The population today is approximately 7,000 people. According to my grandfather, there were many businesses in Carlisle several years ago with a much smaller population. There were several grocery stores, a clothing store, and even a very busy tobacco market and stockyards. With this amount of business, Nicholas County would have had a very busy economy. Money would have been flowing in and out of banks and businesses. Today, there are very few businesses to support the larger population. Many people are losing jobs in our area, so they are moving to bigger cities or out of state to find better paying and secure jobs. Over the years, our farming economy has decreased also. Tobacco sales are down because fewer people are smoking, so the demand is less.

Resources currently available in Nicholas County that might encourage businesses to move here are our historical buildings and productive farmland. Smaller businesses would be more appropriate because of our limited resources in our small community. Because of our limited resources such as utilities, good roads, and educated/skilled workers, we would not be able to support a large business or manufacturer like Toyota. We have many historical buildings which may attract tourists, which would encourage us to start more businesses such as restaurants, gift shops, and museums. In the summer, when the farmers are producing their crops, they are selling them in town at the farmers markets to local residents and out of town visitors.

Did you know that according to the *History of Nicholas County*, Carlisle was one of the leading tobacco markets at one time? Our farmers need to diversify, because tobacco is not in demand as it once was, and there are fewer growers. There are many other crops that we can rely on such as corn, tomatoes, peppers, and potatoes. These crops grow well in our environment and they are some of our main groceries. Many other farms have beef cattle, and we also have a few dairy farms. My family raises beef cattle, some of which we sell in the fall. The calves I help raise are sold for money that goes towards my college fund. In 5 to 10 years, I see less farming in Nicholas County because it does not pay as well as it used to. People will be moving to bigger cities to find better paying jobs.

There are fewer businesses now than there were many years ago, but we still have doctors, banks, farming supply stores, gas stations, furniture stores and gift shops. Some of our businesses will grow and some of them will be gone due to the economy. Gas stations will continue to grow because of the use of fuel in cars to go to work in other counties or cities. If we concentrate on tourism, visitors will be coming into the county to stop at gas stations, restaurants, and retail stores while passing through or visiting our tourist attractions. If our tourist traffic increases, we could build a hotel so people could stay and enjoy our attractions longer.

Our limited resources cause us not to be able to start larger manufacturing businesses. We need to focus on tourism and different farming plans, because these will bring us more money and jobs. We have to work hard in our community to make things happen and be successful. We have to look at our resources and see what we have to offer to make our community a better place.

Eighth-Grade Students

Ashlee Garcia
Nicholas County to Come

"Small town with a big heart"; this is what Nicholas County represents. In this county everyone knows everyone, and we wouldn't want it any other way. Residents in Nicholas County who have been here all their lives try to leave, but they always return to give back to the community that gave them everything. This town gives every resident something to carry throughout their life that they will never forget. This town is full of hardworking people who give to their community rather than take from it. Nicholas County may not be the perfect place to work, but it is a great place to live. Most people would say that this town depends on its agriculture, but that isn't entirely true. This town also depends on the residents that have pride for living in this county.

Nicholas County is mostly known for its growth of tobacco. Although a vast majority of Nicholas County's crops are tobacco, not everything we grow here are cash crops. We also grow some staple crops. Nicholas County's farming history is mainly in tobacco, because back then the residents had to grow it for a living. Now you don't have to necessarily grow tobacco or any other crops to put food on the table; you can if you choose to, and can sell a majority of your crops. In 2000, over seven million dollars were sold in tobacco in Nicholas County. Now in 2009, only about three million dollars were sold in tobacco. Most farmers of tobacco have a second occupation so as to ensure that their family will not end in poverty. The reason that their family might end in poverty is due to the fact that there is no quota system that guarantees that they can sell tobacco here in Nicholas County. Now, don't get me wrong. Most families here are not in poverty if they just farm, but they realize before they decide to just farm that there is a possibility of that happening. The problem with growing tobacco here is that there was a law made that tobacco farmers can only grow a certain amount of tobacco. I do not believe that farming in the county will decrease, due to the fact that it has always been here. To help farming prosper, Nicholas County farmers could always transfer to growing staple crops instead of tobacco. Tobacco farms may then decrease in number, while produce farms then will increase in number, as time passes in Nicholas County. This would help supply Nicholas County with fresh crops and farmers could earn more money.

Business in Nicholas County has changed immensely in the past few years. There are about one hundred businesses in Nicholas County, and about three thousand people employed. The largest employer in Nicholas County is the government. There are a fair amount of family-owned businesses in Nicholas County. They started out their businesses by learning how to manage money, and they also learned that you have to sell your product and not have your product sell itself. They need to keep in mind that you need to do something for yourself, but also help others in the process. You can start a business with a small amount of money, and your business can grow and gain money, if you are business savvy. The largest change in our county was when the Jockey Industry left. This left a lot of Nicholas County residents jobless, which then in turn made them have to go out of the county for work, or move out of the county entirely. I predict that the future of business in Nicholas County will probably stay at a constant, or increase slightly. In my opinion, in order for Nicholas County to increase job availability, a large company would have to come to our county.

The future of our county depends on our residents, and our economy. If our residents do not try to help make the future of our county better, then it won't change. The adults aren't the only ones who can change the future; the young adults and children can even help, because the young adults and children are the future. If they don't make the choice to help within their power, then I doubt that there will be enough change to affect everyone in the county. The economy makes a huge impact on who helps and how much they help, because the economy scares most people. They are afraid that if they spend too much money, then they won't have enough to feed their family or pay their bills. This is understandable, but you don't have to invest a huge amount into your community to help it. You can just give a small amount every once in a while when you have more than enough; small amounts add up. The future of Nicholas County looks bright and full of potential. It will take time, but I believe that it is completely possible for us to reach our personal and community goals.

In conclusion, the future of Nicholas County looks as bright as ever, and full of people who love their community and the people in it. The farming industry in Nicholas County will probably change in the future, but it will not disappear. Business in Nicholas County should change in the future if more people start their businesses, or large companies decide to move to Nicholas County. The only way to change a county for the better is for the people in it to believe and work hard to achieve the goal in mind.

Katie Myers
Where Farming Has Come From and Where It's Going

Nicholas County, Carlisle, Kentucky, is a small farming community with a population of less than 2,000. Our community, you might say, is a large family. We live in a quiet community where everyone knows and cares about each other. With farming being 99.9% of our income, we all have the same interest. Most families are fortunate to have 2 to 3 generations that work each day together side by side.

Burley tobacco, corn, hay, wheat, and vegetables are the most common crops for this area. The majority of farm families depend on the tobacco income in order to support their family. The corn and hay crops are harvested to feed livestock; vegetable gardens are grown for food and resale; and beef cattle are raised for resale, and to slaughter in order to provide food.

Farming provides a natural way to live off the earth. We are able to raise our own food, live among our extended families, and enjoy the life of the country, but farming does not provide any healthcare benefits. This presents a disadvantage for most families.

With the government enforcing tobacco use restrictions, it is harder to sell the crops for a profit. With little to no jobs available in our community, young adults are going to college and working in larger cities. With the expense of farm equipment, difficulty in finding seasonal workers for harvesting, long hours, hard work, and a fading market, farming is becoming a life of the past.

I am a daughter of a third-generation farmer. I am proud of my heritage and of my family. My dad works long hours to provide for us. The land we purchased and on which we built our home belonged to my dad's grandfather, who handed down farming to his son, my grandfather. The Myers' have farmed and lived on Cassidy Creek Road, Nicholas County, Carlisle, Kentucky, since the early 1900s. Farming has been the way of life as far back as my dad remembers. My dad has come to realize that my sister and I will not farm the land. We will attend college and find a career other than farming.

There is little to no future for small town community farmers. We are at the government's mercy in their stand for tobacco and we are hoping for support in another cash crop. Farming has been the way of life for Nicholas Countians for many years. It saddens me, my family, and community to see farming come to an end.

Kaitlyn Wells
The Future of Nicholas County

Nicholas County, since its early history, has relied mainly on agricultural activities by raising livestock such as beef, swine, and poultry, and growing crops such as hay, corn, and burley tobacco. Although the other agricultural activities have made a huge impact on the local economy, nothing has produced an income or way of living for the county's residents like tobacco. Raising tobacco crops has supplied a way and means of providing jobs, and a financial security for its residents and landowners. Farmers and tenant farmers understood that growing tobacco was in demand, not only locally, but worldwide. This also allowed them a way to get the most out of their land. Growing tobacco on their farms allowed farmers to generate a greater income which, in turn, provided a better way of life for their families than any other legally grown crop or agricultural activity.

In past generations, there has been a large number of family farms in Nicholas County that were experienced in raising tobacco and selling it as a way to pay the bills. Occupations with educational opportunities, as we have today, were not available in the earlier years. Over time, this has changed, due primarily to the increased costs to produce tobacco. The cost of land, equipment, fuel and labor has continued to increase while the sale price has decreased and has not kept up with the expense to produce the crop. The price has actually dropped since the government no longer offers a support system. There are other factors that have played a part, such as demand has decreased and there have been studies that have found that tobacco causes health problems to those who use it. Since this has happened, the numbers of tobacco growers have continued to decline. Due to these reasons, farming, and growing tobacco as a cash crop, has become more of a hobby than a source of income. This is the main reason why you see larger farms with hundreds of acres more than you see small family farms. This is due to the amount that is needed to spend to operate a larger farm such as equipment, labor, etc.

When education became more available, many Nicholas County farmers were able to train in other jobs to make a living without relying on growing tobacco. Many Nicholas County farmers now find themselves and their families working in other areas of employment including sales, factories and customer service jobs.

Many of the families now work out of the county, due to a shortage in employment. Nicholas County does not have enough service jobs or factories. If Nicholas County provided more of these jobs, it would bring in a growth of income for the county and a growth of population. Nicholas County is located in the center of many large cities, including Paris, Lexington, Winchester, Mt. Sterling, and Maysville, all within a small driving distance. Many people from Nicholas County travel to these different cities to find jobs, due to short driving distances.

Nicholas County alone, in past years, has relied on the income of tobacco. Many of the areas around us are moving to the advance of technology to bring jobs and income into the county. If we also do the same, this will help expand the growth and production which our county needs to help us expand and grow into a thriving community.

Ninth-Grade Students

Finn Brutsman
Using the Facts of the Past

Although I have only lived in Nicholas County for three years, I proudly call Nicholas County my hometown. When I first moved here, I quickly discovered that Nicholas County was made up of a tiny, hardworking, and caring community, but I also realized that it had a very small population and workforce. I think that in order to predict the future of our county, we must first look to our past. All of the records and human references show that Nicholas County was once a booming county. However, over the years, it has become a non-progressive town due to factors such as: loss of population, lack of jobs, and the need for local business which can boost the economy of our county. All of these things have caused our development to slowly come to a halt, and we need to do something drastic in order for our future to be more successful.

During the late 1800s, Nicholas County was a very prominent county; it was a great place to live, with movie theaters, factories, and hotels among the numerous businesses that created the many recreational and occupational opportunities. The train depot located in the heart of Nicholas County which provided the transportation and brought many people passing through the county, contributed to the economic success of Nicholas County. Nicholas County supported an even better agricultural area, consisting of tobacco, vegetables, livestock, and other crops that were sought after during those times.

Nicholas County's success was short-lived, though; all of these accomplishments started to expire, as every county experiences, during the early 1900s. On account of NAFTA, Jockey was shipped overseas due to the inexpensive costs of production in foreign countries compared to the costs of producing products in the United States. Things really began to take a turn for the worst when Cincinnati and northern Kentucky began to grow with factories and corporations. The hotels, theaters, and even railroads gradually fell apart in Nicholas County, so they decided to move to Cincinnati and northern Kentucky where there was a need for employees and the jobs paid better rates.

Although all of that has happened, and factories have become a major part of employment, agriculture has always been a major part of Nicholas County's culture. When the families no longer had employment, and needed a source of income, they often looked to farming as that source. Therefore, tobacco played a key role in Nicholas County, and it was an easy crop for everyone to grow. There was also a demanding market for tobacco, seeing that nearly everybody smoked, and it was sold everywhere. The only problem with farming for most people, however, is that it doesn't allow families to obtain a large enough income to support their family, so they need an additional job to fill that need, which was very hard to find back then. Even in today's economy, it's hard to just own a farm and get by; the costs are becoming more and more expensive, and the demand for farming products is constantly falling.

So after examining the past, my belief about Nicholas County's future is that it will remain stable unless factories or something else people have a demand for comes to Nicholas County and produces more jobs for the area, but I don't think that the residents will move, either. That's another thing that makes Nicholas County great: the community. The people are always there for one another, and they would help each other out under any circumstances. I also share the opinion with many longtime citizens that there will always be farming in Nicholas County. It has become something that holds together the residents, and it's more of a lifestyle than a job for the majority of Nicholas County's populace, but it doesn't allow for our county to be able to progress as well as it could. Nevertheless, people will always "follow the money." That's true for wherever you go. Consequently, that is why I think that Nicholas County will only have a stable future ahead of itself.

Ethan Smith
Farming in Nicholas County

My name is Ethan Smith and I am 15 years old. I have lived in Nicholas County, on a farm, all my life. My grandfather has been a farmer all his life, and his father as well. My papaw has made his living raising tobacco ever since he started working as a young boy. I was raised to help out, as much as I could, with the raising of the tobacco. I have helped him prepare and plant seeds to grow the tobacco plants, set the tobacco, top and spray it, cut and harvest the tobacco, and, finally, strip it. My papaw will tell me how things have changed over the years, and I have seen the different things that have changed in my life so far. There are a lot of farmers that can't make a living raising this crop any more. Help setting and harvesting the crop is very difficult to find. Many farmers hire Mexicans to assist them in raising tobacco. It is not as easy to sell your crop now as it was 10 years ago, either. My papaw has sold his tobacco through a contractor for the past several years. However, their rules change year to year, and it has become much more difficult to satisfy them.

I believe that within the next few years, raising tobacco will be a thing of the past for most farmers, including my papaw. It is difficult to make a profit raising tobacco and much harder to sell. Many tobacco warehouses have closed, and farmers are not getting contracts with the tobacco companies. The companies that are still open are thinking about making farmers change the way they sell the tobacco they raise. Most farmers in the past have had what is known as "little bales" of tobacco that weigh 80 to 100 lbs.; tobacco warehouses are now deciding whether to move to big bales of tobacco, which can't be moved by hand. The big bales range from 300 to 400 lbs., so most little farmers would have to buy and build new stripping rooms, and buy a tractor or bobcat, just to raise something that they have raised their whole life. I believe it will be very difficult for many farmers that quit raising tobacco, because that is all they have known. It has been their life for many years. Most of the farmers are older, and it may be hard for them to find a job to support their family. This will cause problems for the families as well as the community.

If raising tobacco becomes extinct in Nicholas County, the whole county will suffer. There will be numerous people without jobs and an income. This causes many hardships for the families. I believe it will affect the businesses in the county as well. People may not be able to buy groceries, clothes, etc., in the county like they have in previous years. They may have to go out of the county to buy at larger stores for cheaper prices, or they will start raising gardens again like in the past. This affects everyone. I would like to believe that another crop will be able to be raised in Nicholas County that will enable farmers to continue working and keep up with their current lifestyle; however, I am not sure. I don't know what the crop would be: maybe soybeans, tomatoes, blackberries, anything. I don't think Nicholas County will become a ghost town, but everyone that lives here will be greatly affected.

Arris Stacy
Working Together to Preserve Nicholas County

How will Nicholas County continue to grow without relying so heavily on the farmer? Most believe without farming, Nicholas County will eventually be absorbed by a neighboring county or become just another statistic of the "little county that couldn't." However, I believe that with the proper education of our youth, continued education of our adults, and community involvement, Nicholas County will prosper through the years.

For many years, Nicholas County was the booming small town life. We really had the best of both worlds. We had industry, Jockey International, Inc., and we had the tobacco and cattle farmer. Residents were employed and local governments prospered, as well as retail businesses from the revenue produced. Small town life in Nicholas County wasn't that bad. Education was not the most important item on the minds of teenagers and adults. They didn't hesitate to drop out of school early to secure a job on the family farm, local clothing/grocery store, or factory to increase the family income. Fast forward 30 years, the factory is gone as well as most of the retail businesses, and farming is at its lowest.

Living in a small town has its pro's and con's. The pro's are actually knowing the name of your bank teller, gas station attendant, or the person you pass by on the street. The con's are minimal jobs to choose from and low pay scales, thus forcing the resident to seek employment outside of the county. Most employers in Nicholas County only require a high school diploma, but those jobs are few in number. However, to secure a job in another area may require technical school or a college degree. Low pay scale jobs such as a fast food establishment or grocery store in another area will require only a high school diploma, but the individual must take into respect travel expenses, thus the low paying job may not be economical for them. Will this individual continue his/her education to obtain the higher paying job to support the family, or will he/she decide it's easier to stay in the small town, hope for a job of their skill level to open, and choose to live free on government money, a path which so many find to be easier? This is where education begins.

Education of our youth is of the utmost importance. It's not just teaching them to read, write, and solve math problems. It is teaching them responsibility, resourcefulness, and respect. The three "R's" are very important, as has been proven for hundreds of years. But responsibility to take action for their lives is extremely important. They have a responsibility to obtain and absorb the much-needed information that they will receive in school to obtain a job in their chosen career. Teaching resourcefulness to use every opportunity they have to grow as a person. Teaching youth to be resourceful to know that if one particular action doesn't bring forth the wanted result or correct answer, they know where to go or what to do to resolve the problem. Respect for self and others is taught in schools, but much more emphasis should be devoted to this area. Education should place first in our community.

Most adults do not understand the importance of continuing education, even those with minimal reading, writing, and math skills. As parents, they want more for their children than they have achieved themselves. However, with little to no industry and the farming career at its lowest in Nicholas County, now is the time to increase their knowledge. Whether it be the tobacco farmers who can no longer rely on top dollar per pound for their tobacco or the individual who is mainly skilled at working in a factory. The farmer must be open to expanding the crop from mostly tobacco to growing vegetables. With the proper information, the farmer may be able to sell his vegetable crop not only to the local farmers market, but the larger stores. This will increase, or at least continue, the family income, in turn bringing money back into the community. Those who are skilled mostly in factory work should look into taking a computer or writing class to increase their knowledge to assist in finding a job outside of the factory. With industry finding its way overseas more and more, now is the time to add to their skill.

Community involvement is a must in order for Nicholas County to prosper. Government officials need to urge the community to unite as one. This could be done by asking local school teachers to assist the local GED agency to assist adults with reading, writing, and math skills, implement computer classes to teach the basics and expand the knowledge of computers and different software, and ensuring that Internet is available to all areas of the county. Computers and the Internet have endless opportunities and possibilities for everyone, if they know how to use them. This is why community involvement is so very important to assist Nicholas County to continue to grow throughout the years.

Farming will always be a part of Nicholas County, but without continued education and community involvement, it will decrease even more. It is the responsibility of all members of this community to work together to ensure that we continue to prosper or possibly suffer a drastic fate.

References Cited

Aamodt, Agnes M. 1981. "Neighboring: Discovering Support Systems among Norwegian-American Women." In *Anthropologists at Home in North America: Methods and Issues in the Study of One's Own Society,* edited by Donald A. Messerschmidt, 133–149. Cambridge: Cambridge University Press.

Adams, Jane. 1994. *The Transformation of Rural Life: Southern Illinois, 1890–1990.* Chapel Hill: The University of North Carolina Press.

Anglin, Mary K. 2002. *Women, Power, and Dissent in the Hills of Carolina.* Chicago: University of Illinois Press.

Associated Press. 2001. "Farmers over 65 Form Largest Group." *Lexington Herald-Leader,* December 22, C3.

Axton, W. F. 1975. *Tobacco and Kentucky.* Lexington: The University Press of Kentucky.

Badger, Anthony J. 1980. *Prosperity Road: The New Deal, Tobacco, and North Carolina.* Chapel Hill: The University of North Carolina Press.

Baesler, Scotty. 1994. "Straight Talk." Washington, DC. Letter mailed to constituents.

Batcheldor, Matt. 2000. "Tiendas y Restaurantes Reviven Área Comercial en Lexington." *Lexington Herald-Leader-Business,* August 21, 13.

Batteau, Allen W. 1990. *The Invention of Appalachia.* Tucson: The University of Arizona Press.

———, ed. 1983. *Appalachia and America: Autonomy and Regional Dependence.* Lexington: The University Press of Kentucky.

Benson, Peter. 2008a. "El Campo: Faciality and Structural Violence in Farm Labor Camps." *Cultural Anthropology* 23 (4): 589–629.

———. 2008b. "Good Clean Tobacco: Philip Morris, Biocapitalism, and the Social Course of Stigma in North Carolina." *American Ethnologist* 35 (3): 357–379.

Berry, Wendell, and John Berry. 1998. "Rural Areas Must Survive, Even if Tobacco Doesn't." *Lexington Herald-Leader,* May 27, A17.

Billings, Dwight B., Gurney Norman, and Katherine Ledford. 1999. *Back Talk from Appalachia: Confronting Stereotypes.* Lexington: The University Press of Kentucky.

Blessing, Stephanie All. 2007. "'Appalachian Ingenuity' in Action: Activists Reach Beyond Traditional Economic Development in Kentucky." MA thesis in Geography. Lexington: University of Kentucky.

Bond, Hank. 1988. "Priority: Reviving the Farm Economy." *Carlisle Mercury,* July 14, 1.

———. 1987. "Fiscal Court Passes County Tax Ordinance." *Carlisle Mercury,* April 9, 1, 3.

173

Bortz, Margaret. 1993. "Robertson Farmer Turns from Growing Tobacco to Raising Exotic Birds." *Lexington Herald-Leader,* April 13, B2.

Braden, Maria. 1990. "Toyota." *Kentucky Living,* February, 18–20, 32.

———. 1986. "Kentucky's Far East Connection." *Rural Kentuckian* 40 (7): 6–9, 21–22.

Brim, Risa. 2001. Publisher Plans Monthly Issue of *La Voz. Lexington Herald-Leader,* May 19, B1, B8.

Brown, James S. 1988. *Beech Creek: A Study of a Kentucky Mountain Neighborhood.* Berea, KY: Berea College Press.

Brown, Wendy. 2006. *Regulating Aversion: Tolerance in the Age of Identity and Empire.* Princeton: Princeton University Press.

Buck, Pem Davidson. 2001. *Worked to the Bone: Race, Class, Power, and Privilege in Kentucky.* New York: Monthly Review Press.

"Burley Imports: Kentucky Farmers Find They Like These Tobacco Laborers from Afar." 1989. October. *Kentucky Farm Bureau News* 53 (1): 1.

Campbell, Tracy. 1992. "The Limits of Agrarian Action: The 1908 Kentucky Tobacco Strike." *Agricultural History* 66: 76–97.

Capehart, Thomas C., Jr. 2003. "U.S. Tobacco Industry Responding to New Competitors, New Challenges." *Amber Waves* (a publication of the United States Department of Agriculture Economic Research Service) 1 (4): 14–21.

Carlisle Mercury. 2004. "Jockey International Closing Three Facilities in Kentucky: 137 Will Lose Jobs in Carlisle," March 5, 1, 10.

———. 1992. "Marshall Named to Central Kentucky Development Roundtable," October 15, 3.

———. 1988. "Kentucky Nursing Homes: A Growing Industry in Need of Attention," February 25, 1, 6.

———. 1986. "Mum's the Word as Heads of State Meet with Jockey," October 16, 1.

Carter, Jimmy. 1998. "Big Tobacco Isn't Helping Farmers: Meddling Hurts Efforts to Secure Better Future." *Lexington Herald-Leader,* November 30, A9.

Chriss, Catherine. 1988. "Kentuckians Don't Want Imported Trash." *Lexington Herald-Leader,* January 31, A1, 12.

Clark, Thomas D. 1977. *Agrarian Kentucky.* Lexington: The University Press of Kentucky.

Collins, Glenn. 1995. "Generation Gap Cited in Farmer Views on Tobacco." *Lexington Herald-Leader,* November 1, A1, A11.

Collins, Jane. 2003. *Threads: Gender, Labor, and Power in the Global Apparel Industry.* Chicago: The University of Chicago Press.

Collins, Patricia Hill. 2000. *Black Feminist Thought: Knowledge, Consciousness, and the Politics of Empowerment,* 2nd ed. New York: Routledge.

Collins, Samuel Gerald. 2008. *All Tomorrow's Cultures: Anthropological Engagements with the Future.* New York: Berghahn Books.

Copley, Rich. 1999. "Out, Standing: In Their Fields, State's Barns Endure to Mark Life, Times." *Lexington Herald-Leader,* October 3, K1, K3.

Dirlik, Arif. 1996. "The Global and the Local." In *Global/Local: Cultural Production and the Transnational Imaginary,* edited by Rob Wilson and Wimal Dissanayake, 21–45. Durham, NC: Duke University Press.

Donaldson, Susanna. 2009. "From Neighbors to Migrants: The Shifting Organization of Agricultural Labor in East Tennessee." Paper presented at the annual meeting of the Society for Applied Anthropology, Santa Fe, NM, March 21.

Douglas, Mary. 1966. *Purity and Danger: An Analysis of Concepts of Pollution and Taboo.* London: Routledge and Kegan Paul.

Duncan, Cynthia L., and William A. Duncan. 1985. "Guest Editorial: Water and Economic Development in Rural Kentucky." *Water Watch* 2 (2): 3, 23. Frankfort: Kentucky Division of Water.

Duncan, Janie R. 1987a. "Vice Dairy Operation a Family Affair." *Carlisle Mercury,* June 25, 1–2.

———. 1987b. "Hensley Fighting to Help Farmers with Farm Aid." *Carlisle Mercury,* August 20, 3.

———. 1987c. Garrett Works from Inside—Out." *Carlisle Mercury,* July 23, 4.

Edmonson, Jacqueline. 2003. *Prairie Town: Redefining Rural Life in the Age of Globalization.* Lanham, MD: Rowman & Littlefield.

Eller, Ronald D. 2008. *Uneven Ground: Appalachia since 1945.* Lexington: The University Press of Kentucky.

Ellis, William E. 1995. "Small Towns in Transition: The Small Town in Kentucky Oral History Project." *Small Town* (March–April), 22–27.

Estep, Bill. 2010. "Doctor Charged with Trafficking: South Florida Practice Allegedly at Heart of Eastern Kentucky Pain Pill Epidemic." *Lexington Herald-Leader,* May 27, A3.

Estep, Bill, and Linda J. Johnson. 1999. Tobacco Quotas Are Dilemma for Schools. *Lexington Herald-Leader,* June 6, A1, A8.

Feldman, Eric, and Ronald Bayer. 2004. *Unfiltered: Conflicts over Tobacco Policy and Public Health.* Cambridge, MA: Harvard University Press.

Fitchen, Janet M. 1981. *Poverty in Rural America: A Case Study.* Long Grove, IL: Waveland Press.

Flora, Cornelia Butler, and Jan L. Flora. 2008. *Rural Communities: Legacy and Change,* 3rd ed. Boulder, CO: Westview Press.

Foley, Douglas E. 1990. *Learning Capitalist Culture: Deep in the Heart of Tejas.* Philadelphia: University of Pennsylvania Press.

Forstall, Richard, compiler and ed. 1995. Kentucky. Population of Counties by Decennial Census: 1900 to 1990. Washington, D.C.: U.S. Bureau of the Census, Population Division. Accessed September 11, 2009. http://www.census.gov/population/cencounts/ky190090.txt.

Foster, Stephen William. 1988. *The Past Is Another Country: Representation, Historical Consciousness, and Resistance in the Blue Ridge.* Berkeley: University of California Press.

Foucault, Michel. 1979. *Discipline and Punish: The Birth of the Prison.* Translated by Alan Sheridan. New York: Vintage Books.

Frank, Dana. 1999. *Buy American: The Untold Story of Economic Nationalism.* Boston: Beacon Press.

Friedman, Milton. 1962. *Capitalism and Freedom.* Chicago: University of Chicago Press.

Futamara, Taro. 2007. "Toward the Construction of 'Kentucky Food' in the Twenty-first Century: Food Localism and Commodification of Place Identity under Post-Tobacco Agricultural Restructuring, 1990–2006." PhD dissertation in Geography, University of Kentucky, Lexington.

Galbraith, Gatewood. 2004. *The Last Free Man in America Meets the Synthetic Subversion: The Autobiography of Gatewood Galbraith.* Lexington, KY: Gatewood Galbraith and Mark Perkins Press.

Gannon, Renee. 1996. "Editor's Memo: Resolutions for 1996." *The Burley Tobacco Farmer,* January 15.

Gaventa, John. 1980. *Power and Powerlessness: Quiescence and Rebellion in an Appalachian Valley.* Urbana: University of Illinois Press.

Geertz, Clifford. 1973. "Thick Description: Toward an Interpretive Theory of Culture." In *The Interpretation of Cultures: Selected Essays*, 3–30. New York: Basic Books.

Gibson-Graham, J. K. 1996. *The End of Capitalism (As We Knew It): A Feminist Critique of Political Economy*. Cambridge, MA: Blackwell.

Goodman, Jordan. 1993. *Tobacco in History: The Cultures of Dependence*. London: Routledge.

Goonatilake, Susantha. 1995. "The Self Wandering between Cultural Localization and Globalization." In *The Decolonization of Imagination: Culture, Knowledge, and Power*, edited by Jan Nederveen Pieterse and Bhikhu Parekh, 225–239. London: Zed Books.

Gray, Mary L. 2009. *Out in the Country: Youth, Media, and Queer Visibility in Rural America*. New York: New York University Press.

Greene, Randy. 1992. "Global Factors May Constrain Burley Prices." 1992 Burley Sales. Special supplement to *Carlisle Mercury*.

Greenhouse, Carol. 1986. "History, Faith, and Avoidance." In *Symbolizing America*, Edited by Hervé Varenne, 142–158. Lincoln: University of Nebraska Press.

Griffith, David. 2009. "The Moral Economy of Tobacco." *American Anthropologist* 111 (4), 432–442.

Halfacree, Keith. 2003. "Landscapes of Rurality: Rural Others/Other Rurals." In *Studying Cultural Landscapes*, edited by Iain Robertson and Penny Richards, 141–164. London: Hodder Arnold.

Hall, Joan. 1988. "Jockey Schedules Union Vote." *Central Kentucky Times*, February 11, 1, 6.

Halperin, Rhoda H. 1991. *The Livelihood of Kin: Making Ends Meet "the Kentucky Way."* Austin University of Texas Press.

Hartigan, John, Jr. 1999. "Establishing the Fact of Whiteness." In *Race, Identity, and Citizenship: A Reader*, edited by Rodolfo D. Torres, Louis F. Mirón, and Jonathan Xavier Inda, 183–199. Malden, MA: Blackwell.

Harvey, David. 1990. *The Condition of Postmodernity: An Enquiry into the Origins of Cultural Change*. Cambridge, MA: Blackwell.

Hensley, Lida Ruth. 1992. "River View Farm Approved as Historic Farm." *Carlisle Mercury*, August 20, 3.

Honeycutt, Valarie. 1998. "Advocate: Hispanics Work, Live Like Slaves." *Lexington Herald-Leader*, June 17, A1, A7.

Jordan, Kari. 1999. "Carlisle Couple to Produce from Three Springs Farm." *Carlisle Mercury*, April 1, 1.

Kauffman, Elisabeth. 2010. "In Murfreesboro, Tenn.: Church 'Yes,' Mosque 'No.'" *Time*, August 19. Accessed August 20, 2010. http://www.time.com/nation/article /0,8599,2011847,00.htm.

Kearney, Michael. 1995. "The Local and the Global: The Anthropology of Globalization and Transnationalism." *Annual Review of Anthropology* 24: 547–565.

Kemmis, Daniel. 1990. *Community and the Politics of Place*. Norman: University of Oklahoma Press.

Kentucky Christian. 1994. "KAM and LTS Sponsor 2nd Tobacco Church Workshop," December 1, 5.

Kingsolver, Ann. 2010. "Talk of 'Broken Borders' and Stone Walls: Anti-immigrant Discourse and Legislation from California to South Carolina." *Southern Anthropologist* 35 (1): 21–40.

———. 2007. "Farmers and Farmworkers: Two Centuries of Strategic Alterity in Kentucky's Tobacco Fields." *Critique of Anthropology* 27 (1): 87–102.

————. 2001. *NAFTA Stories: Fears and Hopes in Mexico and the United States.* Boulder, CO: Lynne Rienner Publishers.

————. 1992a. "Contested Livelihoods: 'Placing' One Another in 'Cedar,' Kentucky." *Anthropological Quarterly* 65 (3): 128–136.

————. 1992b. "Development Districts: Buying and Selling Rurality in Kentucky." Paper presented at the World Rural Sociology Congress, Pennsylvania State University, August.

————. 1991. "Tobacco, Toyota, and Subaltern Development Discourses: Constructing Livelihoods and Community in Rural Kentucky." PhD dissertation in Anthropology, University of Massachusetts, Amherst.

Kingsolver, Barbara, with Steven Hopp and Camille Kingsolver. 2008. *Animal, Vegetable, Miracle: A Year of Food Life.* New York: HarperCollins.

Kitchell, Anne, Erin Hannan, and Willett Kempton. 2000. "Identity through Stories: Story Structure and Function in Two Environmental Groups." *Human Organization* 59 (1): 96–105.

Kroll, Harry Harrison. 1965. *Riders in the Night.* Philadelphia: University of Pennsylvania Press.

Lane, Rob. 1976. "Education and Schools." In *History of Nicholas County,* edited by Joan Weissinger Conley, 299–308. Carlisle, KY: Nicholas County Historical Society.

Levitas, Ruth. 1993. "The Future of Thinking about the Future." In *Mapping the Futures: Local Cultures, Global Change,* edited by Jon Bird, Barry Curtis, Tim Putnam, George Robertson, and Lisa Tickner, 257–266. London: Routledge.

Lynd, Robert S., and Helen Merrell Lynd. 1965. *Middletown in Transition.* New York: Harcourt, Brace, & World.

Masterson, James. 1986. "Toyota and Automation: Are They Friends or Foes?" *Carlisle Mercury,* May 1, 15.

Mathes, Heather. 1988a. "Nicholas Native Mattox, a Toyota Employee." *Carlisle Mercury,* June 9, 13.

————. 1988b. "Changing Crops May Offer a Fruitful Future." *Carlisle Mercury,* June 9, 13.

————. 1987. "Carlisle's Main Street Is Loaded with History." *Carlisle Mercury,* November 26.

Mathias, Frank F. 2000. *The GI Generation: A Memoir.* Lexington: The University Press of Kentucky.

Mattox, Charles. 2007. "CORE Group Meets." *Carlisle Mercury,* August 8, 1, 10.

May, Timi P. 1988. "Lt. Governor Gives Revitalization Plans for State's Economy." *Central Kentucky Times,* August 11, 9.

Maynes, Mary Jo, Jennifer L. Pierce, and Barbara Laslett. 2008. *Telling Stories: The Use of Personal Narratives in the Social Sciences and History.* Ithaca: Cornell University Press.

Meehan, Mary. 1999. "326 Jockey Employees to Lose Jobs Dec. 30." *Lexington Herald-Leader,* November 3.

Miller, Daniel. 1997. *Capitalism: An Ethnographic Approach.* New York: Berg.

Miller, Penny M. 1994. *Kentucky Politics and Government: Do We Stand United?* Lincoln: University of Nebraska Press.

Mintz, Sidney. 1985. *Sweetness and Power: The Place of Sugar in Modern History.* New York: Penguin Books.

Moffet, Barbara S. 1985. "Life on the Farm after the Year 2000." *Carlisle Mercury,* January 10, 9.

Mullins, Rebecca. 1993. "Economic Reform Reaches Nicholas County in Planned Town Meetings." *Carlisle Mercury*, February 18, 1, 3.

Murdoch, Jonathan, and Andy C. Pratt. 1997. "From the Power of Topography to the Topography of Power: A Discourse on Strange Ruralities." In *Contested Countryside Cultures: Otherness, Marginalisation and Rurality*, edited by Paul Cloke and Jo Little, 51–69. London: Routledge.

Nadel-Klein, Jane. 1991. "Reweaving the Fringe: Localism, Tradition, and Representation in British Ethnography." *American Ethnologist* 18 (3): 500–517.

Naipaul, V. S. 1989. *A Turn in the South.* New York: Alfred A. Knopf.

Narayan, Kirin. 1993. "How Native Is a 'Native' Anthropologist?" *American Anthropologist* 95 (3): 671–686.

Nesbitt, Roger. 1987. "Textile Plant Moves from Underwear to Down Under Wear." *Lexington Herald-Leader,* August 30.

"Next Year's Leaf Crop Could Be a Whopper Despite Tiny Quota Hike." 1990. *Kentucky Farm Bureau News* 54 (3): 1.

Nicholas Countian. 1999. "Legislators Come to Talk and to Listen to Nicholas Countians about Tobacco," February 19, 1, 10.

Nietschmann, Bernard. 1974. "When the Turtle Collapses, the World Ends." *Natural History* 83 (6): 34–43.

Norberg-Hodge, Helena, Todd Merrifield, and Steven Gorelick. 2002. *Bringing the Food Economy Home: Local Alternatives to Global Agribusiness.* West Hartford, CT: Kumarian Press.

O'Bannon, Lottie. 1976. "Henryville." In *History of Nicholas County*, edited by Joan Weissinger Conley (Section 3: Sections and Post Offices), 79–82. Carlisle, KY: Nicholas County Historical Society, Inc.

O'Boyle, Thomas F. 1991. "New Neighbor: To Georgetown, Kentucky, Toyota Plant Seems a Blessing and a Curse." *Wall Street Journal,* November 26, A1, A5.

Ogawa, Jillian. 2007. "Farms Forward: Planners Look to Save Agricultural Heritage from Developers." *Lexington Herald-Leader,* October 29, A1, A12.

Olivera, Oscar, with Tom Lewis. 2008. *¡Cochabamba!: Water War in Bolivia.* Boston: South End Press.

Omi, Michael, and Howard Winant. 1994. *Racial Formation in the United States: From the 1960s to the 1990s.* New York: Routledge.

Ortner, Sherry. 1973. "On Key Symbols." *American Anthropologist* 75 (5): 1338–1346.

Patton, Janet. 2000. "Philip Morris to Try Buying Tobacco Directly." *Lexington Herald-Leader,* February 2, A1.

Peacock, James L. 2007. *Grounded Globalism: How the U.S. South Embraces the World.* Athens: The University of Georgia Press.

Peebles, Alistair, and Laura Watts. 2009. *Orkney Futures: A Handbook.* Stromness, Scotland: Brae Editions.

Perin, Constance. 1988. *Belonging in America: Reading between the Lines.* Madison: The University of Wisconsin Press.

Poole, Annette. 1988. "Shortage of Farm Labor Is Critical for Tobacco Growers." *Central Kentucky Times,* September 15, 1.

Poplin, Dennis. 1979. *Communities: A Survey of Theories and Methods of Research.* New York: Macmillan.

Prather, Paul. 1989. "Toyota and Georgetown: The Boom that Wasn't." *Lexington Herald-Leader,* December 31, A1, A12.

Rawick, George P. 1977. *The American Slave: A Composite Autobiography.* Supplement, series 1. Westport, CT: Greenwood.

Rawlings, William. 2009. "Destruction by Tobacco." *Carlisle Mercury,* School section, February 11, 6.

Resnick, Stephen A., and Richard D. Wolff. 1987. *Knowledge and Class: A Marxian Critique of Political Economy.* Chicago: The University of Chicago Press.

Rios, Brenda. 1992. "A Growing Role for Migrant Workers: Kentucky Farmers Look South for Help with Crops." *Lexington Herald-Leader,* October 4, A1, A14.

Robbins, Richard H. 2008. *Global Problems and the Culture of Capitalism,* 4th ed. Boston, MA: Allyn & Bacon.

Roberts, Sam. 1995. "The Mythical Appeal of Small Towns." *Lexington Herald-Leader,* September 3, E2.

Roser, Mary Ann. 1987. "400,000 Kentuckians Lost in a Sea of Words." *Lexington Herald-Leader,* September 20, A11.

Rothstein, Frances Abrahamer. 2007. *Globalization in Rural Mexico: Three Decades of Change.* Austin University of Texas Press.

Sacks, Karen Brodkin. 1988. "Gender and Grassroots Leadership." In *Women and the Politics of Empowerment,* edited by Ann Bookman and Sandra Morgen, 77–96. Philadelphia: Temple University Press.

Salamon, Sonya. 2003. *Newcomers to Old Towns: Suburbanization of the Heartland.* Chicago: The University of Chicago Press.

Schacter, Harry W. 1949. *Kentucky on the March.* New York: Harper.

———. 1947. "Report on Manufacturing." *Reports of Committee for Kentucky (President).* Lexington, KY: Agricultural Experiment Station, University of Kentucky.

Schipper, Lori L. 2001. "Show Me the Money: What's Happening with Phase I and II Funds?" *The Burley Tobacco Farmer,* May 15, 10–11.

Schirmer, Peter, and Melissa A. Taylor. 1995. *Farms, Factories and Free Trade: Rural Kentucky in the Global Economy.* Frankfort: The Kentucky Long-Term Policy Research Center.

Scott, Shaunna L. 1995. *Two Sides to Everything: The Cultural Construction of Class Consciousness in Harlan County, Kentucky.* Albany: State University of New York Press.

Sen, Amartya. 1992. *Inequality Reexamined.* Cambridge, MA: Harvard University Press.

Shannon, Jasper B. 1976. "Nicholas County in General." In *History of Nicholas County,* edited by Joan Weissinger Conley, 23–45. Carlisle, KY: Nicholas County Historical Society.

Shepherd, Josh. 1991. "From Philippines to Carlisle: Villaflors Come Home." *Carlisle Mercury,* August 15, 8.

———. 1989a. "Mexicans Join Nicholas Workforce." *Carlisle Mercury,* September 28, 1.

———. 1989b. "The Year: 1907—Night Riders Filled the Highways." *Carlisle Mercury,* October 12, 6.

Shiva, Vandana. 2002. *Water Wars: Privatization, Pollution, and Profit.* Boston: South End Press.

Smith, Christa. 2007. "Managing Downtown Revitalization Projects in Small Cities: Lessons from Kentucky's Main Street Program." In *Beyond the Metropolis: Urban Geography as if Small Cities Mattered,* edited by Benjamin Ofori-Amoah, 269–292. Lanham, MD: University Press of America.

Smith-Mello, Michal. 1995. *Reclaiming Community, Reckoning with Change: Rural Development in the Global Context.* Frankfort: The Kentucky Long-Term Policy Research Center.

Spradling, Jeff. 1990. "Organizers Seek to Bring Tourism Dollars to the County." *Carlisle Mercury,* March 1, 1.

Stamper, John. 1998. "Homegrown History Lesson." *Lexington Herald-Leader,* August 6, A1, A12.

Stewart, Kathleen. 1996. *A Space on the Side of the Road: Cultural Poetics in an "Other" America.* Princeton: Princeton University Press.

Stone, Leigh. 1994. "Local Farmers Talk Tobacco." *Carlisle Mercury,* June 23, 1, 3.

Stull, Donald D. 2009. "Tobacco is Going, Going . . . but Where?" *Culture and Agriculture* 31 (2): 54–72.

———. 2000. "Tobacco Barns and Chicken Houses: Agricultural Transformation in Western Kentucky." *Human Organization* 59 (2): 151–161.

Sumner, Jennifer. 2005. *Sustainability and the Civil Commons: Rural Communities in the Age of Globalization.* Toronto: University of Toronto Press.

Swanson, Mark A. 2001. "No Substitute for Tobacco: The Search for Farm Diversification in Appalachian Kentucky." PhD dissertation in Anthropology, University of Florida, Gainesville.

Swasy, Alecia. 1990. "It's a Nice Place to Live, but They Just Don't Want to Visit There." *Wall Street Journal,* June 18.

———. 1987. "Toyota to Get Controversial Trade Subzone." *Lexington Herald-Leader,* November 17, A1, A7.

TamilNet. 2005. "Navalady—a Village Turned Graveyard." January 8. Accessed January 9, 2005. http://www.tamilnet.com/art.html?artid=13910&catid=79.

Thomas, Kedron. 2009. "Structural Adjustment, Spatial Imaginaries, and 'Piracy' in Guatemala's Apparel Industry." *Anthropology of Work Review* 30 (1): 1–10.

Thomas-Houston, Marilyn M. 2005. *"Stony the Road" to Change: Black Mississippians and the Culture of Social Relations.* Cambridge, UK: Cambridge University Press.

"Tourism Talk." 1990. *Carlisle Mercury,* November 29, 5.

Tsing, Anna Lowenhaupt. 2005. *Friction: An Ethnography of Global Connection.* Princeton, NJ: Princeton University Press.

———. 2000. "The Global Situation." *Cultural Anthropology* 15 (3): 327–360.

Tuan, Yi-Fu. 1977. *Space and Place: The Perspective of Experience.* Minneapolis: University of Minnesota Press.

Turner, William H., and Edward J. Cabbell, eds. 1985. *Blacks in Appalachia.* Lexington: The University Press of Kentucky.

Vice, Tribby. 2000. "CFA Members Only People to Testify Before the Senate Appropriations and Revenue Committee on HB 611." *CFA News,* May, 6–7.

Vidich, Arthur J., and Joseph Bensman. 1958. *Small Town in Mass Society: Class, Power and Religion in a Rural Community.* Princeton, NJ: Princeton University Press.

Vos, Sarah. 2008. "Tobacco-Related Cancers High in Kentucky: State Has Highest Smoking Rate in U.S." *Lexington Herald-Leader,* September 6, D1–2.

Wall, J. K. 2000. "Softer Sell Finds a Market." *Lexington Herald-Leader,* April 20, C1.

Weber, Max. 1958. *The Protestant Ethic and the Spirit of Capitalism.* Translated by Talcott Parsons. New York: Dover Publications.

Weinbaum, Eve S. 2004. *To Move a Mountain: Fighting the Global Economy in Appalachia.* New York: The New Press.

Wolf, Emily A. 1983. "Shumates Attribute Teamwork to Success of Marriage and Careers." *Carlisle Mercury,* December 8, 1.

Yoneyama, Lisa. 1999. *Hiroshima Traces: Time, Space, and the Dialectics of Memory.* Berkeley: University of California Press.

Subject Index

181